CAUGHT BETWEEN AMBITIONS

THE UNITED STATES AND IRANIAN DEVELOPMENT POLICY TO WIN THE COLD WAR

Safeer Tariq Bhatti

Preface

Caught Between Ambitions is a historiography thesis on the United States' development

policy towards Iran, and Iran's political, economic, and military developments. Most

importantly, this thesis is to serve as the victory of the Cold War- *or at least that is what*

Americans thought between 1950 and 1959. This project started as a review essay for my class in

Middle Eastern politics. Each week throughout the semester we discussed the contributions of

the authors we read to the overall theme and subject of political science. My dissertation advisor,

friend, mentor, and professor, Dr. Vitalis, educated me on the resources that we had in the library

of Iran files from the U.S. State Department. He also explained to me in simple, separated

sentences that *no one has done research* on this time period before, and this study would be

beneficial not only to me, but to academia as a whole. I wanted to do something creative and

"new" for the understanding of analytical history and political science and felt this would be my

best bet. After finishing the semester and submitting my review essay for this thesis, I

immediately began researching. After graduation, all summer, I read just about every document

on microfilm listed for the time era. At the end of researching the time period from 1950 to 1959

I concluded that America wanted to do whatever it would take to win the cold war-*and that was*

the essence of their development policy.

Caught Between Ambitions is also a personal feat as well since I took ample coursework

to refine my understanding of international relations and diplomatic history. My political science

coursework in comparative and IR literature helped me further develop the nature of this thesis.

Dr. Granieri taught me the love of diplomatic history, which I have included in this thesis as well. This thesis has incorporated the history of decisions made by both the foreign policy advisors of the United States and foreign policy dignitaries of Iran. These foreign policy decisions impacted the shape of the cold war and the strengthened the position of the United States, allowing it to win the cold war much later. Studying contemporary politics of Iraq, I learned small bits of Iranian history as well as about the conflict of Iran and Iraq. In our Middle East politics class we studied how Aramco, the Saudi Oil company selling to America reacted to the American request that U.S. oil companies invest in Saudi oil so the American economy would benefit. In my Globalization class, Dr. Spooner taught us the theories of modernization and westernization and how these theories impact culture and erase heritage. In order for Iran to be an active player in the international arena, the Shah wanted Iran to modernize its practices, its ways, and its infrastructure and began to export more oil internationally as a result of this modernization. My focus at the University of Pennsylvania College of Liberal and Professional Studies was International Studies. I feel that I have achieved a global education. This thesis is for others like me who are interested in international affairs and doing something to contribute to international relations.

Research Design

The design of this research project became uprooted mainly through my research of the State Department Files for Iran from 1950–1959. I considered a few secondary sources. The main theme of this paper is to show the reader how the United States wanted to win the Cold War. They felt Iran was the answer and gave Iran life, support, money, military advancements, and infrastructure so that the United States could create a stronghold in hegemony in the Middle East. If Britain and the Soviet Union were out of the Middle East, then the United States could assume the role of sole hegemon, controlling the exports of oil coming out of a powerful state.

By limiting Soviet involvement, they weakened the Soviet's position in the Middle East, deterred the influence of Communism, created U.S. regional defense bases to respond to any immediate threat by Soviets, and took away their monopoly of sugar, so that the United States could benefit from Iran's monopoly of sugar. Essentially, it was whatever one could do to advance in the technological race and be ahead, and if that meant giving more than a billion dollars to Iran, all military equipment, and receiving $9.8 billion USD in profits from Iran, then *so be it*. Through American hegemony, economic aid and weakening of the Soviet influence, the US won the Cold War in the second revolution in 1959. The first signs of victory in the regional Cold War were in 1953 when the U.S. defeated the Soviet Union influence. The next remaining years were to maintain that hegemony.

The topics that will be considered are threefold: political developments, economic developments, and military developments. Each topic area will concentrate on two eras. The first time period covered is 1951–1953 (first revolution), while the second is 1953–1959 (second revolution). Each time period will comprise of certain highlighted events that occurred during the relationship between Iran and the United States and how the foreign policy decisions of 1951–1953 impacted events in 1953–1959. These events will be looked at in great detail, analyzing together how the United States was on their way in winning the global Cold War. In the introduction, there will be a brief history of the landscape of the Middle East in the 1950s by various authors. Once the landscape is portrayed, the introduction will delve into the history of the political situation in Iran, focusing on the character of the Shah and Iranian oil. The time era of 1951–1953 will also be known as the Mossedegh era. This era was the first revolution in Iranian politics because Iranians protested against British and Soviet control of their oil. They used United States assistance for their liberation and later the overthrow of Prime Minister

Mossedegh. During this time, the United States became very interested in the political dynamics of Iran and provided political, economic, and military developments to seek an American position there. The politics of oil was their major motivation. The second time period that this thesis will look at is 1953 to 1959 or called the second revolution. This time period is the crux of this thesis because there has been ample research on the Mossedegh era and the White Revolution of 1961. However, there has not been much research on the pre-White Revolution era. Many historians and State Department files have concluded that this time period was *uneventful* in Iranian history. Yet, many developments occurred during this time period known as the second revolution. This period heavily involved President Eisenhower and the Shah on many levels. It was a developmental period in history. I believe that the root of developmental foreign policy was born during this period.

Statement of Problem

In Elton Daniel's literature of the *History of Iran,* he states: "the rest of the 1950s were relatively uneventful for Iran," making a comment on the post-Mossedegh era. He dedicates less than a paragraph to this time period. In the report summaries of many State Department files, the text also supports Daniel's claim that the post-Mossedegh era showed no progress, no event, no change, and nothing of importance to report. This statement of *uneventful history* is quite contradictory because all history is comprised of past events, and though the authors acknowledge that events took place, in their minds they were of no importance. My research project advisors told me to *run with it* and tell them during my defense where I ended up. I ran with the research of this project for four months and at many intervals, I felt I was ending in a ditch, but there were many passages in the ditch that allowed me to continue my journey until 1959. This thesis is to explore the problem and absence in worldwide historical literature on the period of 1954 to 1959. The general story is that the United States poured millions of dollars into a state far along the Middle East for oil, but I assure you in this thesis, the politics of oil was not the only initiative that drove the United States into Iran and to maintain a good relationship with the country for more than twenty years. Further, developmental policy does not only comprise of economic developments, but political and military developments too. I want to figure out why historians have stated that this time period was uneventful and find out how to change the description of the Second Revolution into: *eventful history.*

Table of Contents

Table of Contents

Introduction

The United States did not win the Cold War in 1991. After the overthrow of the

Mossedegh regime in Iran and the installation of the Shah of Iran in August, 1953, the United

States initially felt they were going to win the Regional Cold War against the Soviet Union. The

stipulation to this victory was the maintenance of the American hegemony in the Middle East

throughout the 1950s. During the Truman and Eisenhower administrations, the United States

weakened the Soviet Union's position, hegemony, and oil diplomacy in Iran, which at the time

was the most powerful nation in the Middle East. The United States won the Cold War in the

second revolution of Iran's history in 1959 by weakening Soviet aggression, trade, and

communist influences through American foreign policy and economic aid, the sugar monopoly, and trade agreements with Iran, the United States and other allies. The United States needed Iran to win this Regional Cold War so that they can win the Global Cold War against their bi-polar partner: the U.S.S.R. The Middle East was the key to power and hegemony. In the 1950s, there were many complex issues. The regional Cold War and the involvement in the Arab Cold War was a clash between American and Communist identity. The goal was to supersede one identity over another to potentially control the Middle East and gain unipolarity in the world. Both imposed identities came into a battle with local Iranian/Arab nationalism. Nationalism was their biggest threat- if nationalism succeeded, then the identity of Communism or Americanization would not have even been able to influence this region. In order to defeat nationalism, the goal was oil diplomacy-oil politics. Oil politics was the cause of the detachment from Arab and Iranian nationalism; it was the reason the United States was able to gain influence in Iran and later the Middle East. The goal was: whoever controlled Iran would control the Middle East. In the 1950s, both the Soviet Union and the United States were at their height of competition. After the United States defeated the Soviet Union in the 1950s, it created an imbalance in the Cold War, weakening the Soviet Union in the 1960s and leading to its subsequent fall in 1991. If the reverse had occurred, then history would have been different and perhaps the United States would not hold the World Soldier position it holds today.

Many historians would argue that the statement of winning the Cold War for the first time in the second revolution seems idiotic and not academically based in the history of American foreign policy. But the history of American foreign policy during the Cold War has limited and inaccessible primary sources. In American foreign policy, historical writing is premised on a country's relationship with the United States.[1] A historiography essay is also

---

[1] Nathan Citino *Middle East Cold Wars: Oil and Arab Nationalism in U.S.-Iraqi Relations, 1958-1961 (Oxford: Rowman and Littlefield Publishers, Inc, 2006) 245*

difficult to complete because of the difficulties of discovering accessible sources and political knowledge of the past. Diplomatic historians studying American foreign policy conduct historical and archival research on *experiences* of the past funneled through experiences of the present. Sometimes the objectives are reached, but American historians then face the problem of many unanswered questions. There needs to be more academic research on American diplomacy in the Middle East for these two reasons: 1) to understand our foreign policy decisions made with leaders of the Middle East; and 2) to learn from our mistakes and prevent future conflict based on incomprehensible decisions of the past. This in fact is the purpose of this study.

During the struggle for independence of many Middle Eastern countries, there was a lot of post-war Arab nationalism. States like Egypt with Nasser and other regional rivals began the Arab Cold War. This was a struggle among the first generation of revolutionary Arab leaders to control their dramatic changes of identity.[2] The United States and the Soviet Union were also components of the Arab Cold War because they tried to converge a western identity or a communist allegiance. The Cold War in the Arab world and the Regional Cold War between the Soviet Union and the United States was a clash of identities. Whoever's identity would win in Iran would control the Middle East and history to come. History showed that Americanization was the supreme identity in Iran and later imposed the supreme hegemony of the Middle East. This paved the way for later movements like the Arab Union and sects preaching Arab nationalism. But, while nationalism was at its height, the Shah of Iran wanted to suppress such nationalistic movements so that the influence of American foreign policy, the American dream, and American aid could flourish in Iran. If Iranian nationalism took shape, then the United States would never have achieved hegemony in the Middle East, and never would have had control of

---

[2] Nathan Citino *Middle East Cold Wars: Oil and Arab Nationalism in U.S.-Iraqi Relations, 1958-1961 (Oxford: Rowman and Littlefield Publishers, Inc, 2006) 247*

Iran, its oil and its money. Nationalism was a local threat-a local identity that would have both threatened the American and Communist outlook. But, nationalism in Iran would have probably changed the current political situation we have today. If the Soviets with their powerful communist influences spread into Iran, the country today would have been totally different. Cold War is usually understood at a global level, but there were some regional Cold Wars that impacted the goal of winning the Global Cold War in history. This regional Cold War in the Middle East was between the obvious actors: the United States and the Soviet Union.[3] The source of the conflict was Iran and its resources because Iran had the potential of being the most powerful nation in the Middle East. It was Eisenhower's commitment to lead an overt aggression after any controlled International communism. The ideology of American imperialism, westernization, and modernization was in direct conflict with Communism and its influence. The defeat of the Soviet Union in the Superpower Cold War of the Middle East was followed by America's attainment of hegemony and oil. Further, the foreign policy of the post-war Middle East was American-based and Iran was pulled into the global economy. The United States did not feel it was important that the infrastructure, nationalism, and the *Myth of Middle Eastern Mad-Men* (a theory crafted by Historian R. Stephen Humphreys discussing the illogical decisions of Middle Eastern leaders because they were against the United States attitude), was a result of the victory of the cold war.

The reason oil diplomacy was pledged in Iran by the Eisenhower administration and that any motive for regime change of the Baghdad Pact was because oil politics detached from pan-Arab nationalism. Oil politics allowed the United States to defend its access to oil and achieve its diplomatic goals in the Middle East.[4] Oil politics was the impetus that battled against Arab

---

[3] Nathan Citino *Middle East Cold Wars: Oil and Arab Nationalism in U.S.-Iraqi Relations, 1958-1961 (Oxford: Rowman and Littlefield Publishers, Inc, 2006) 247.* (This theory of the superpower Cold War and the Arab Cold War was first crafted by historian Malcolm Kerr).

nationalism. It helped suppress the Iranian nationalistic ideals and was the main cause for the American victory in August, 1953. There is *existing scholarship (that) has established a clear connection between the superpowers' contest to win allies in the Middle East and the radicalization of Arab politics.*[5] This policy began to take form in 1953 when Secretary of State John Foster Dulles went to the Middle East to find a suitable location for the United States' Cold War strategy. Once Dulles and Eisenhower confirmed that Egypt and its nationalism could not help them win the Cold War, they went out and sought the *northern tier* countries of Turkey, Iran, Pakistan, and Iraq. With these countries, they were able to formulate the Baghdad Pact and start a Middle East Defense Organization. Once Great Britain joined, Arab nationalists felt it was another move for colonialism and America did not join.[6] By Nasser not joining the Baghdad Pact and accepting military aid from the Soviet Union, foreign policymakers knew him as an ally of the Soviet Union. He also allied Arab nationalism with communism, and the United States took this as a threat. The Soviet Union showed signs of Arab nationalism acceptance and Eisenhower stated after sending a lot of economic aid to the Middle Eastern countries, "we simply could not stand around and do nothing and see the whole area fall into the hands of communism." He increased military aid to Middle Eastern countries.[7] Dulles knew that if Arab nationalism spread, it will be "a flood that cannot be stopped but only contained by building sand-bags around vital U.S. assets in the Middle East."[8] The control of Arab nationalism later and the suppression of the Soviet Union and communism led to the United States' victory and becoming the hegemon of

---

[4] Nathan Citino *Middle East Cold Wars: Oil and Arab Nationalism in U.S.-Iraqi Relations, 1958-1961 (Oxford: Rowman and Littlefield Publishers, Inc, 2006) 247-248*

[5] Nathan Citino *Middle East Cold Wars: Oil and Arab Nationalism in U.S.-Iraqi Relations, 1958-1961 (Oxford: Rowman and Littlefield Publishers, Inc, 2006) 248*

[6] Nathan Citino *Middle East Cold Wars: Oil and Arab Nationalism in U.S.-Iraqi Relations, 1958-1961 (Oxford: Rowman and Littlefield Publishers, Inc, 2006) 248*

[7] Nathan Citino *Middle East Cold Wars: Oil and Arab Nationalism in U.S.-Iraqi Relations, 1958-1961 (Oxford: Rowman and Littlefield Publishers, Inc, 2006) 249*

[8] Nathan Citino *Middle East Cold Wars: Oil and Arab Nationalism in U.S.-Iraqi Relations, 1958-1961 (Oxford: Rowman and Littlefield Publishers, Inc, 2006) 251*

the Middle East. Being a hegemon and victorious in the Middle Eastern superpower Cold War actually means what? How important was the Middle East?

Importance of the Middle East

Masud Foruqi, the Master of Princess Shams' household stated in 1957:

> After 15 years on the throne, Mohamad Reza Pahlavi has not lived up to the high expectations as Crown Prince….the present Shah must be persuaded to withdraw from politics.[9]

Mr. Foruqi believed that the Shah of Iran was a *staunch monarchist* and that the position of king had to be stabilized for the stability of the country. He described the Shah as both *devious* and *vacillating*.[10] Foruqi describes that the Shah of Iran, Mohamad Reza Pahlavi, as the *spectacle of oriental intriguer surrounded by such sycophants as his wife's worthless Bakhtiari relatives*.[11] The conditions in Iran in 1957 were getting worse. The numerous amounts of aid

---

[9] Masud Foruqi to Philip Clock & T.A. Cassilly, 6 February 1957, General Records of the Department of State, Record Group 59, 1955-1959, 788.00/2-657, National Archives, Washington DC (hereafter cited as RG 59, with filing information).

[10] Masud Foruqi to Philip Clock & T.A. Cassilly, 6 February 1957, RG 59, 788.00/2-657

received from the United States had seen no effect in Iran. The United States provided economic and military assistance, but Foruqi angrily asserted that the present government "can't even balance the budget".[12] Iranians began comparing the current King of Iran to his father Reza Shah and only saw failure. The situation in Iran further showed rampant corruption and the cost of living was at the brink of popular discontent. Foruqi says, "Unless something is done about it, in six months or one year there will be riots in the Tehran bazaar which could spread rapidly to the gates of the palace."[13] The *main obstacle to the development of Iran was the present shah.[14]*

The Middle East is a very confusing term. It represents many sects of faith, culture, and traditions along its vast boundaries. One such state with a rich heritage is has an increasingly complicated alliance with the Middle East.[15] Iran, a state with a 3,000 year history, and the analysis of its developmental policies in the 1950s is the focus of this paper. Historians like Elton Daniel and State Department briefs state that the 1950s was an uneventful period of history. This thesis aims to debunk their theories and persuade the educated reader that the post- Mossedegh pre-White Revolution era has a lot of history. In 1957 for example, Iran was powerful than ever. It achieved much military advancement, political infrastructure developments and economic aid, yet Iranians were still displeased with the Shah's leadership, feeling it was the cause of the ill-development of Iran. If the Shah represented the destruction of development, then the question regarding my thesis could be: what developmental policy was in Iran if there was no development?

---

[11] Masud Foruqi to Philip Clock & T.A. Cassilly, 6 February 1957, RG 59, 788.00/2-657
[12] Masud Foruqi to Philip Clock & T.A. Cassilly, 6 February 1957, RG 59, 788.00/2-657
[13] Masud Foruqi to Philip Clock & T.A. Cassilly, 6 February 1957, RG 59, 788.00/2-657
[14] Masud Foruqi to Philip Clock & T.A. Cassilly, 6 February 1957, RG 59 788.00/2-657
[15] Firuz Kazemadeh, *Review: The West and the Middle East* (Baltimore: The John Hopkins University Press, 1959), 467.

The development policies of all countries had many strings attached. Initially development policies were the ones that the United States agreed and acted upon since Iran was dependent on American foreign policy. Iran's foreign policy and their developmental policies in the 1950s were aligned with the interests and policies of the United States. Thus, one can intelligently claim that Iran did not have developmental policies- that their policies were American developmental policies. The few strings attached with the developmental policies of Iran were that the country was to cease all support of communism. It was also hoped that the policies would give Iran a better society economically and militarily create a regional defense tract against the Soviets. Besides the politics of oil, economic benefits, and political and military developments, the United States wanted to become the hegemonic authority in the Middle East and most importantly, they wanted to win the Cold War. Kazemzadah further elaborates and says, "Thus American foreign policy in the Middle East must be seen as a part of global strategy in the long, arduous, and dangerous struggle between Russia and the free world."[16] If a state's foreign policy mirrors the foreign policy of America, then America can assert its influence and right to be the sole controller, receiving many economic benefits on the side. Winning the Cold War was the goal of America and despite numerous pleas of domestic political intervention; the United States only intervened out of investment interests. If developmental foreign policy of Iran and the United States cared about its internal dynamics, then perhaps Foruqi would never have made his statement about the potential of riots in Tehran. How did such statements even evolve in Iran? The United States had firm faith that Iranians were pleased with the Shah and continued to give economic and military aid, assuming that the aid was improving the development of Iran.

---

[16] Firuz Kazemadeh, *Review: The West and the Middle East* (Baltimore: The John Hopkins University Press, 1959), 468.

Caught Between Ambitions is a case-study of the ambitions of the United States asserting a developmental foreign policy in Iran. It is a case study of Iran exporting its developmental foreign policies and becoming a world-wide powerful nation. And it is a case study on how to win the Cold War, defeating the Soviet Union. The purpose of this research is to fill the gap in history during the post-Mossedegh and pre-White Revolution era. The goal is to discuss and analyze the decisions of foreign policy makers in the 1950s to see why scholars assumed this period is uneventful and to educate the reader about the developmental policies of the Truman and Eisenhower administration toward Iran in the 1950s on the path to winning the Cold War. Hence the thesis statement is the developmental policies of Iran and the United States in the 1950s were only motivated to win the Cold War. This paper will briefly introduce a sketch of the Middle East in the 1950s, giving the reader perspective and understanding of placement of time. It will also provide a brief sketch of Mohamad Reza Pahlavi's character analyzed by many sources and accounts, and provide information on the importance of Persian Oil. The thesis will be primarily organized into three parts: Pre-Revolution (1950-1951), First Revolution (1951-1953), and Second Revolution (1953-1959). In the Pre-Revolution, it will state the events leading up to the First Revolution, which is the era of Mossedegh. During the First Revolution of 1951-1953, it will discuss the successes and failures of the Mossedegh regime leading up the Second Revolution. In the Second Revolution of 1953-1959, it is the Post-Mossedegh era; it is an era of the Shah's rule. It was in the second revolution (known as the Quiet Period) that the United States won the Regional Cold War against the Soviet Union. The thesis will focus on a Pre-White Revolution time period. Revolutions change a country's landscape and it will be shown how the contrast between the first and second revolutions impacted developmental policies. Even Prince Colam Reza Pahlavi, the oldest of the Shah's half-brothers said in 1959, "we're very interested in avoiding here in Iran, one of those silly revolutions like the one which took place in Iraq,"-we will just have to wait and see how silly the first and second revolution really was in Iranian history.[17]

Each part will comprise the political, economic, and military developments of the pertaining revolution. In a part, there will be a political, economic and military section. The purpose of the political section is to discuss the political events, infrastructure, agreements, and importance of oil during that time period. The entire thesis will be organized to show that the United States maintained diplomatic relationship with Iran because they wanted to win the Cold War. The political development section of 1950 -1951 will concentrate on the mediation of an oil agreement with Great Britain. It was also to suppress the Iranian nationalistic influences that were to undermine both the Americans and the Soviets in Iran. During 1951-1953, the political development policy of America was to avoid communist influence. The two reasons for this statement are that the United States did not want a Tudeh communist influence to spread locally or by the Soviets; and they wanted to weaken the Soviets' position, money, oil diplomacy, and status in Iran. During the Second Revolution (1953-1959), the Iranian foreign policy depended on the United States. The result of Iran's alliance to United States policy was faced with a heavy American presence. The goal was to suppress nationalism and gain supremacy in Iran to potentially gain hegemony in the Middle East. **If the United States' power was not maintained, they would lose their hegemony in the region.** The economic section will comprise elements of the politics of oil, economic aid, mismanagement of funds, corruption, trade, trade of opium, and American influences. During the Pre-Revolution, America's economic goal was to nationalize Iran's oil that would result in a forego of British properties and oil

---

[17] Colam Reza Pahlavi to Embassy Officer, 28 February, 1959, General Records of the Department of State, Record Group 59, 1955-1959, 788.00/2-2859, National Archives, Washington, DC (hereafter cited as RG 59, with filing information).

investments to Iran and a lack of Soviet influence. During 1951 to 1953, the economic target was to get the United States involved as the mediator of the oil agreement, nationalize the oil industry, and get oil from Iran. If Iran refused, then the United States wanted to cease economic aid and later planned to install the Shah. The politics of the oil diplomacy would span out importance during this time. These politics also weakened the Soviets' position, limiting their access to oil, creating more oil production in Iran for the United States, and creating trade and foreign investment programs, and stopping all influence of Tudeh. In the second revolution, Eisenhower's economic foreign policy was established. It was economic aid that would defeat the Soviet Union's influence in Iran. The economic policy was to prevent communism. Communism was prevented through controlled trade, controlled diplomacy, the push for more oil and foreign investments, export of opium and the sugar monopoly of Iran. The third section is military development. This section will portray the training and education of Iranian armed forces by the U.S. military, especially the U.S. Air Force and U.S. Navy. In the Pre-Revolution, there are only minor negotiations trying to get involved into the military dynamics of Iranian politics. The U.S. military mission was already present in Iran and they wanted to expand their military role. The first revolution was to create a regional defense arrangement in the Middle East in Iran targeting the Soviets. This defense arrangement also brought in a lot of aid to train the Iranian armed forces, educate personnel, create SAVAK, and weaken the strategic military position of Soviets. During the second revolution, the two policies were to make the U.S. defense systems complete and stabilize U.S. military missions in Iran. The defense system created a security mechanism in Iran against the Soviet Union and U.S. military missions brought in American bases and American military all over Tehran for purposes of training and military combat. This section will also analyze military aid and show reasons why the defense of the Middle East is important. It will also discuss the hegemony of America. The majority of these sections will be heavily derived from Confidential State Department Files with a few secondary sources.

The Middle East in the 1950s

The Middle East is a term coined to represent the stretch of land from the Near East at the western border of Egypt to the western border of India. The Middle East contains land from the Black and Caspian Seas of the North to the Arabian Sea and Indian Ocean in the south. It is a mundane region to the average person, but to the international community, it is a region important to the defense of the world.[18] It represents freedom, a bridge between three continents, and a strategic location for each and every empire since Peter the Great, who said that "anyone who ruled the Persian Gulf and the Black Sea would rule India and Europe."[19] This region was

---

[18] N.Saifpour Fatemi, *The United States in the Changing Middle East* (Annals of he American Academy of Political and Social Science :Sage Publications, Inc., 1954), 151.

afflicted with British, French, and Russian suffering. During World War II, there were 70,000 American soldiers and more than 6,000,000 tons of lend-lease goods sent to Tehran to help Russia. Iranian roads and railroads prevented the destruction of Russia.[20] President Roosevelt also visited the Middle East and sent General Hurley to study Iran. Hurley proposed the first independent American foreign policy in Iran, believing that Iran could achieve self-government and free enterprise. FDR replied:

> I am thrilled with the idea of using our efforts in Iran as example of what can be done by an unselfish American policy. If we can get the right kind of American experts who will remain loyal to their ideals, I feel certain that our policy of *aiding* Iran will succeed.[21]

In June 1947, President Truman said, 'we are faced with the danger of a shortage of petroleum products. The United States is now using more oil each day than the entire world did before the war.'[22]After World War II, the United States led the fight for independence in many Middle Eastern countries. This step was taken in order to stop Russian aggression and proliferate U.S. military bases in all parts of the Middle East.[23] In 1951, President Eisenhower addressed the Senate Armed Services Committee:

> As far as the sheer value of territory is concerned, there is no more strategically important area in the world than the Middle East. This area is tremendously important in terms of what it could contribute for our whole effort. We should use our resources, our power, our organizational ability and above all, our leadership- to get some kind of organization that would rally all of them to go in with us.[24]

---

[19] N.Saifpour Fatemi, *The United States in the Changing Middle East* (Annals of he American Academy of Political and Social Science :Sage Publications, Inc., 1954), 151.

[20] N.Saifpour Fatemi, *The United States in the Changing Middle East* (Annals of he American Academy of Political and Social Science :Sage Publications, Inc., 1954), 153

[21] N.Saifpour Fatemi, *The United States in the Changing Middle East* (Annals of he American Academy of Political and Social Science :Sage Publications, Inc., 1954), 153

[22] Sir Arthur Hearn, *Oil and the Middle East* (International Affairs: Royal Institute of International Affairs, 1948), 67.

[23] N.Saifpour Fatemi, *The United States in the Changing Middle East* (Annals of he American Academy of Political and Social Science :Sage Publications, Inc., 1954), 151

[24] N.Saifpour Fatemi, *The United States in the Changing Middle East* (Annals of he American Academy of Political

It was in 1901 that D'Arcy, a British businessman, obtained a sixty-year concession to explore for oil and sell whatever he found. After seven years of exploration and 100,000 pounds later, he found oil.[25] The strategic location and understanding of the vast importance of the Middle East erupted after 1908 when the world found oil at Masjid e Sulaiman. Oil was the motivator for them to achieve their presence in that region. Until very recently, oil was only known as a substance seeping on the surface, useful in the old days for chariot axles or the scalps of Red Indians. But even in 1859 when the first mechanical drill was erected, oil's value was not known until much later.[26] The Middle East in fact contains 80 billion barrels of oil, some 63 percent of the world's petroleum resources.[27] The oil fields in Iran produced 8,000 barrels a day and 30,000,000 tons of oil in 80 wells in 1950 at a low cost.[28] It means that it cost the Anglo-Iranian Oil Company less than $0.15 to produce a barrel of crude oil compared to $1.70 a barrel in the United States. In 1954 these wells were owned by five American oil companies: Standard Oil of New Jersey, Gulf Oil Corporation, Standard Oil of California, Sacony-Vacuum Oil Company, the Texas Company; and two British companies: Anglo-Persian Oil Co. and the Royal-Shell Company. There were also some Dutch companies and one French company invested in this oil project. The income of oil was more than 1,500,000,000 dollars.[29] There are more than 180,000,000 people inhabiting this region.[30] Iran is the largest and the first oil Middle

---

and Social Science :Sage Publications, Inc., 1954), 151

[25] Tehran to the Secretary of State, 13 June, 1951, General Records of the Department of State, Record Group 59, 1950-1954, 888.2553/6.1351, National Archives, Washington, DC (hereafter cited as RG 59, with filing information).

[26] Sir Arthur Hearn, *Oil and the Middle East* (International Affairs: Royal Institute of International Affairs, 1948), 63.

[27] N.Saifpour Fatemi, *The United States in the Changing Middle East* (Annals of he American Academy of Political and Social Science: Sage Publications, Inc., 1954), 151

[28] N.Saifpour Fatemi, *The United States in the Changing Middle East* (Annals of he American Academy of Political and Social Science: Sage Publications, Inc., 1954), 151

[29] N.Saifpour Fatemi, *The United States in the Changing Middle East* (Annals of he American Academy of Political and Social Science: Sage Publications, Inc., 1954), 151

East producer.[31]But the independent foreign policy for Iran did not remain accurate. Today's foreign policy is described as *schizophrenia*. Today, the five problems facing the Middle East for the United States are 1) revolt of the people of North Africa against French colonialism; 2) the Anglo-Egyptian dispute; 3)the Arab-Israeli conflict; 4)the Anglo-Iranian dispute and 5) the poverty and backwardness of the area.[32] Unless changes are not extended to the people, and the grievances of these nations against colonial powers are not solved, *there can be no stability and security and no defense system in that region.[33]* The Middle East will remain a challenge to the United States and the Shah of Iran needs support from outside his country and the ruling class. The best thing that the United States can do to operate effectively in Iran and the Middle East is to create partnerships, a common interest, and settle all disputes and conflict. The people of the Middle East expect an illustrious American foreign policy.[34] Due to illiteracy, none of them understand the implications of the oil problem and neither the government nor the press tried to educate the public. If the illiteracy rate is low, then people cannot read or listen to the story of the Anglo-Iranian Company.[35] It will be interesting to see if the United States carries out Fatemi's recommendations for a successful American foreign policy in Iran. Now we have understood the landscape of the Middle East and the most valuable product of oil that brought America into Iran. Next we will find out that when they got there, and who were they dealing with?

---

[30] N.Saifpour Fatemi, *The United States in the Changing Middle East (*Annals of he American Academy of Political and Social Science: Sage Publications, Inc., 1954), 152

[31] Sir Arthur Hearn, *Oil and the Middle East* (International Affairs: Royal Institute of International Affairs, 1948), 66.

[32] N.Saifpour Fatemi, *The United States in the Changing Middle East (*Annals of he American Academy of Political and Social Science: Sage Publications, Inc., 1954), 156

[33] N.Saifpour Fatemi, *The United States in the Changing Middle East (*Annals of he American Academy of Political and Social Science: Sage Publications, Inc., 1954), 156.

[34] N.Saifpour Fatemi, *The United States in the Changing Middle East (*Annals of he American Academy of Political and Social Science: Sage Publications, Inc., 1954), 157

[35] Tehran to Secretary of State, 13 June 1951, RG 59, 888.2553/6-1351.

Ethnicity Clashes in Iran

There were many types of ethnicities that came under the umbrella of an Iranian. The main clashes were among the Jewish ethnicity. The Jewish population was becoming a serious concern for Iran. The Jews lived in misery, ignorance, and many at near starving conditions. Some of them were living in horrible housing. Though the Iranian government was known for being tolerant to minorities, the persecution of Jews had been increasing. The persecutions became rampant in Kurdistan where Jews are forced to flee from their homes. The government had done very little to control the Kurds. Due to hunger and despair, this could turn into violence against the Jews. Further, this potential threat was growing due to the mass migration of Jews from Iraq and Kurdistan into Iran. They represent Zionism and are among Iranian Jews. In August 1950, the accommodations were causing difficulties in Iran. With 3,000 Jews living in two refugee camps, there was no shelter and it was very much anarchy. The Jews moving from Iran to Israel were limited to an immigration quota of 1,500 to 1,800 Jews a month and only a small percentage of Jews would go when it was feasible. Though there was no objection for Jews to go to Israel, there were restraints.[36] Furthermore, the relationships between Muslims and Jews had been good in Kurdistan until the creation of the State of Israel.[37] Sunni Kurds who are close to the Palestinian Arabs, then the Shi'a Persians stirred anger and Arab propaganda. This anger showed through beatings, stoning, kidnapping, and sometimes mob violence against the Jews in Kurdistan. They have stories of oppression and "hope of return to Israel (as) the solution of all their problems." At first, they made a synagogue of 1,000 square yards, but that soon became filled with more than 800 people. When the roads were made in 1950, 3,000 of them poured into Tehran into camps made for 1,200 people. The cost to maintain the camp was $1,000.00 that

---

[36] Restricted Tehran Summary, 24 August 1950, General Records of the Department of State, Record Group 59, 1950-1954, 788.022/8-2450, National Archives, Washington DC (hereafter cited as RG 59, with filing information.

[37] Restricted Tehran Summary, 24 August 1950, RG 59, 788.022/8-2450

only prevents starvation and epidemics. Warm food was served only to children age fifteen and under. There were feeding programs and clothing for more than 2,500 children. Then Jewish refugees came from Iraq and in fifteen months, there were more than 12,000 Jews in Iran. This was a problem for Iranians.[38]

The Jewish population was 80,000 Jewish people living across Iran. The conduct and care of the Jews became a concern for the Iranian government and American governments. The American Embassy reported that they were living very well with a high tolerance of their religion, but strong prejudice still existed among Shia Muslims. Many Jews in Tehran lived in the ghetto in poverty and the government stepped in and offered $600,000 a year to improve the health and living conditions of Iran. The Iranian government cooperated with the Israeli government to offer services and clinics to Jewish families.

[39] Many were now immigrating to the United States, to Tehran from Meshed and some to Israel claiming their birthrights. The Jewish people in Iran were some of the wealthiest businessman in all of Iran. They were honest, shrewd, and very hard-working. Most of them did not speak Hebrew, but Farsi and Arabic were their tongues. The faith and life was supported by only three synagogues in Meshed. Until some of the threats started happening, the Jews lived there quite peaceably and the Shia community were very friendly.[40]

---

[38] Restricted Tehran Summary, 24 August 1950, RG 59, 788.022/8-2450
[39] Department of State to American Consulate, 6 December 1955, RG 59, 788.00/12-655.
[40] Department of State to American Consulate, 6 December 1955, RG 59, 788.00/12-655.

The Character of the Imperial Purple

Mohamad Reza Pahlavi was known as the *Imperial Purple*. He was made an Emperor after the birth of a son, and referred to as His Majesty in correspondence. The Shah of Iran was a *politically-conscious, weak, spineless,* and *indecisive* man. With an incredible smile, Iranians understood that the *Shah's character was capable of changing.*[41] But his present behavior can only be judged with a clear understanding of his background. He went to school in Switzerland at a very young age under the care of Moadeb-ed-Doleh Nafisi, a very frightened old man.[42] His teacher enforced very stringent rules. For example, Nafisi would not let the prince go to a party after 10:00 PM because that was bedtime for the prince unless he wanted to telegraph Tehran for orders. Back in Tehran he lived under the shadow of his father.[43] At the age of 18, the King sent the young prince to Egypt to marry Fawzieh, the sister of Former King Faruq. She was a beautiful woman, considered "even lovelier than Queen Soraya."[44] The young prince and Fawieh were attached to each other and very much alike, but the vigor of Princess Ashraf broke them apart. In his lifetime, he had "an innate distrust of strong and capable men." Foruqi relates that his complexes "are grafted on certain Iranian character weaknesses and on a marked propensity to deviousness and intrigue."[45] He enjoys flattery, but cannot bear to be lied to. He cannot stand against anyone who is as firm as he is, and will work to undermine the other person's firm status. "Furthermore, he can be vicious and vindictive to men who have served him loyally." In between his two marriages, "the Shah led the life of a gay bachelor and had a number of mistresses, at

---

[41] Embassy Tehran to The Department of State, 22 August, 1957, General Records of the Department of State, Record Group 59, 1955-1959, 788.11/8-2257, National Archives, Washington, DC (hereafter cited as RG 59, with filing information).

[42] Masud Foruqi to Philip Clock & Christian Chapman, 9 March, 1956, General Records of the Department of State Record Group 59, 1955-1959, 788.00/3-0956, National Archives, Washington DC (hereafter cited as RG 59, with filing information.

[43] Masud Foruqi to Philip Clock & T.A. Cassilly, 9 March 1956, RG 59, 788.00/3-956.

[44] Masud Foruqi to Philip Clock & T.A. Cassilly, 9 March 1956, RG 59, 788.00/3-956.

[45] Masud Foruqi to Philip Clock & T.A. Cassilly, 9 March 1956, RG 59, 788.00/3-956.

least two of them whom he rendered pregnant."[46] Mr. Eshraqi who at that time in 1959 was reluctant to describe the Shah because of his status at the Consul of Iran decided to confide his feelings on the Shah of Iran to the American consulate. *He then began a very discouraging summary of the present state of Iran…*

The single greatest problem in Iran was corruption. Corruption is at the top and at the bottom of the government. At one time, he wanted to pay his taxes before coming to the United States. He spoke to the Ministry of Finance who looked at him distraught and uttered 'Are you crazy?' to the most ambitious gentleman. He further insisted and received answer that the Shah was the one responsible for reducing his corrupted allocation to reduce the taxes. He, the Shah, *had a very good deal:* **money, trips all over the world, and a different girl every night.**[47] In June 1958, he escorted a model and an airline hostess with him in San Francisco. It ended his relationship with Queen Soraya.[48] This was a very brief synopsis of the Shah's character and more details will appear throughout this thesis. This was a brief overview of who the United States was dealing with in the 1950s, not necessarily, who they *wanted* to deal with. Our next section will be looking at the political developments in the Pre- Revolution.

---

[46] Masud Foruqi to Philip Clock & T.A. Cassilly, 9 March 1956, RG 59, 788.00/3-956.

[47] Hosein Eshraqi to Franklin Crawford & Charles Exum, 19 May, 1959, General Records of the Department of State, Record Group 59, 1955-1959, 788.00/5-1959, National Archives, Washington, DC (hereafter cited as RG 59, with filing information).

[48] Hosein Eshraqi to Franklin Crawford & Charles Exum, 19 May, 1959, RG 59, 788.00/5-1959

PART ONE:

PRE-REVOLUTION (1950-1951)

The Pre-Revolution era in Iranian history was an embattlement against colonial imperial rule. It was a revolt against the overarching British control of Iran's oil resources and the political authority of the Soviet Union. Iranian nationalists felt it was time for independence. It was time for an Iranian identity. The political developments in this time period heavily concentrated its efforts on a negotiation of a solid oil agreement. It was to give more money back into the hands of Iran and less to foreign powers. Locally, Iran was experiencing nationalism. Iranian nationalism was growing and it deemed a threat to both America and the Soviet Union. Nationalism will undermine American interests and ruin communist influence. The goal was to also stop Iranian nationalism. The economic policies were to nationalize Iran's oil industry and remove British and Soviet economic influences in the state. The military policies were to continue the U.S. military mission in Iran and investigate possible American influences in Iran.

Part 1:Section 1- Political Developments

Nationalism in Iran

There was also a lot of tension in Iran. At this time, nationalism was beginning to grow. Iranians felt proud of their independence, and for the first time in a very long time: felt like Iranians. But the Shah persisted on his modernization campaign which included giving oil to America, and being subservient to American foreign policy. So many Iranians began to dislike him and America. The Shah of Iran in fact continued to reduce the feeling of nationalism in favor of modernization. But in countries like Iran with a low standard of living, it is imperative to develop nationalism "if they are to advance socially and economically and maintain their political independence."[49] Progress must be understood by the people to insure nationalism. If

---

[49] Henry Francis Grady *Tensions in the Middle East with particular reference to Iran* (Proceedings of the Academy of Political Science: The Academy of political science, 1952) 554.

nationalism like Grady says, *serves the selfish purposes of the few can destroy a county and possibly its friends.*[50] The reason Iran is of much attention and tension is because the country is one of the main points with the struggle with Russia. *What happens in Iran may determine whether we have or avoid World War III.*[51] In 1950 there was no talk of nationalization even when Dr. Mossedegh was Chairman of the Majlis Commission. The Anglo Iranian Oil Co. was the symbol of revolt. Iranians revolted against them for interfering in their affairs against the British and felt if this company could be destroyed, then nationalism could take its due course.[52]

This revolt is presented as a revolution to the world and it is unfortunate the United States had to remain a spectator to this *supreme drama* of history. It is a movement against foreign exploitation, against misery and poverty, and against the ruling class who had impoverished and exploited the poor.[53] In the Pre-Revolution, Iran was rich with culture and heritage and had a national income of $100 per capita per annum.[54] Besides being invaded five times by Russia and living in fear of the Russians, they remember all the grievances of outside powers that have afflicted their people and their lands. The response is the *Pre- revolution,* a chance to rejoice against international rule; and a chance to be Iranian. The reason Britain does not want the Anglo-Iranian Oil Co. to go out of business is because they invested more than $100 million in fifty years and produced 2,508 million barrels of oil, achieving sales of more than $2 billion. In fifty years, only $400 million has been paid to Iran.[55] The reasons for such low payments are that

[50] Henry Francis Grady *Tensions in the Middle East with particular reference to Iran* (Proceedings of the Academy of Political Science: The Academy of political science, 1952) 554.

[51] Henry Francis Grady *Tensions in the Middle East with particular reference to Iran* (Proceedings of the Academy of Political Science: The Academy of political science, 1952) 554.

[52] Henry Francis Grady *Tensions in the Middle East with particular reference to Iran* (Proceedings of the Academy of Political Science: The Academy of political science, 1952) 554.

[53] N. Saifour Fatemi *Tensions in the Middle East.* (Annals of the American Academy of Political and Social Science: Sage Publications, 1952). 53
[54] N. Saifour Fatemi *Tensions in the Middle East.* (Annals of the American Academy of Political and Social Science: Sage Publications, 1952). 53

there were many gaps in payments, and some were never made. The British says the Iranians are anti-west, but Fatemi claims that Iranians are not against anyone- they just love Iran more than the west. Fatemi says, "We desire consideration and respect from those who have always benefited by us. It is a shame to call us fanatics and extreme nationalists. Iran has always advocated the cause of humanitarianism and internationalism." His response to the western countries was: "whatever aid you give to the Middle Eastern countries will be a premium on a peace insurance policy."[56]

American Nationalization of Iranian Oil

The Americans advised the Iranian government to ban the Soviet Union to prevent the spread of communism through their lucrative offers, and to weaken the Soviet's strategic position in the Middle East, especially in Iran. On June 1, 1951, a closed secret communication came from the President of the United States to the Prime Minister of Iran. This has become known as the earliest initiative of a diplomatic relationship with Iran in the 1950s. This message says, "I express to you the serious concern of the government of the United States at the controversy between Iran and British Government concerning operations of the Anglo-Iranian Oil Co. The United States is a close friend of both countries." The United States went on to say how they were extremely eager to seek a solution for the desires of the Iranian people were for the nationalization of their petroleum resources.[57] This early influence, getting involved in the affairs of Iran and trying to suppress Soviet influence was also to limit the influence of Great Britain. All was suggested for United States' purposes. The United States was going to work

---

[55] N. Saifour Fatemi *Tensions in the Middle East*. (Annals of the American Academy of Political and Social Science: Sage Publications, 1952). 55

[56] N. Saifour Fatemi *Tensions in the Middle East*. (Annals of the American Academy of Political and Social Science: Sage Publications, 1952). 59

[57] US President to American Embassy London and American Embassy Tehran, 1 June 1951, General Records of the Department of State, Record Group 59, 1950-1954, 888.22/6-0151, National Archives, Washington DC (hereafter cited as RG 59, with filing information.

hard to secure an agreement between Anglo Iranian Oil Co. and the Iranian government. The goal of these negotiations was to prevent the Iranian government from resuming control over its oil resources and to not publish propaganda against the British and AIOC. The State Department said, "It sincerely hopes no Iranian government notes or public statements by Iran officials will keep delegation from conference table."[58]The oil diplomatic talks were not heavily favored by the State State Department, but if negotiations failed, then the United States would "at that time (take) course of action it would support." Furthermore, the United States was interested in having the negotiations fail between the British and the Iranians, informing them the "consequences of the closing of the refinery and boycott of Iranian oil." Furthermore, the United States believed to choose normative arrangements to replace the AIOC instead of risking revolution, denial of Persian oil, and the "possible loss of Iran to the western world."[59] Though they wanted the negotiations to fail, just in case they did not, they wanted to have a say in the normative arrangements. They still wanted the British to succeed in their plan and encouraged that the negotiations not be broken off. But, the ridiculous proposals of the AIOC were motivating Iran to nationalize their oil.[60]

A newspaper article in 1951 read: "Black Day for Britain." The black day corresponds to their continuing limited role in the humiliating disaster in Persia. They say, "We are chivied and edged out of our own vast vital property by a covey of Persian soldiers." During these negotiations, they were negotiating on a concession and their complete influence and from the negotiations, it looked as if they were going to lose it all. The article identified Mossedegh as the Potter who was a leader of a people "who could not even develop their own country- that is indeed cause for shame and despair." Further, the people in Europe were ashamed of the

---

[58] US President to American Embassy London & American Embassy Tehran, 9 June 1951, RG 59, 888.22/6-951
[59] American Embassy Tehran: Grady to Secretary of State, 20 June 1951, RG 59, 888.22/6-2051
[60] American Embassy Tehran: Grady to Secretary of State, 20 June 1951, RG 59, 888.22/6-2051

ruination of Great Britain's power in the Middle East. The British say, "We may have to make more concessions than we would like to the Persian point of view, but for negotiation to have become possible is a big step forward." The British admitted their foolishness about their social responsibilities "that go with the getting of money and valuable materials in other people's countries." It ends stating the Persians have been expecting nationalization- something the British cannot furnish in negotiation.[61]

Part 1: Section 2-Economic Developments

Pre-Revolution Economic *Spending*

The inception of the Pre-Revolution looks at the underdevelopment, poor communication, lack of technical skills, illiteracy, and disease in the economic summary of Iran. The nationalization of oil in 1950 that raised a lot of shock and limited foreign access actually hurt Iran because two thirds of its foreign exchange revenue and one third of the government income was dependent on the oil program between AIOC and Iran.[62] Since Iran wanted to achieve independence both internationally and domestically, they felt nationalization would allow Iran to keep their oil and get more money for it. But no one wanted it and after spending their reserves, they began to have a budget deficit. It is the budget deficit that raised prices, limited imports and became dependent on deficit financing from the United States. This dependence of a debt-forsaken nation on loans from another source and their decision to be an independent economic nation actually prevented their independence and limited their freedom. If they had not nationalized oil, Iran probably would have been a richer nation today, more independent and free, and the 26 year history with the United States could have been different.

---

[61] Black Day for Great Britain, 20 June 1951, RG 24, 888.22/6-2051
[62] Iran's Economic Summary, 1950, March. General Records of the Department of State. Record Number 59. 1950-1954. 888.15/3-50 (hereafter cited as RG 59, with filing information).

The nationalization of oil was to parade nationalism and Iranian pride. It was to succumb to the masses who wanted to be Iranian. This national Iranian movement economically disabled the country. It later also produced political opposition movements. The people of Iran wanted results. By 1958, Iran could make $180 million and could form a good economic program by 1956, but they wanted immediate results.[63]

The urgency of the demands of a deficit nation and an outspoken public called for drastic changes. Iran begged the United States for assistance. In this regard and to establish an oil diplomatic relationship that could provide the United States a stronghold and stronger economic position than the Soviet Union, the United States agreed to provide $5 million a month starting in August 1953. They helped initiate a $20 million per year program and the Export-Import Bank gave Iran $53 million to buy American imports and use the money to ship exports into the United States.[64] The total request of technical assistance in 1955 came to $69,617,000, economic aid at $24 million, other economic aid at $113.3 million with a grand total of $206,910,000 of aid to Iran by 1955. There were additional amounts added on top of the final grand total.[65] The communications of these funds were heavily shown on the telecommunication rates to call the individual countries. With over $69 million rials of assets in the telephone company, the USSR only cost seven rials cents per minute while London was 21.10 rials cents per minute. There were calls to the United States, to places like Minnesota, New Mexico, Montana, Canada, New Hampshire, Pennsylvania, West Virginia, etc. Interestingly enough, Hoboken, Jersey City, etc, all New Jersey cities were on the bill of an Iranian phone statement.[66] AT & T representative

---

[63] Iran Economic Summary, 1950 March RG 59 888.15/3-50
[64] Iran Economic Summary, 1950 March RG 59 888.15/3-50
[65] M.S.p. Economic Aid to Iran, 7 December 1954. General Records of the Department of State, Record Number 59 888.2614/12-754. Washington DC. National Archives. (hereafter cited as RG 59).
[66] Foreign Service of the USA Unclassified Appendix B to Tehran No. 715. 1951 December. General Records of the Department of State. Record Number 59, 1950-1954 988.2300[988.2100/12-51 National Archives. Washington DC. (Hereafter cited as RG 59, with filing information).

James Earl Jones consulted with Iran to form proper communication facilities regarding their telephone matters. The meeting looked at the existing facilities in the Middle East and South Asia. Also discussed at the Lahore meeting were ways to improve the circuits and routing. Iran wanted to add a European relay point and a second route to the United States. They began forming connections between Paris-Tehran and a New York to Tehran from Paris.[67] In Iran, there were more than 45, 278 motorcycles and 10,550 touring cars. The majority of cars imported into Iran were American with Jeep and Chevrolet at its height and British with Vauxhall and Austin.[68] Another accomplishment that occurred in Iranian political economy was the construction of the Iranian state railways that extended from Shahpur to the Persian Gulf and to the Caspian Sea- a distance of 1,388 kilometers. Between Andimisk and Dohrud, it was a difficult extension because of the ascent, but the Iranians constructed the ascent, together forming the most difficult railway accomplishment in the world. There are also 114 tunnels created across Iran.[69] This small introduction was to provide the reader a sense of what Iran was like economically and what challenges, difficulties, and organizational tasks they faced in the new independent era of Iran.

This independence began with a keen interest by the United States to get involved in Iranian affairs. Though the First Revolution began in 1951 with the rise of Mossedegh, the United States was interested in Iran under the Truman administration in the Pre-revolution era. In February of 1950, the United States was making arrangements to provide military and economic assistance to Iran. The Shah of Iran was concerned that American aid would not reach Iran's borders, but the State Department was insistent that aid would arrive.[70] The State Department

---

[67] AEmbassy Tehran, 1951 December RG 59, 988.2300[988.2100].

[68] Enclosure number 1 to Dispatch no. 655, 1951 December. RG 59, 988.51[988.71];enclosure number 2 to dispatch no. 255, 1951 December. RG 59, 988.51[988.70].

[69] Unclassified to Tehran no. 445 1951 December, RG 59, 988.512(988.712).

[70] From George McGhee to Iranian Ambassador Mr. Ala, 7 February 1950. General records of the Department of State. Record number 59. 1950-1954. 788.5MAP/2-750. National Archives. Washington DC. (Hereafter cited as RG 59, with filing information).

signed the agreement between Iran and the United States stating again in a draft letter of February 8, 1950 that "Upon such terms and conditions as may be agreed upon the two governments, and consistently with the principle…economic (edited as Econ) recovery is essential to international peace and unity and must be given clear priority."[71] This agreement excluded the British and the Soviets. The consequence of the American agreement with Iran was a letter by George McGhee, assistant secretary of state discussing the Anglo-Iranian Oil Co. concession dispute:

> The Anglo-Iranian Oil Company concession agreement which was signed last year has not yet ratified by the Iranian Parliament. The Department has informally been suggesting to the British that the chances of ratification might be enhanced if some public statement of principle were issued indicating that the British did not have a closed mind on certain Iranian desiderate….[72]

The closed mind was because of the lack of Iranian personnel and the majority of Indian workers in the company. What was happening was that Iran was on a path toward mental independence, and mentally prepared to sacrifice everything for nationhood. They were noticing that the British usually accumulated large reserves of oil, giving Iran only a 20 percent share. This share was not enough any more. The State Department told England to give Iranians more concessions to make the deal go through.[73] The economic development and recovery Iran needed was to come from three sources: "additional credit from Bank Melli which rough estimate indicates could be as much as rials 2.5 billion; U.S. loans, or loans and AIOC payment under supplemental agreement." This supplemental payment by AIOC was to be 6 million pounds. The British position is more worthwhile because U.S. funds *still* won't make a difference. But, this all required negotiation and someone from London to come to Tehran from the AIOC London

---

[71] Outgoing telegram: Department of State. 8 February 1950. RG 59. 788.5/MAP/2-850.
[72] From Mr. Hare to George McGhee, 20 June 1950 RG 59. 888.2553AIOC/6-2350

[73] From Mr. Hare to George McGhee, 20 June 1950 RG 59. 888.2553AIOC/6-2350

Office to negotiate and accept an agreement by both parties.[74] This negotiation was flagged in the political section as an oil diplomacy relationship between the United States, Great Britain, the Soviet Union, and Iran. Instead of getting 6 million pounds, the British gave 8 million pounds and Iran was still not satisfied, laying off more than 25,000 rail construction workers. They could not find any more funds.[75]

Even after the advance, Iran hoped that the concession agreement would be satisfied. The British were quite pleased that everything was back on track. In a seven month period they produced 18, 493,000 tons of oil compared to a March 1943 number of only 2,195,000 of oil.[76] The financial benefits for the Iranians to sign this agreement were great. Mr. D'arcy knew the commercial risk was great since it might produce wars or a threat of war and some conditions that would remain fragmented in the Middle East. But this concession brought forth by Mr. D'arcy gave 16 percent of royalties to the Iranian government. In the 1930s, this amount was lower. In fact, under the 1933 agreement, Iran was making 13,589,000 pounds when under the new revision; they could have made 22,890,000 pounds. The AIOC felt that they were a "good and profitable tenant of the Government operating under a lease that will be valid until 1993 when all its properties in Persia will be converted to the government." Great Britain was assured a large increase in payments for its leases. They also admitted they considered the Persian government and its agreement since 1933.[77]

While the negotiations were taking place, the United States got their chance to investigate Iran a bit and see if Iran was a suitable place for further investment and perseverance. A letter dated December 26, 1950 by Andre Delanjian, an owner of an Oriental rug business in

---

[74] From Tehran -2#111. 20 June 1950 RG 59. 888.2553AIOC/6-2350
[75] Tehran to Secretary of State, 14 September 1950, RG 59 888.2553-A IOC/9-1450.
[76] Tehran to Secretary of State, 7 September 1950, RG 59 888.2553-AIOC/9-750
[77] Notes on the benefits derived by the Iranian government and Nation from the operations of the AIOC. 7 September 1950. RG 59. 888.2553-AIOC/9-750.

Massachusetts sent a letter to Dean Acheson, Secretary of State, about a friend from his childhood who was ready to share patents, ideas, and secrets of the Iranian government with the United States.[78] Dean Acheson replied that he thanks Delanjian for writing the letter. He states:

> You may assure Mr. Simonian (astronomer, scholar, man with secrets) that he is most welcome to or to confer personally with officers of the American Embassy at Tehran concerning any matter he said would be of interest to the United States Government…

He stated that Simonian was also requested to send drawings of his patents, but only patents of military defense arrangements would be considered.[79] This sense of having a regional military arrangement was happening in 1950.

In order to compensate for budget deficits and the rising prices for food because of the shortage of agricultural production, on January 27, 1951, the Shah sold crown land that belonged to his father to peasants. The money from the sale was used to create "productive sources and companies useful to farmers, and the profits from these enterprises will go to the same charities which had previously been receiving benefits from the Royal properties." The Shah wrote to Jalal Shademan, manager of the crown lands estates, "Whereas, it has been our heartfelt desire that the arable lands of His late majesty the Shahinshah, our august father, which were transferred to us in conformity with law, should pass ownership of the farmers of each locality themselves."[80] The crown lands are 1,677 villages that would be distributed to 17 communities and the majority of them were located in the Mazanderan province.[81] An example of the cost of living index for food was 816 in November, and 833 in December of 1951. Meat, fruits, raw materials, and clothing were all getting expensive.[82]

---

[78] Andre Delanjian to Dean Acheson 26 December 1950. RG 59. 888.172/12-2650.

[79] Acheson to Delanjian 21 February 1951. RG 59. 888.172/2-2151

[80] HV Geib: Land Reform- Sale of Royal properties. 27 August 1951. RG 59. 888.20/8-2751.

[81] HV Geib: Land Reform- Sale of Royal properties. 27 August 1951. RG 59. 888.20/8-2751.

The Refining of Opium in Iran

Although the story of opium is considered insignificant, it is however considered imperative. Opium was a poppy crop grown in Iran and shipped to the State Department. In exchange, the State Department gave lots of money and funneled extra money through this exchange so Iran could grow and purchase more than 20,000 tons of sugar. The growth of sugar allowed them to become a sugar monopoly, defeating their counterpart the Soviet Union and weakening the Soviet monopoly. The United States also maintained proceeds from the sugar monopoly of Iran. In a dispatch on January 13, 1951, opium began to be refined. This statement was prepared by Stewart Smith who outlined how the American consulate toured the opium factory on January 13, 1951.[83] My inclination is that the opium was used to build America's stable pharmaceutical business that we have today. This poppy crop is raised in the spring in various parts of the country. Its final despot is in Isafahan, the location of the country's "only opium refining plant, where it is purchased by the government." The growers are paid for the net weight of the crop they grow. The raw opium is removed by hand from the transporting tins and placed in large containers for the sampling process. In the sampling, they determine and produce the drug morphine.[84]

And the negotiations continue…

By March 12, 1951, there is growing terrorism, xenophobia and hatred of the AIOC. The State Department recommended to AIOC officials to make a public statement and provide equal terms similar to the Aramco formula.[85] The Aramco formula was for Saudi Arabia to represent

---

[82] Cost of Living index. 1951 November. General Records of the Department of State. Record number 59. 1950-1954. 888.062/11-51 National Archives. Washington DC. (Hereafter cited as RG 59).

[83] John Ordway, American Consul Iran to Department of State. 13 January 1951, General Records of the Department of State, Record Number 59, 1950-1954, 888.3932/1-1351 National Archives. Washington DC; (hereafter cited as RG 59, with filing information).

[84] Stewart Smith *The Refining of Opium in Iran.* 13 January 1951 RG 59. 888.3932/1-1351.

[85] Tehran to Department of State, 28 February 1951, RG 59. 888.3932/2-2851.

the Arabian American Oil Company. Aramco was known as the most important petroleum company and their pricing was of huge importance in the market. Aramco dealt with wholesale motor gasoline, kerosene from Arabia and Kuwait, diesel fuel. In Saudi Arabia, Aramco was selling American gasoline worth at 0.7398 in Al Khobar to 0.8705 in Jeddah in lots of 1,000 gallons or more. Iran wanted a similar equation.[86] At 12:00 noon on March 17, 1951, the State Department was thinking of a re- AIOC nationalization program. Though objecting later to the nationalization since it ceased to benefit the United States, the United States was kind to consider a nationalization program because it would limit British and Soviet interest. The United States says:

> While in general US does not favor nationalization, US recognizes **right of sovereign states to nationalize provided prompt payment [and] compensation made. However, this policy not publicized abroad as it might encourage foreign states to nationalize.** [87]

The United States wanted to economically weaken the Soviet position through American aid and American contracts with oil. Oil, opium, export-import programs and the condemnation of the Tudeh community party were all the works of America. During 1951, the State Department was, however, not opposing nationalization because if such opposition took place, it would ruin the relations between the United States and Iran *and might result in loss of Iran to Soviets.*[88] In an economist article of 1951, it stated that the Iranian government would use the money from its oil revenues to sell nationalized oil, and the new company for Iran would give AIOC 300 million of sterling pounds to be paid in 40 years.[89] This nationalism however turned in to a fanatical movement and if not controlled, law and order would break down, the "well

---

[86] Department of State to Dhahran, 6 May 1950. RG 59. 888.3932/5-650.

[87] Department of State to Tehran, 17 March 1951, RG 59. 888.3932/3-1751.

[88] Department of State to Tehran, 17 March 1951, RG 59. 888.3932/3-1751.

[89] London to Department of State, 5 May 1951, RG 59. 888.00-FA/5-551

organized Communist Tudeh Party, could in doubt says Economist, organize coup d'état and take over the country."[90] Since Iran was working with the United States, Congress approved an Aid Bill giving $25 million grant aid program for Iran. This aid was to help the agriculture, village, and rural improvement program, housing, vocational education, sanitation and water, water in small towns, small roads, and goods. The grant in May 18 was actually $24,882,300, but Iran received on June 6, 24,050,000.00. [I] "would appreciate explanation of difference and also program break-down."[91] In October 22, 1951, the reply came back to Dr. Claude Forkner of New York about the $24 million dollar legislation not yet passed in Congress for the village and agricultural development of Iran. This aid was to attack the major problems and improve rural life, education, health, and productivity.[92]

In a newspaper article of April 1951 just before the United States began their initial and arduous diplomatic relationship with Iran, the newspaper clippings were reading: *Britain reserves the right to act as we see fit to protect British lives and property in Persia.* These clippings were stemming from the order that all British oil properties seceded to Iran. Great Britain was not pleased and made the above declaration in the House of Commons. They continued to say "We hold the Persian Government responsible for all injuries and losses that may be sustained by British nationals and interests."[93] Great Britain became concerned about the lives of British nationals working at British-owned properties in Iran. These riots came from a crowd of 4,000 in contact with the Persian military and resulted in injuries and deaths of British citizens.[94] Three hours later, the Shah responded to Herbert Morrison's statement by dismissing

---

[90] London to Department of State, 5 May 1951, RG 59. 888.00-FA/5-551
[91] Tehran to Secretary of State, 12 June 1951 RG 59 888.00-FA/6-1251.
[92] Claude Forkner, 22 October 1951, RG 59 59 888.00-FA/10-2252.
[93] Embassy at London to Tehran, 13 April 1951, RG 59, 988.6241/4-1351
[94] Embassy at London to Tehran, 13 April 1951, RG 59, 988.6241/4-1351

the Governor of the oilfield province and sent an army commander, General Shahbakht, to stop the riots.[95] In another newspaper article, the "high diplomacy procedures" told AIOC to withdraw its $585,000,000 dollars worth of properties to the government of Iran. The Iranian Parliament said: *or else take the responsibility for starting world war III. This is no shallow threat what the oil-hungry Soviet Russia just across the mountains.* [96] America and Europe received a constant World War III threat, which the United States responded calmly and most energetically to, while Britain tried to insert their own views. The reason for this nationalization of oil was to nationalize the country to be Iranian.[97] In a Los Angeles *Times* article dated May 16, 1951, the Iranian government says the British government must take steps to abandon their commitments to the Abadan refineries of the AIOC- *an international clash might follow and precipitate World War III.*[98]

Many critics of Britain's foreign policy with China and their limited role in the Korean War say that Great Britain must pull out and surrender their interests because their interests could lead to total destruction of the Middle East. Iran has claimed that the refineries are the national properties of Iran. But, besides prestige and an ongoing assessment of imperialism, Great Britain- as the article claims- needs the daily production of 400,000 barrels of oil from Abadan because it is their single largest investment.[99] There is an additional 100,000 barrels refined at a refinery in Bahrain that is under United States control. The property is valued at $585 million *as the fact that the British government controls between 52 percent to 54 percent of company stock.*[100] Moreover, this Iranian oil supplied to the Army, Navy, and the British war

---

[95] Embassy at London to Tehran, 13 April 1951, RG 59, 988.6241/4-1351
[96] Embassy at London to Tehran, 13 April 1951, RG 59, 988.6241/4-1351
[97] Embassy at London to Tehran, 13 April 1951, RG 59, 988.6241/4-1351
[98] United States to Tehran, 17 May 1951, RG 59, 988.6241/5-1651
[99] United States to Tehran, 17 May 1951, RG 59, 988.6241/5-1651

[100] United States to Tehran, 17 May 1951, RG 59, 988.6241/5-1651

machines of the Queen of England. This agreement signed in 1933 between Iran and England provided an average gross revenue of $200 million dollars a year. But the royalties given to Iran were considerably lower compared to the royalties given to other oil-rich Middle Eastern countries from the United States.[101] In just 1951, Iran only made 214, 905,002.80 million rials in their last quarter.[102] This agreement would end in 1993, but now the country faced religious fanatics and the Communist Tudeh party, two forces binding the government. The two options that Great Britain had: complain to the UN International Court for breach of contract, or not complain about the decision and work to modify new terms. The new terms were: *lock, stock and barrel, run it themselves and sell the oil to 11 companies.* This nationalization was also going to potentially hurt American investment in Bahrain as the Tudeh party informed Bahrain to nationalize their oil, weakening the American position in the Middle East and destroying their access to 10 million barrels of oil a day and $237,476,547.95 of revenues from Bahrain. It may not have happened since Bahrain was not part of Iranian territory, but any hasty decision could lead to serious repercussions.[103]

Seven Year Plan

In May, 1951, Charles Stein Jr. from Beverly Hills, California wrote a letter to Dean Acheson inquiring about the United States' position on the seven year plan. In his letter he stated that *Fortune* magazine called the State Department "vacillating and inconsistent" because the State Department did not fight hard enough to get money from Congress. He calls the data

---

[101] United States to Tehran, 17 May 1951, RG 59, 988.6241/5-1651

[102] Dispatch No 470 4 October 1951 RG 59, 888.2553/10-451
[103] United States to Tehran, 17 May 1951, RG 59, 988.6241/5-165; Dispatch 822. 2 May 1951 RG 59 888.2553/5-251

"vague and undocumented" and liberal magazines support the State Department's policies.[104] Acheson responds in 1951 that the seven year plan was the work of the Iranian government in 1949, who allocated their revenues for the achievement of this plan. But, "the budgetary and administrative difficulties as well as the financial consequences of the unresolved oil dispute [weakened their success]." Acheson further notes that the United States would economically and socially develop Iran by "providing military aid under the Mutual Defense Assistance Act, providing over $1 million for rural development, and by the export-import bank, give $25 million for agricultural and highway development."[105] A concerned Iranian friend wrote to Henry Dawes that the seven year plan required the United States to give Iran $250 million according to American advisors who surveyed the situation in Iran and paid them $3.5 million dollars, but no aid had arrived. "Now two years of our Seven Year Plan have passed and still there is no sign of loan." [106]

Part 1: Section 3- Military Developments

Political developments showed America's goal was to establish a solid oil agreement between all the parties. The goal was to get America's foot in the door. Economically, the United States wanted the oil industry to nationalize and remove British and Soviet influences in Iran. Militarily, the United States wanted to continue their missions in providing military aid and training to Iran. In these few years, the United States extended military aid, training, and a defense system to the Iranians. The U.S. military mission was present in Iran and the United States wanted to expand their military influences in Iran for a potential regional defense system against the Soviets.

---

[104] Charles Stein to Dean Acheson. 23 May 1951 RG 59 888.00/5-2351
[105] State Department to Stein. 25 June 1951. RG 59 888.00/6-2551
[106] Henry Dawes to State Department, 12 January 1951, RG 59, 888.00/1-1251

The biggest factor motivating the United States to enter Iran was that *Iran was one of the few countries along the Russian border that has remained outside the Communist fold.*[107] The United States wanted to maintain this and did not want the Tudeh party or other communist elements from turning Iran into a communist nation. But ever since World War II, Iran had been under pressure from Moscow. With the help of the UN, it forced the Red Army to withdraw from Iranian soil known today as Azerbaijan. In April of 1950, the Tehran American Embassy says that *Iran is in the midst of a cold war.*[108] The whole idea of this thesis is to show how the United States won the Cold War by using Iran and its political, economic, and military developments to win the Cold War in the Middle East and defeat the Soviet Union. Iran *constitutes part of a front upon which that cold war is conducted.*[109] It is further known that Iran was standing *firm* in this war and *wished to preserve its independence and hopes for the aid of like-minded countries in attaining that end.*[110] Already in 1950 the Shah was negotiating for medium tanks. But the United States felt that these medium tanks were difficult to maintain and did not have many spare parts. The United States did not want to give Iran more complicated machines as the country already had a track record of not being able to maintain complicated machinery.[111] In addition to the cost of parts, $1.3 million dollars, Iran had to buy 50 tanks.[112] But in 1950 when food and hunger were at their height, the Shah was negotiating for more military might. General Azizi believed there was no reason for an Iranian army if the country had no food or sanitation. The unrest in the government also spread to army officers who lost confidence and "for a few

---

[107] Tehran to Secretary of State, 23 April 1950 RG 59 788.5 MAP/4-2350
[108] Tehran to Secretary of State, 23 April 1950 RG 59 788.5 MAP/4-2350
[109] Tehran to Secretary of State, 23 April 1950 RG 59 788.5 MAP/4-2350
[110] Tehran to Secretary of State, 23 April 1950 RG 59 788.5 MAP/4-2350
[111] Tehran to Secretary of State, 24 March 1950 RG 59 788.5 MAP/3-2450
[112] Minutes of the United States Iranian Meeting 25 April 1950 RG 59 788.5 MAP/4-2550.

rials, both civil and military officials are ready to sell themselves to foreigners."[113] Loyalty existed no more in Iran. General Rukhi stated that Iran was in a deteriorating state.[114]

The other main concern was the border routes. Despite strengthening Turkey or Greece, the Russians could take three routes into Iran and through Iraq. On these routes the military should be present and if the Russians did over extend themselves, then the Iranians could fight back. But in order for the resistance movement to be successful, Iran needed supplies to fortify its strategic locations. Also the Shah stated that the people would fight against communism. In order to combat these violent threats, the Shah told of British and American aid that would come to the rescue.[115] But what came to the rescue was not only aid, but also the influx of military bases in Iran and military training. The Department of Defense was interested in performing a list of training exercises and films needed. In all, the Defense Department wanted to also include an equipment list for Iran. It was through a program with the U.S. Army that the funding and execution of these lists occurred. Another program that was occurring was the MDAP program, which was the mutual assistance program providing assistance to Iran and its military.[116] In May of 1950, the Mutual Defense Assistance Act was established and diplomatic notes mention that there will be an understanding that the United States would manufacture military items given to Iran. The purpose of these military weapons was to protect Iran from any foreign threat. The State Department suggested, *the policy of our two countries is to work for peace, prepare for war*. It is similar to the pre-WWI notation that if you want peace, prepare for war. Peace in the mindset of Americans was not surrendering before aggression; *it was the right and duty of free nations to deter aggression*. The United States felt that the best way to defeat aggression was for

---

[113] Department of State to Tehran 1 May 1950 RG 59 788.5/5-150.
[114] Department of State to Tehran 1 May 1950 RG 59 788.5/5-150.
[115] Department of State to Tehran 1 May 1950 RG 59 788.5/5-150.

[116] Tehran to Department of State 13 May 1950 RG 59 788.5 MAP/5-1350.

the aggressor to recognize that *his prey* had economic and military strength to resist. The US

government said, "The purpose of our military assistance program is to help to [achieve] such

strength."[117]

In light of the Mutual Assistance program, the Government of Iran in exchange, agreed to

produce, transport, export, and facilitate the transfer of raw and semi-processed items to the

United States. Iran would engage in these affairs without threatening the security of their nations.

Both governments would take precautions and the United States would transfer military

assistance to Iran. The terms of the agreement would not be transferable and both governments

would grant tax exemption to the export of their products. Iran also agreed to receive United

States personnel to discharge their processing of raw and semi-processed materials.[118] In essence,

before the United States became interested in the politics of communism and the oil diplomacy

of Iran, its first inclination was to achieve their victory through military means. It was military

power and the early development of military aid and assistance that garnered their political and

economic strength in the region. So, oil politics was the main thing that got the United States

involved as later espoused, it was military power that interested the country initially. After

Military Assistance was passed, it was confirmed that the U.S. Army would supply equipment

and training. Any surplus C-47 spare parts from the army and Material Department of the U.S.

Air Force were to be made available to the Iranian State Airways.[119]

Another fundamental step the United States took in the military affairs of Iran was the

issue of transferring Iran from Title III to Title II in the Mutual Assistance Program. Senator

Knowland of the Senate Foreign Relations Committee examined the issue and Title III countries

---

[117] Department of State to Tehran 19 May 1950 RG 50 788.5 MAP/5-1950.
[118] Department of State to Tehran 19 May 1950 RG 59 788.5 MAP/5-1950.

[119] Ohly to Department of Defense 9 June 1950 RG 59 788.5 MAP/6-950.

were those outside of the North Atlantic Pact considered Far Eastern countries and military aid received by them was less than Title I and Title II. Iran advocated that they were a strategic location for the United States and belonged in Title II with Greece and Turkey. In this way, more aid could also be given to them. The other reason for entitlement under Title II was that Greece, Turkey, and Iran were independent nations and their territorial integrity was a concern. The State Department says, "It is logical that the three countries should be held together in our military assistance program in the manner they are in the political matters within the Department."[120] Following this amendment, in June 1950, the United States gave more than $60,000.00 for the training program for the Iranian Air Force.[121] These moments became quite impressive for the Shah as he was consolidating his power and building a military stronghold in Iran. In early August the Shah stated his approval of the President providing him with additional military aid. He told President Truman that he was overjoyed about his awareness and *the strategic importance Iran and of realization military aid to Iran* was inadequate.[122] The Shah however was saying that the weakest link was in the north where the country was vulnerable to Russian expansionists. The Shah also advised the Americans that the United States should only grant light arms to South Korea to build up their armed forces for internal security. He complimented the success of North Korea and said that South Korea would be inadequate to withstand any Soviet aggression.[123] When General Evans left, the Shah told him how much he wanted a larger army, and would request more funds.[124] In 1950, the Air Force material program cost about $1, 172,072 while training was $59,946.00. Aircrafts, spare parts and equipment cost $987,333.00.

---

[120] Claxton to Rountree 16 June 1950 RG 59 788.5 MAP/6-1650.
[121] Ohly to Department of Defense 28 June 1950 RG 59 788.5 MAP/6-2850.

[122] Tehran to Secretary of State 3 August 1950 RG 59 788.5 MAP/8-350.
[123] Tehran to Secretary of State 3 August 1950 RG 59 788.5 MAP/8-350
[124] Tehran to Secretary of State 3 August 1950 RG 59 788.5 MAP/8-350

In total, the army and Air Force Material program totaled $10,579,867.00.[125] The material program for the army included small arms, machine guns, jeeps, armored cars, artillery, bombs, and supplies. This signaled a cycle of dependence.[126]

In June 1951, Prince M Pahlavi was arrested in Ann Arbor, Michigan for speeding and many traffic violations. He ignored four speeding tickets, got his license revoked, and then drove without a license, spending two nights in jail. The Prince was a U.S. student and did not have immunity, but because of the excellent relationship the United States had with Iran on a military basis, the State Department got involved and tried to keep the case from going to court. Any bad publicity would hurt the ongoing relationship with Iran and the United States.[127]

---

[125] Tehran to Secretary of State 3 August 1950 RG 59 788.5 MAP/8-350

[126] Tehran to Secretary of State 3 August 1950 RG 59 788.5 MAP/8-350

[127] Department of State to Amembassy Tehran 23 June 1951 RG 59 788.5/6-2351

PART TWO:

FIRST REVOLUTION: (1951-1953)
MOSSEDEGH ERA

Part 2: Section 4: Political Developments
The First Revolution
1951 to 1953
Mossedegh Era

The political developments of the pre-revolution focused on resolving the oil dispute with

Great Britain, the Soviet Union and the United States. The initial impetuses of American

involvement in Iran were the economic repercussions that removed British and Soviet's

economic influence. It led to a U.S. military buildup and defense strategies in Iran. The time

period of 1951 to 1953 will be known as the *First Revolution*. After Iran began to grow and

Mossedegh led the nationalization of oil campaign, the *First Revolution* in Iran started with Mossedegh at the helm. It is during this revolution that Iranians revolted against British and Russian control of their oil resources. This section will focus on the premise that America did not want any Soviet influence in Iran. The reasons for the Soviets limited role in Iranian affairs were to: 1) limit communism, and 2) weaken the Soviets. In the Pre-Revolution, we learned that nationalism was the threat against American and Russian infiltration. In order for the U.S. to win the global Cold War, it had to limit the influence of communism and in fact weaken the Soviet organization in Iran. These two sub-fields will be elaborated further in the paper. It primarily limited communism through the American political developments of Iran and weakened the Soviet Union through the American economic and military foreign policies of Iran.

In a May 15, 1951 poll, George Gallup asked the American public a question:

> Do you think the United States should start an all out war with Communist China, or not?

	Who's Who	General Public
Should:	9%	30%
Should not:	84%	61%
No opinion:	7%	9% [128]

The majority of the population did not agree with going into a foreign communist nation and starting a McCarthy-like war against them. Perhaps the response would be similar if Iran was communist…

It was Mossedegh along with other Iranians who joined forces with Americans and helped Iran gain independence, self determination, and created a free enterprise. The United States wanted a percentage of oil in return for their independence. In the beginning the United States supplied economic and military aid while receiving oil proceeds. Mossedegh nationalized oil proceeds, feeling all oil profits should benefit Iran. As a result the United States retracted

---

[128] George Gallup *Gall up survey funds professional*… (Princeton: 1950)

their commitments, ceased all economic and military aid, and through the CIA and important actors in the federal system, overthrew Mossedegh and installed the Shah. The motivations for these acts were oil and money. Throughout this time period, the discussion centered on what Iran wanted. Iran was gaining independence, so America was concerned about Iran joining the CENTO pact with Pakistan and Turkey. Most importantly, America wanted Iran to cease all ties with the Soviets. The Soviets provided very handsome offers and agreements, but to prevent Tudeh Communist and Soviet influences to continue in Iran, all ties had to be broken. But there was a deeper understanding that the United States was at *war* with the Soviets in the Cold War, and the United States wanted to be the regional hegemon and to be more powerful in oil resources than the Soviets. It was a race against not only technology, but hegemony, and power. The United States wanted to beat the Soviet Union economically, militarily, but also politically. By being the sole supplier of goods to Iran, Iran had no other choice but to follow U.S. foreign policies. Iran maintained relationships with Israel for trade, Turkey, Italy, and Japan for rice, and India for textiles. It was also a time that the United States could introduce its military bases into Iran, have American companies and banks invest in Iran to further their revenues, and further the American economy. All and all, there was oil, drug imports and exports, and money into Iran. There were also a significant number of Jews helping the Iranian economy. There were a lot of problems in Iran and the United States wanted to curb their problems with United States money because it was profitable for them to do so.

First Revolution Infrastructure Politics

In 1951, the infrastructure was sporadic. There was a dispute over the electricity rates pending settlement on the low price of fuel. Right now, in 1951, there is a 25 rials or $0.32 cents a month discount and only 18,000 Iranians use private electricity out of 250,000 in Tehran. If the low price of oil was enacted, it oil could be exported at a competitive price, but it would hurt the infrastructure because the lower rates of fuel at a rate of 200 rials ($2.56) per ton at 50 tons a day would total $3,840.00 a month and the loss would be $4,320.00 a month. Though the company would survive, they would make very low profits. There was also a lack of water supply and there was a need for the planning and storing of resources.[129] The Karaj dam project was costing $32 to 36 million for five years giving 33,000 KW capacity and this project was fully funded by the bills that people would pay.[130] But water was lacking and only agricultural expansion of the 65 percent of land that was able to be cultivated and provide irrigation water, was possible. The total area of Iran is 164,000,000 hecatares where 10 percent is cropland and 20 percent is cultivable.[131] In 1951, early developments for infrastructure also included 21,000 tons of rails delivered to the Iranian port for about $2,500.00. Currently, more than half of the population was connected by the Tehran-Tabriz line and a bad gravel road. There are politics going on with Azerbaijan, who feels separated from Iranian culture, both linguistically and ethnically. The solution to this would be to build a railroad to Azerbaijan so they could feel more connected with Iran. The fundamental interest in completing the railroad framework was sneered at by the United States, but with little money, the United States "can share immediately in the credit for the whole railroad." The unfinished section is about 500 kilometers and it will take 1,000 million rials and 35,000 tons of rails later to complete it.[132]

---

[129] Economic Section Office of Great Turkish and Iranian Affairs to Mr. Statesman office, 10 September 1951, RG 59, 888.15/9-1051.

[130] Economic Section Office of Great Turkish and Iranian Affairs to Mr. Statesman office, 10 September 1951, RG 59, 888.15/9-1051.

[131] Embassy Tehran, September 1951, RG 59, 888.15/9-1051

[132] Tehran to the Department of State, 31 August, 1951. , RG 59, 888.15/8-3151

Mossedegh is born....

Before the senate adjourned for the summer session, politicians were speaking of a successor government. They were concerned that Mossedegh wouldn't allow a successor. The government was indecisive on how to handle the situation if he opposed removal.[133] In 1952 Great Britain took Iran to The Hague over an Iranian land dispute. Mossedegh felt the only way to reduce high taxation and remove corrupt financial officials was to have an oil settlement with Great Britain. This settlement aroused much criticism because it appeared that Iran was known again to be enslaved to another colonial power.[134] When the prime minster returned from The Hague, he gave the Shah two choices. The first choice was to keep him, his policies, and his drastic economic changes, or accept a new government. He was ready to offer his resignation. If no decision was made, Prime Minister Dr. Mossedegh was to give responsibility to Parliament. But, Parliament also felt that they were unable to continue politically without oil revenues.[135] Newspaper articles called for Mossedegh's retirement. No one knew if he was to be re-nominated. Whatever decision was made, it was agreed that it needed to be made by Iranians for their future, not foreign interests. *Mosadeq* was identified as the "Fuhrer" who would sell his oil to "*commies.*" He said, "Owing an imbalanced budget, I would be compelled to sell its oil to *any interested customer.*" [136]What occurred was the opposite. Mossedegh resigned and was subsequently re-appointed as Prime Minister of Iran. The Mossedegh government resigned on July 5, and the next speaker was to be Moazami, a leader strongly opposed to Mossedegh, but

---

[133] Tehran to Department of State, 23 June, 1952 General Records of the Department of State, Record number 59, 788.00/6-2352, National Archives, Washington DC (hereafter cited as RG 59, with filing information)
[134] Tehran to Department of State, 23 June, 1952, RG 59, 788.00/6-2352

[135] Tehran to Department of State, 2 July 1952, RG 59, 788.00/7-252.

[136] Tehran to USAFE 2 July 1952, RG 59, 788.00/7-252

Enami was elected.[137] The Shah in fact wanted to have Mossedegh back in power in 1952. He said that only Mossedegh could deliver a national oil program.

The nationalization of oil was a perfect example to weaken the influence of the U.S.S.R. in Iran. Also, in order to use Mossedegh popularity, the Shah made a plan to have him lead the efforts on a national oil program, then nationalize the oil and the United States will terminate aid to Iran. In result, Mossedegh will lose his popularity and the Shah and the United States can easily overthrow him later. It was in the interest of both the Shah and the United States to nationalize the oil and remove all Soviet and British influence from Iran.

The Tehran Bazaar also threatened to close if Mossedegh was not elected. In essence, 52 votes from the Majlis went to him over 2 to Qavam. The quick response of the lower house pocketed the bill and gave it to the Shah who decided to vote for Mossedegh. So the senate assumed "Mosadeq would be granted a vote of confidence only on the merits of his proposed future course of action."[138] But later there were not enough votes for the Shah with nineteen casting blank ballots and fourteen were in favor. The senate was very much opposed to Mossedegh, but the Shah insisted and reprimanded them for an inconclusive vote. They went to Mossedegh who later presented a bill for plenary powers for six months.[139] Also, Dr. Enami was elected as Speaker. But, during this election, Iran witnessed three new opposition parties. But, the election of the House speaker 'broke dictatorship of Mosadeq and Kashaniu.' People in Iran believed that Mossedegh had to retract from his impractical views; though the force of his support was great. In order to generate revenue, Mossedegh initiated strategies that included "heavier taxes, budget without oil revenues, circulation of new bank notes, dismissal of half of government employees." He also planned to reduce a number of government servants' salaries.[140]

---

[137] Tehran to USAFE 8 July 1952, RG 59, 788.00/7-852
[138] Tehran to Department of State, 8 July 1952, RG 59, 788.00/7-852
[139] Tehran to Department of State, 15 July 1952, RG 59 ,788.00/7-1552

Iran could live a little longer without *oil diplomacy,* but sold its first share of oil on July 8, 1952 to Waldron and Nelson Co. in Denver, Colorado for $500,000. The delivery would be made before the end of the year, even though a United States agreement would not be available. American technicians also assisted in the construction of a new oil well that would give 1,000 barrels a day. The Soviet government also protested to the Americans giving U.S. military aid to Iran.[141]

In 1952, trade began between USSR and Iran. The goal of the economic -trade policy between the Soviet Union and Iran was to in fact limit the conduct of communism in Iran. The soviets felt that a trade policy would bring them closer to Iran, but it actually brought them farther apart. Iran wanted to import sugar and other goods of Iran to in essence make them weak against their own product. Later, the Iranians developed a sugar monopoly and a trade dependent policy which the Soviet Union had no other choice but trade with Iran. In 1952, the Soviets had a monopoly on newsprint, *sugar,* cheap cotton goods, and cement. This trade grew Iran's economy and benefitted the country. Indeed, later in Iranian history, Iran became the sole producer and supplier of sugar, creating a sugar monopoly, which the United States received proceeds from Iran.[142] Despite Mossedegh being re-elected, Mossedegh wanted plenary powers for six months and the Shah refused to give them. Mossedegh gave the Shah an ultimatum: to accept his proposal of plenary powers by 8:00 PM or accept his resignation. At 8:30 PM, the Shah made the decision and the following day announced to the Majlis that Mossedegh had resigned. They appointed Qavam who had received only two votes, prime minister. Iran returned to violence, calling Qavam a traitor as he began ways to bring the British back into Iran. Iran had "demonstrations and riots all over the country." Qavam told the Shah to dissolve the majlis,

---

[140] Tehran to USAFE, 8 July 1952, RG 59 , 788.00/7-852
[141] Tehran- Department of State 8 July 1952, RG 59, 788.00/7-852
[142] Tehran- Department of State, 1 July 1952, RG 59, 788.00/7-152

arrest those departments and restore order. The Shah complied with hesitance.[143] Riots and violence swept through Iran and the people demanded the return of Mossedegh. The Tudeh communist party took advantage of the situation and along with the National Front collaborated and destroyed Tehran. Qavam was forced to resign, but the Tudeh party still continued their violence and the National Front decided not to associate themselves with such leftist elements of society. Then Mossedegh was "swept back into power on the wave of the popular uprising," 61 members out of 64 voted for the former prime minister. The ICJ declared themselves incompetent because of the AIOC allegations that Iran "lifted [Mossedegh] prestige to unprecedented height." The opposition was slowing down, but the Tudeh communist party was greater than ever.[144] After returning to power, Mossedegh began the rise of himself. His government fought unemployment by balancing the budget, charging a levy of 2 percent on real estate, and increasing the price of sugar and other *monopoly items.* The levy on real estate would bring in about 3 billion rials, covering their deficit. Also, foreign aid would be a new possibility, but it would undermine the currency. The rise of the Mossedegh government was on its way. Now they felt independent and Iranian. The next thing was to get more money into Iran and review their foreign aid options.[145]

The Foreign *Exchange*

In September 1952, Iran's major political concern was the United States and the United Kingdom August 30 oil proposal, which would allow the export of oil to generate some oil revenues. Iran said, that we continue to have the "utmost interest" in the oil dispute. In exchange

---

[143] Tehran to Department of State, 22 July 1952, RG 59, 788.00 (W) 7-2252

[144] Tehran to Department of State, 29 July 1952, RG 59, 788.00 (W) 7-2952

[145] Tehran to Department of State, 12 August 1952, RG 59 788.00/(W) 8-1252

for oil, Iran would receive $10 million, but should've in fact gotten $1 billion.[146] The goal of this *exchange* was a shift in power politics. While the West were making segway into Iranian politics, the Soviet Union strategies in Iran were weakening because of Western influence. With the decision pending, Great Britain threatened to use force if the decision did not go their way and would come to the Iraq-Iran frontier. In October, the United States and United Kingdom's replies finally arrived regarding Iran's request for nationalization of its oil. These were joint proposals that they would consider further compensation and negotiations between the AIOC and Iran. The United States and United Kingdom were surprised by Mossedegh's proposals, especially the United Kingdom who wanted to settle the matter in a very courteous and kind way. Due to this oil proposal, Bank Melli transferred 300,000 rials to 3 billion rials into different reserves of capital.[147] In a reply to President Truman regarding the oil proposals, Mossedegh thanked Truman for his solution to and acknowledged the procrastination of Iran. When Mossedegh replied to the British, he offered them one to three weeks of negotiations within the limits of the agreement. He asked them to give 20 million pounds initially and several million pounds later. Tehran was indeed optimistic about this proposal and expected more negotiations, but Great Britain was not pleased. This news reached Iran and Iran decided to sever diplomatic relations with the United Kingdom. Also in October, the Iran-Polish agreement was signed which was to "export oil, lead oxide, manganese and agricultural products".[148] In the month of November, Iran showed America's interest in purchasing U.S. oil and aid. They began prosecuting Qavam, and seized his properties while he was awaiting trial. There were talks that Iran was beginning negotiations with the Soviet Union through the Caspian Fisheries agreement,

---

[146] Tehran to Department of State, 12 September 1952, RG 59, 788.00/ (W)9-1252

[147] Tehran to Department of State, 1952 October, RG 59, 788.00.10-1952
[148] Tehran to Department of State, 1952 October, RG 59, 788.00/10-1952

the return of Iran gold, and the 1921 USSR-Iran treaty and its revisions.[149] These oil negotiation was a strategy to limit communism.

In January 1953, the oil negotiations began between Ambassador Henderson of America and Prime Minister Mossedegh. On January 13, a bill was proposed to extend Mossedegh's plenary powers for another year and on January 19, the Majlis extended his powers beyond the six month cutoff date of February 9th . The national response to the extension of his powers in newspapers were:

> Full powers should be extended 1 year so Mosadeq can succeed in obtaining just claims of Iran (Kayhtc-Independent). Granting powers will mean dictatorship. No single person should possess such powers (Siasate Me court). Mosadeq has condemned our constitution to slow death. Man who claims liberal breeding has become absolute despotic ruler (Dad- anti-govt). Imperialistic US Dept State interferes in what only entirely domestic concern.[150]

In 1953, the Muslim year was 1332 and the budget was 2,552, 278, 500.[151] After the powers of Mossedegh were extended, Mossedegh became a very strong man in Iran. The nation loved him. Despite being criticized by Majlis President Kashani for "violating rights of people," he asked the nation to remain united and was happy that his one year subsequent plenary power extension reduced the power of the Majlis president.[152] Externally, the USSR acknowledged that the fisheries problem was a problem shared between Iran and the Soviets. They wanted to begin new trade in that area, an encouragement being opened through Tudeh. There were U.S. reports that the United States was publishing anti-Soviet propaganda about the fisheries problem. In response, the Soviets said to respect all rights of sovereign nations.[153]

---

[149] Department of the Army, 19 November 1952, RG 59, 788.00/11-1952
[150] Department of the Army, 1953 February, RG 59, 788.00/2-1952
[151] Tehran to Department of State, 1953 20 January, RG 59, 788.00/1-2052
[152] Tehran to Department of State, 27 January 1952, RG 59, 788.00/1-2752
[153] Tehran to Department of State, 27 January 1952, RG 59, 788.00/1-2752

While the potential oil agreements between the United States and Iran were in the process, concerns began to rise from local oil producers. Here is such a concern from a corporation trading company in the United States in February of 1953 to the U.S. State Department:

> We are interested in finding out if a United States Citizen, or a Corporation, organized under the laws of any of the states here, could *legally* hold title to any or all of the oil, both crude and refined oil products, now in dispute between Great Britain and Iran.

The response by Stanley Neteger, Assistant Legal Advisor for Internal Affairs:

> Under present circumstances, this Government believes that the decision whether or not the purchase of oil from Iran should be left to the individuals or firms [acquiring them], and to be depended upon their own judgment.

Essentially, the legal recourse was left to the firms or individuals who were acquiring oil from Iran. All legal happenings thereafter were also the responsibility of the acquiring entity. The United States took no legal measures to promote the acquisition of Iranian oil or capital investments in Iran.[154] In Iran, the rising tension of the nationalist movement had begun to calm down as Mossedegh produced an atmosphere of acceptance that "political developments in near future would either ease political position of Mosadeq." In February, the heightened tension between the Shah and Mossedegh as prime minister led the king to "cease all contact with military figures and with persons deemed unfriendly, give revenues of crown lands and Meshed Shrine properties to government." The Shah agreed to give the crown lands revenue and this weakened any opposition against Mossedegh. Kashani supporters said that this would "delay any attempt to oust Mosadeq, essential factors which have produced this opposition to Mosadeq remain."[155] One of the vocal opponents of Mossedegh was Baqai who had wanted to destroy

---

[154] Industries Corporation to US State Department, 14 February 1953, RG 59, 788.00/2-2553; Department of State to Mr. Glumicich, 20 February 1953, RG 59, 788.00/2-2053.

[155] Tehran to Department of State, 23 February 1953, RG 59, 788.00/2-2352.

him since he was on the Afshartus case. Martial law was paramount in Iran and there were reports that General Zahedi was denying applications for passports to leave Iran. Many government circles and newspapers were optimistic about Iran's financial future because Dulles promised economic aid and a solution to the oil problem. "Pro papers announced Iran's problems would be considered and new policy US toward Iran in offing. But, later Dulles retracted and reports came that his visit to Iran failed. The anti-government papers believed that Mossedegh was unable to maintain a public eye; the US Secret Service also labeled Iran unsafe to visitors".[156] This label came after Mossedegh's letter to Former President Harry Truman in 1953 about his 1951 visit to the United States. President Truman sent him a photograph album. In response, Prime Minister Mossedegh wrote:

> I shall never forget the courteous and friendly treatment which I received from
> you and from many other Americans, both in official and private life, while I was
> in the United States. May I wish for you and your family much happiness in your
> retirement?[157]

In a telegram from Tehran to London, the securities of the borders were imperative. The United States was committed to the security of the Middle Eastern borders, borders that were being trespassed by the British. The British had overwhelming interest in their obligations to Turkey and the commonwealth obligations to Pakistan. The "British fear if Iran moves forward defensive matters and arrangements it might be awkward for them to extend treaty commitments to Iran similar to those they already elsewhere in Middle East." Iran was also reluctant to persuade the British to make a decision earlier in the process on this matter.[158]

---

[156] Department of the Army, 1953 February, RG 59, 788.00/2-1953.
[157] Mossedegh to Truman, 4 February 1953, RG 59, 788.00/2-453

[158] Tehran to London, 4 March 1953, General Records of the Department of State, Record Group 59, 1950-1954, 788.34/3-453, National Archives, Washington DC (hereafter cited as RG 59, with filing information.

The Fall of Mossedegh: July 1953

The period July 1953 to August 1953 was a period known in Iranian history as the *fall of Mossedegh.* This popular leader that swept back into power through popular support was losing his prestige. In fact the American Embassy was receiving reports that the popular prime minister of Iran was losing his popularity. Mossedegh was popular at the time when he took office. His struggle against the Anglo Iranian Oil Co. was paramount and received widespread support from everyone who hated the British. Mossedegh then nationalized oil, giving full control and profit margins to the Iranians. Both the United States and the United Kingdom were deeply upset. But the nationalization of oil also increased his popularity and he was known later as a "demi-God" by some. It was an era that Mossedegh was particular to Iran. The American Embassy said,

> The figure of an old man, in an Oriental country where of itself commands respect, who are to be successfully winning a battle against tremendous odds, aroused by the sympathy of all Iranians. In a country where political corruption had been the accepted norm, there now appeared a man whose patriotism and financial honesty was unassailable.[159]

Despite his personal prestige, the economic and financial position of Iran continued to plummet. It became known in his speeches and oral deliveries that his promises and statements of a better future was farce. It was an "oil-less economy" with not enough gas to fight the resistance against his promised reforms. The Embassy said, "The much promised oil solution which was constantly dangled before the people failed to materialize." His power was encouraged and the means for him to stay in power was further in place. The public saw that the Shah left in July because of the differences between Mossedegh and himself. The differences lay in the imperialism of Iran. Imperialism was better than nationalism. The Shah wanted imperialistic governments to extend their interests and exploit the needs of the country while other incidents suggest that Iran should

---

[159] American Embassy Tehran to The Department of State, 3 July 1953, General Records of the Department of State, Record Group 59, 1950-1954, 788.13/7-353, National Archives, Washington DC (hereafter cited as RG 59, with filing information.

begin to take control of itself. In fact, "the past 150 years, those who have risen to defend the interests of history of the past century clearly shows a sinister policy of foreigners in Iran." Mossedegh even asserted that for the last 32 years the British were trying to spread their imperialistic policy, but Mossedegh did not allow Great Britain to continue their imperialistic notions or to get rid of him. Mossedegh was blaming the British for destroying an effective cabinet and "nullified every measure of reform." Mossedegh was hurt by his encounters with the British during the fifth and sixth terms of the Majlis. He was placed "under police surveillance and under house arrest in my village for fourteen years and also caused my imprisonment in Birjand."[160]

Mossedegh was under surveillance when he mentioned that two women, (one was a mother) stopped his car, and that two men were watching him from a distance. This act 'compelled me to stay in the Majlis for awhile." But this prevented Mossedegh from leaving his home. He feared the crowds and feared of his life. The remaining speeches during his time as prime minister were delivered from his bed and transmitted over Radio Tehran. He was "no longer able to address the people in Parliament square." The Embassy reported, "Mosadeq was no longer the popular here." But, the prime minister did not give up, still intending to remain in office regardless of his lack of popular support. He was to remain as long as Parliament was *one half plus one,* a simple majority he was garnering. He did not have to obtain votes of confidence anymore, and if the threat of the dissolution of the majlis was not given, the majority would have gone against him. Furthermore, Mossedegh curtailed his problems resolving the oil crisis because of his problems with the Shah. The Embassy says, "There seems to be no doubt that the Prime Minister did in fact "suggest' that the Shah leave Iran." Also, Mossedegh underestimated the Shah's popularity. Though he was not popular, his roots and his position as the Shah of Iran

<hr>

[160] American Embassy to The Department of State, 3 July 1953, RG 59, 788.13/7-353.

impressed people. Mossedegh did not know that his failures with the Shah would lead to a major blow against his position as prime minister. He failed in this issue and began to realize that for the first time in his life, he had failed at a domestic issue. The protest at the Shah's departure led the Majlis to limit the Shah's powers from the "Majlis Eight-Man Committee Report," and the Shah "appeared to have discredited himself with some of those who wished him well." The Shah's opponents were very smart to limit the Shah's powers, but simultaneously, they limited Mossedegh's powers too "i.e. cancellation of the Majlis grant of plenary powers."[161]

Besides his population plummeting domestically, Prime Minister Mossedegh was having difficulties abroad regarding international citizens representing Iran. On July 10, there was an exchange between President Eisenhower and Mossedegh. The exchange led to the rejection of aid by President Eisenhower to help their oil-less economy. No one in Iran knew how Mossedegh was going to retaliate. The comment set forth was to "sit extremely confused," while the United States government was "not supporting Mossedegh personally."[162] There was ongoing friction between Mossedegh and Kashani, but in July 1953, Kashani was defeated by another person who would take lead of the affairs of the Majlis. The *DAD* reports: "Mosadeq-Kashani and dispute can grow into conflagration that may engulf whole country and lead downfall Mosadeq."[163]

Despite the opinion against Mossedegh, on July 27 the prime minister *called upon the Iranian people to indicate in referendum to be held shortly their choice between dissolution of the Majlis and continuation of his government or the resignation of his government.* His choice was to

---

[161] American Embassy to The Department of State, 3 July 1953, RG 59, 788.13/7-353.

[162] US Embassy to Department of State, 14 July 1953, RG 59, 788.00 (W)/7-1453

[163] American Embassy to The Department of State, 14 July 1953, RG 59, 788.00 (W) /7-1453.

dissolve the majlis and elect a new body. Mossedegh intended to secure the dissolution of the Majlis. Mossedegh's members were also thinking of forming a new party that would include all national elements and suppressing any opposition. While this was going on and the Shah was out of the country, Princess Ashraf, the Shah's twin sister returned to Iran.[164]

Overthrow of Mossedegh: August 1953

Throughout Mossedegh's tenure as Prime Minister, the political tenants of Iran's government and the severe inequitable leadership secured Mossedegh's position as leader of a contemporary society. Iran was developing into a modern constitutional state, but many political scientists have asserted that unless a society is ready for democratization, an imposed democracy on a disconnected country will be troublesome. Iran represented a medieval social order that was disconnected with cleavages between classes. "Neither social, economic, or political power is, therefore, distributed equitably or uniformly throughout the nation."[165] Westernization, inability to successfully experience its own governmental process, and an economic factor really tightened Mossedegh's rule. It was on August 3, 1953, that the results of the referendum came in and 544 were in favor of the Majlis dissolution while 115 were against it. From the provinces in Tehran, 400,000 people voted in favor to dissolve the majlis and 180 against it. How do you overthrow a government that the people and the government support? The Shah swept back into power to consolidate his rule and limit communism. But, the *new* Iran began without the support of the population. If a new government takes shape and it does not have the support of the populous, then that government will likely fail and lead to a revolution against the government one day…..

---

[164] American Embassy to The Department of State, 27 July 1953, RG 59, 788.00 (W) /7-1253
[165] N Marbury Efimenco *An experiment with civilian dictatorship in Iran; the case of Mohammed Mossadegh (The Journal of Politic: Southern Political Science Association, 1955) 390.*

Since the government of Mossedegh was not supported by the Shah and the United States, it was an American obligation to imperialize the nation and put who they wanted in power. The press confirmed that Mossedegh would dissolve the 17th Majlis and open elections for the 18th Majlis. Mossedegh had plans to continue curtailing the Shah's military powers. The pro-Mossedegh government criticized the United States for "withholding financial and substantial economic aid." The elements supporting Mossedegh also felt that the United States was helping the British blockade, but still reprimanded Iran for not being able to remove the spread of communism due to the severe economic conditions. The Tudeh party also blamed the United States for intervening in Iranian affairs. In a pro-Mossedegh paper, the Niruye Sevon said, "neither US, London or Moscow but only Mosadeq is victorious. Once again nation punched nose Dulles and Churchill. *Iran now laughing foolishness Dulles and Wall Street magnates.* "[166] Unfortunately, Iran could not laugh long enough. But, Mossedegh knew that he had enemies in the royal court that were plotting against his authority. Despite shaking up the military, possessing civilian control of the military, and replacing lead officers in the army, the Shah was still the commander in chief. By dismissing unreliable officers, Mossedegh created a big gap of hypocrisy and found out that Zahedi, the president of the retired army association wanted to replace him.

The Shah stated that days ago he issued a statement appointing General Zahedi as the new Prime Minister of Iran. While the referendum was about to be voted on and before the results came in, the Shah was planning to remove Mosadeq from power. It was Colonel Nasiri of the Palace Guards that delivered this decree to the general, but faced imprisonment as he attempted to deliver it to Mosadeq. The news never reached Prime Minister Mossedegh. On the night of August 15, news were received that Zahedi and some Army officers were attempting to

---

[166] American Embassy to The Department of State, 03 August 1953, RG 59, 788.00 (W) /8-353.

take over the government. The Shah and Queen left to go to Baghdad during this time. He took a plane to Baghdad and then to Italy while tanks went into Iran. In an interview with an Egyptian newspaper, *Al-Mussavar,* the Shah stated that his plane was ready to fly out and was supposed to give the false impression to Mossedegh that everything was alright and the dissolution of the majlis would bring a new majlis led by Mossedegh. Though Zahedi was the current chief of police, the Shah appointed him as Prime Minister before his departure. The departure was seen as the Shah running away.[167]General Riahi took control of the situation and tried to quench anti-shah sentiments. His men arrested some key figures. Colonel Nasiri wanted to arrest Army Chief of Staff General Riahi, but he had already fled. The Minister of Roafs, Foreign Minister Fatemi, and other notable figures were detained. They went to arrest Mossedegh who was at his residence, disarmed, and the Imperial guards apprehended Prime Minister Mossedegh. Tanks arrived at his home and he surrendered to Zahedi. On August 16, a broadcast at 7:30 AM said: *Imperial decrees dated 13 August dismissing Mosadeq and appointing retired General Fazlollah Zahedi [Prime Minister], first of which Nasiri stated carrying Mosadeq at time arrested.[168]*

The CIA-SIS operations in Iran were controlled by three secret agents: Anthony Cuomo, (American Embassy Political Secretary), Ernst Peron, (Swiss Confidant of the late Shah), and Shapour Reporter, who was a Zoroastrian Iranian. Ernest Peron was a friend of Mossedegh and helped him get released from prison. He also studied with the Shah in Switzerland.[169] They were responsible for a network of Iranian nationals that included newsmen, bank officials, active, and retired military officers. The overthrow of Prime Minister Mossedegh was heavily funded by the CIA. A special report of 1954 entitled *America's secret agents,* by Richard and Gladys Harkness,

---

[167] Homa Katouzian. *Musaddiq's Memoirs.* (London: The National Movement of Iran, 1988). 281
[168] American Embassy to The Department of State, 03 August 1953, RG 59, 788.00 (W) /8-353.

[169] Homa Katouzian. *Musaddiq's Memoirs.* (London: The National Movement of Iran, 1988). 275-276

relays Eisenhower's commitment to the overthrow of Mossedegh. The first signs of this strategy were initiated with Mossedegh's rejection of American economic aid in February 1953. Around February 28, the Shah left Iran based on an urgent note from Ambassador Henderson for a meeting and a quick departure. At 1:00 PM, Mossedegh went to see the Shah to say good-bye and noticed a crowd at the main gates ready to kill him. The people felt Mossedegh was sending the Shah away. He saw the Shah collect all the birth certificates for his family and royal party for the issuance of passports. Mossedegh replied in his memoirs that he would have had the Shah leave in July of 1952 and was no mastermind behind the Shah leaving in February 1953. It was that very night that Henderson called Mossedegh over to his house and said nothing of importance to him. Mossedegh felt the entire day of the Shah's departure and the planned failed assassination was a set-up in which Mossedegh was never supposed to make it to the Ambassador's residence.[170] Before the Shah's planned departure, Mossedegh told the Shah how he respected him and would help his government with any unpleasant incidents. The ongoing events displeased the United States and Henderson became more of an ally to the Shah than to Mossedegh. Mossedegh knew that after the death of Stalin on March 7, 1953, the United States had a clear path to take over Iran.[171] Right before the coup on August 10, CIA director Allen Dulles, U.S. Ambassador Loy Henderson and the Shah's twin sister, Princess Ashraf met in a Swiss resort to discuss the plan. Brigadier General Norman Schwartzkopf went to Iran to see "old friends." He was responsible for Iran's police force from 1942 to 1948. He visited Zahedi and Hassan Arfaa and went to the Shah's summer palace on the Caspian Sea. It was the royal elements and the American strategists that defeated Mossedegh. The principal CIA operative in Iran was Kermit Roosevelt who bribed pro-Shah leaders with money to march into the Prime

---

[170] Homa Katouzian. *Musaddiq's Memoirs.* (London: The National Movement of Iran, 1988). 274-277.
[171] Homa Katouzian. *Musaddiq's Memoirs.* (London: The National Movement of Iran, 1988). 274-276

Minister's residence.[172] Zabih says, "All responsibility for this event [attributes] to the Central Intelligence Agency."[173]

The overthrow was marked by heavy criticism and demonstration by the public. On August 17, Henderson saw Mossedegh and persuaded him that nothing was wrong in society. After Mossedegh was banished to prison, the Henderson told the Shah not to kill Mossedegh.[174]On the eve of the 18th of August, the Tudeh Party began their demonstration seeking no recourse from the ousted Mossedegh. A small, yet rapid pro-Shah demonstration spread throughout the city. Rioters began to roam the streets and army and police began to suppress the crowds. There was considerable destruction of government offices by anti-Shah, pro-Mossedegh and pro-communist supporters. There were considerable numbers of pro-Shah slogans. The radio began transmitting pro-Zahedi speeches to the public. Rioters looted and destroyed the houses of Mossedegh and his sons. Former Chief of Army Staff stated the troops had no control of the military. The Prime Minister had already fled the scene. An 8:00 PM curfew was imposed and streets were cleared.[175]At any moment of rebellion or revolution, a small antagonist usually forms in popular demonstrations. In order to successively carry out a coup, the incoming government needs to quickly establish order and limit the influence of that small antagonist demonstration. If the small demonstration is not controlled, then the small demonstration can multiply in numbers and potentially take over the newly established government. One of the first tasks of the Shah was to arrest members of the Tudeh party, execute them and break their branches in Iran. Once the root is broken, then the demonstrations will cede. On October 19,

---

[172] Sepehr Zabih *The Mossadegh Era.* (Chicago: Lake View Press, 1982). 150;124-125
[173] Sepehr Zabih *The Mossadegh Era.* (Chicago: Lake View Press, 1982). 124-125

[174] Homa Katouzian. *Musaddiq's Memoirs.* (London: The National Movement of Iran, 1988). 285.
[175] US Tehran to Department of State, 25 August 1953 RG 59 788.00/8-2553

Edward Donally gave check number 53145 dated August 22 to the Development Bank of Iran (Bank Melli) for a sum of $390,000.00. That was the cost of the overthrow. The amount equaled 32, 643,500 rials. No one found out who Edward Donally paid off to get rid of Mossedegh.[176] On August 22, 1953, the Shah returned to Iran and was blessed with a state that supported him. Mossedegh argued with the Shah that there was no constitutional amendment and that the Shah had to replace him (Article 64 of Iran's Constitution).[177]

Mossedegh failed due to many reasons. Trying to limit all sources of opposition is problematic. A government cannot please everyone and cannot depend on the *emotional aspirations* of people. A leader like Mossedegh reformed the constitution to stay in power, but by undertaking this task, he circumvented the constitutional process of Iran. A big downfall to Mossedegh's control was that he underestimated the strength of the monarchy. He did not know how much the population really was impressed by the Shah of Iran. At the highest crisis, the army's loyalty was more toward the Shah than Mossedegh. Street demonstrations, riots, and crowds also can weaken the political process, and before the overthrow the crowds were giving signs of the impending coup.[178]

Furthermore, the United States was a huge supporter of the overthrow of Mossedegh's regime. Ever since the nationalization law of 1951 that limited oil to foreign investors and gave complete control over the oil to Iran, the United States had wanted to weaken the Soviet's position and control the oil themselves. The royalties and profits from the AIOC was 12.9 percent of the revenues of Iran. Iran was making 38,000,000 dollars per year and also giving jobs

---

[176] Homa Katouzian. *Musaddiq's Memoirs.* (London: The National Movement of Iran, 1988). 281.

[177] [177] N Marbury Efimenco *An experiment with civilian dictatorship in Iran; the case of Mohammed Mossadegh (The Journal of Politic: Southern Political Science Association, 1955) 403.*

[178] N Marbury Efimenco *An experiment with civilian dictatorship in Iran; the case of Mohammed Mossadegh (The Journal of Politic: Southern Political Science Association, 1955) 403-405.*

to more than 175,000 workers with 67 million in wages. But, "Iranians felt that the profits were in no measure commensurate with the prevailing practice in Saudi Arabia."[179] There were tight battles between Britain and the United States over oil. It produced an uncertainty over the coordination of their policies. Also, the USSR had no stake in the matter. In order to pressure the Mossedegh government and show Iran that it had lost a powerful ally, the United States suspended some military aid in 1952 followed by a suspension of all economic aid unless the *oil question was arbitrated or settled peacefully.* This aid was helping Iran meet its budget deficits, but a suspension of this aid dug a deeper financial hole for Iran. This suspension of aid went against the agreement between the United States and Iran signed on May 23, 1950 in Seoul, Korea. This was confirmed as public law in the 81st Congress of the United States. The 81st Congress confirmed that 'economic recovery is essential to international peace and security must be given clear priority." Since Iran was not meeting the United States' criteria for profitable investment, the United States turned against this international legal agreement as well. The United States promised to help Iran with any material, service, or need- consistent within the UN charter. Iran also promised not to transfer any materials received by the United States to another party and to export to the United States a production or raw and semi-processed materials in exchange for payment. In the agreement, it said, "the Government of Iran will take appropriate measures which are not inconsistent with security and the interests of the country to keep the public informed of operations pursuant to these understandings." Iran also agreed to duty-free exemption and to receive technical support from the United States. In fact, it legally states, "nothing herein shall be construed to alter, amend, or otherwise modify the agreements between the United States of America and Iran."[180]

---

[179] N Marbury Efimenco *An experiment with civilian dictatorship in Iran; the case of Mohammed Mossadegh (The Journal of Politic: Southern Political Science Association, 1955) 393.*

Due to these concerns, the United States felt the Tudeh Party was becoming stronger and increasing its strength. They wanted to intervene before the Tudeh communist party took over the government and potentially handed it over to the Soviets: "the threat of a possible victory of the Tudeh elements endangered American efforts to keep Soviet influence out of Iranian corridor at the head of the Persian Gulf."[181] If the Tudeh government controlled Tehran, then Moscow would create a satellite and would seek the Arabian Peninsula, *the area of American oil interests.* This was the reason why the United States wanted the Shah to have more power in the United States. Due to Iran's nationalization of oil, Iran weakened its political position and became even more dependent on foreign aid. These "changes within the Iranian political scene aptly demonstrate why the Shah and the Army ousted Mossadegh from power."[182]

Part 2: Section 5 Economic Developments

First Revolution

---

[180] *Agreement between the United States of America and Iran* (American Journal of International Law: American Society of International Law, 1951) 76-78.

[181] N Marbury Efimenco *An experiment with civilian dictatorship in Iran; the case of Mohammed Mossadegh (The Journal of Politic: Southern Political Science Association, 1955) 405-406.*

[182] N Marbury Efimenco *An experiment with civilian dictatorship in Iran; the case of Mohammed Mossadegh (The Journal of Politic: Southern Political Science Association, 1955) 406.*

The First Revolution began in 1951 when Mossedegh assumed stature in Iranian politics. In this revolution, political developments discussed that the United States wanted to win the cold war by weakening the Soviet position in the Middle East. This political victory was achieved through the limitation of communist influences, limiting Soviet intake of oil, deposing Mossedegh and conspiring to install the Shah, and numerous other factors mentioned in the political development section. Though the Soviet influence was great, money and the politics of oil diplomacy drove the United States into Iran with the intention of winning the cold war. The main intention of the economic developments of the First Revolution was to weaken the influence of the Soviet Union. The influence weakened because through the economic decisions that revolved around oil politics. Earlier, it was stated that oil politics detached Iran from pan-Arabism and an Iranian nationalism. This path was purely economic as the American persuasion and economic efforts around the oil industry of Iran was to weaken the Soviets and grow Iran. Frankly, the United States needed oil to build its oil industries in the United States. Iran had plenty of it and needed economic assistance. The relationship worked out. American political policies showed how the United States wanted to win the cold war in the Middle East, so that they can become a hegemon and resourceful profitable ruler controlling the oil. The control of the oil led them to the mindset of making profits and giving economic aid to Iran for their needs. During this time, the United States was trying to persuade them to make more oil, and to have a strong export-import development program in which Iran buys American imports and uses the money to export into the United States. Stopping the spread of communist influence was also on the minds of American government officials. Iran would do anything to have an economic aid package.

The Oil Debate Team

This economic development garnered *free flow of Iranian oil* to the west. In a July 28, 1951 article by *Natural Resources,* the author said the free oil is vital to the American economy because it prevents American depletion of domestic oil and builds up other dependent Marshall Plan nations with this oil. By supplying oil to the west and Marshall Plan nations, these nations' economies were being strengthened and required less aid from the United States. Negotiations still continued between AIOC and the United States to keep the oil flowing from its first drill in 1902 in western Iran. From that one well in 1902, many wells followed and the AIOC produced more than 663,700 barrels of oil a day in 1950. The biggest suppliers were Iran, Iraq, Saudi Arabia, Kuwait, Bahrein, and Qatar. These nations had American and British contracts producing larger quantities of oil. The single largest investment was in Iran, which was the debate.[183] Besides the US and AIOC feeling frustrated about the debates, the Shah of Iran was also depressed because the oil under Mossedegh would be nationalized and Iran would own the oil. The Shah was in favor of protecting Great Britain's oil interests and their properties in Iran.[184] But, the next day on June 23, 1951, the *Civil and Military Gazette,* the pro-Soviet and anti-west and the *Pakistan Times,* told the Iranian government about their appreciation of the nationalization of the oil. They were pleased that Iran took over the oil installations and in the *Pakistan Times,* it said: "following final break down of the negotiations between the Government of Iran and the Anglo-Iranian Oil Company, *orders have been issued to the Government's representatives at Abadan for immediate assumption of control over the Company's installation.*[185]

---

[183] *Free Flow of Iranian Oil.* (Natural Resources: Science News Letter, 1951). 53.
[184] Tehran to Secretary of State, 22 June 1952, RG 59, 888.2553-AIOC/6-2251
[185] Tehran to Secretary of State, 22 June 1952, RG 59, 888.2553-AIOC/6-2351

Everybody was getting involved with these debates. A letter addressed to the President of the United States in July 1951 originally by Howard Cowden, President of the Cooperative League made the following suggestions:

> 1. Recognize Iran's right to nationalize its petroleum industry. 2. AIOC retains ownership and marketing facilities. 3. Organize international oil cooperative to produce, refine, transport and market under long-term contract with Iran and AIOC. 4. Directorate to consist of three Iranians, three British and three from consuming countries. [186]

In response to his letter, someone from the State Department wrote back congratulating his role in containing communism, nationalizing Iran's oil with a company managing the oil wells and distribution. The United States was pleased that the nationalization showed the United States' respect for laws, encouraged acquirement of natural resources, and "we could work for the development of the principle of international cooperation in the development and administration of basic natural resources, and this *I think might serve as one of the most effective means of curbing the growth of communism."*[187] Meanwhile, Iran's economic council was creating three bills: 1) a bill to encourage exports 2) a bill to encourage foreign capital investment in Iran 3) a bill that all restrictions of imports and exports were to be lifted.[188]

The month of November 1951 was very boring because Iranians were waiting on the negotiations between the Prime Minister of Iran and Washington regarding the oil dispute. Many were depressed that there would not be an oil settlement and that Iran would face another ruler of its oil, but Iran was in a desperate situation because it needed American financial assistance. Local businesses were also suffering, with less goods, high prices, and an economy at a standstill and "with no oil sales in sight, businessmen wondered how long this sum would last (a sum of

---

[186] Jerry Voorhees to the President of the United States 25 July 1951, RG 59, 888.2553-AIOC/7-2551
[187] State Department to President of Cooperative League, 25 July 1951, RG 59, 888.2553-AIOC/7-2551
[188] Department of State to High Economic Council,5 December 1951, RG 59, 888.00/12-551

$8,750,000 was provided by IMF to Iran)." The financial decline of Iran continued as new taxes brought little revenue. There was also an implementation of a 50 percent monopoly tax for new imported automobiles that sat and rotted in car dealerships across Iran. [189]

The Economic Verdict

In a February 21, 1952 correspondence, the economic summary of Iran was poor. Before the nationalization of the oil and the dispute with the British government, Iran used to receive 30 percent of its revenues from the British-owned oil industry. But consequently, Iran's nationalization and dispute with Great Britain left the country without income since April of 1951, though payroll was still provided by the AIOC.[190] In order to compensate their losses, Iran borrowed 14 million rials from the currency reserve. The foreign exchange and gold held against the notes were also reduced and the termination of the dollar convertibility from Iranian sterling was also rampant. In September, the rate jumped from 47.25 rials for a dollar to 60 rials to a dollar in November.[191] The government reduced expenditures by 15 percent, and limited only one car for one ministry. The money in surplus, the carpet decorated buildings were sold, and salaries reduced. Taxes on liquors and tobacco increased. There were also proposals of a 2 billion rials bond to be created. In November they refined more than 25 million gallons of crude oil, but the oil remained- it was not sold to anyone. There were many strikes and a fear of unemployment.[192]

The other problem for Iran was that sugar was widely used throughout Iran and is the country was dependent on Soviet Russia for sugar, giving them money and a stronger sugar

---

[189] Monthly Economic Report. 22 October 1951 RG 59 888.00/10-2251

[190] No.1 to Dispatch No. 939. 21 February 1952 RG 59 888.00/2-2052

[191] No.1 to Dispatch No. 939. 21 February 1952 RG 59 888.00/2-2052

[192] No.1 to Dispatch No. 939. 21 February 1952 RG 59 888.00/2-2052

economy. Sugar was one of the basic items necessary. Iran needed 180,000 metric tons against a small domestic production of 60,000 metric tons. The goal was to have Iran produce sugar, not buy it from the Soviets and create their own monopoly against the Soviets.[193] The money Iran would get for the sugar production in Iran was through opium sales to the United States. The Iranian government sold $1,750,000 worth of opium to the United States in exchange for 10,000 tons of sugar at a value at $1,480,000. This sugar shortage caused great problems to the country. Also, Iran was negotiating with a Dutch interest company shipping more than 20,000 tons of Iranian barley in exchange for 10,000 tons of sugar well-priced at 30 pounds sterling.[194] In result of this exchange, Iran was on its way in weakening the economic influences and decreasing trade with the Soviet Union.

The railroads owned by Iranian State railways and general transportation increased. The country met the demands of the people. The clothing industry with wool and cotton was flourishing and the amount of exports increased, especially for carpets which increased significantly. The United States also received a portion of the profits in the carpet business and the agreement with Western Germany on trade was effective.[195]

According to a June 16, 1952 report, the beginning of 1951 produced 16,177,000 tons of oil which was 15,573,000 less than the oil produced in 1950. Kuwait, Iraq, and Qatar all increased their oil imports. AIOC now owned only 24, 255,000 tons of oil compared to a 31,507,000 ownership. There was only 12,258,000 processed in 1951. Oil had significantly dropped.[196] However, a late fall report of 1951 said that a dividend payment of 1,600,000 pounds

---

[193] No.1 to Dispatch No. 939. 21 February 1952 RG 59 888.00/2-2052

[194] No.1 to Dispatch No. 939. 21 February 1952 RG 59 888.00/2-2052

[195] No.1 to Dispatch No. 989. 8 March 1952 RG 59 888.00/3-852

[196] American Embassy in London to Department of State, 16 June 1952 RG 59 888.2553 AIOC/6-1652

was made to Iran as part of the concession agreement.[197] The deficit continued and Bank Melli gave 150 million rials to cover the 120 million rials deficit.[198]

Due to the financial crisis of Iran, the local newspapers were publishing reports of a planned military coup by officers in relation to the Tudeh communist party. Though they claimed the story was unfounded, leaders were encouraging the Shah of Iran to take more of *"energetic action"* against Mossedegh.[199] Just then a report came in from the International Court of Justice at The Hague. Mossedegh presented his case on nationalization. Iran planned to deliver oil to Italy and extend trade with Germany and Soviet Union, but the Rose Mary, the ship carrying Iranian oil was seized because it went into a wrong port and Iran claimed ownership of the oil. Italy still strived to renew commitments and to get more oil from Iran.[200] There was an increase in funds in Bank Melli and foreign trade increased. The Soviet Union became Iran's leading customer and third largest supplier of oil. The trade with Germany increased as well and also got attention in South Asian countries as the export of Iranian rice would receive 9 million dollars of revenue.[201]

By July 1952, the State Department determined that Iran would have a monopoly of sugar, cheap cotton goods, cement, and of course newsprint. The Irani-Soviet trade had become quite important because USSR was Iran's best customer and in return received many Russian imports. If trade did continue, Iran would become very dependent on USSR and *hence more amenable to Soviet pressure.* Iran was concerned, but right now, they had no other choice. The oil intended for Italy never reached them and Iran was speculating on who would be Iran's next

---

[197] London to Department of State 19 July 1951, RG 59, 888.2553 AIOC/7-1951.
[198] Tehran to Secretary of State 17 June 1952, RG 59, 888.00/6-1752
[199] Tehran to Secretary of State 17 June 1952, RG 59, 888.00/6-1752
[200] Amembassy to Tehran, 5 July 1952, RG 52, 888.00/7-352.

[201] Amembassy to Tehran, 5 July 1952, RG 52, 888.00/7-352.

purchaser of oil. *There are persistent rumors that American interests will participate in next transaction and that US flag tanker will be used.*[202] The economy was currently undergoing drastic economic reforms and the Tudeh party reported that "American military and civil advisors be banished." The Hague verdict also came through that Great Britain or the United States did not have authority over another sovereign oil and property and Great Britain was to surrender its properties to Iran. The Hague court wanted to keep Iran's unity and this unity would increase the nationalization law. One newspaper even reported that it was the responsibility of the United States to "preserve our unity until we attain our aims."[203]

This verdict was seen as a "first example of fairness toward small Asiatic nations of an international body." Interestingly enough, American judges dissented. This decision would remove some of Iran's difficulty to sell oil to small purchasers and take delivery of oil.[204] The lack of money in Iran deteriorated the highway conditions in Iran. There were only a few that were asphalted, but maintenance and no policy was written for this year. In June 1952, the responsibility of highways was given to railways.[205] Transocean Airways (Air Jordan) was negotiating to buy Iranian Airways, giving management control to Air Jordan. The Transocean affiliates would offer flights from the United States to Germany and then to the Middle East by Iranian Airways. This would allow operations in Cairo, Beirut, Jerusalem, Amman, Baghdad, Kuwait, Abadan, Kabul, and other places in Iran. Iran was further requesting $5 million dollars to fix up the airports but Nelson, a State Department official, said no more than $500,000 was needed for minor runway damage, and much would go to Transocean and its build up of Iranian

---

[202] Tehran to Secretary of State 9 July 1952, RG 59 788.00/7-952.
[203] Tehran to Secretary of State 29 July 1952, RG 59 788.00/7-952.
[204] Tehran to Secretary of State 29 July 1952, RG 59 788.00 (W)/7-2952.
[205] Tehran to Department of State, 28 July 1952 RG 59 888.2612/7-2852.

airways stock and capital. From March 1953 to 1954, the balance sheet for Iranian Airways was 36, 674,924 rials. [206]

In late October 1952, Prime Minister Mossedegh expressed President Truman's great interest in finding a solution to the oil problem. He wanted to resolve the dispute between the United States and the United Kingdom, now that Iran had leverage over its oil. He set a time of three weeks with one week of counter proposals to settle the oil dispute.[207] He requested a 20 million pounds payment before the AIOC began the negotiations. The people in Tehran were pleased that AIOC could reach a deal with Iran. There was also an Iranian and Polish agreement signed on October 8 that would include exports of oil, lead oxide, manganese, and agricultural products. The replies came back from the United States and United Kingdom that both understood and supported Iran's nationalization policies, but Mossedegh was still shocked by their proposals, as were both countries. Both seemed to utterly reject the proposals. The capital in Bank Melli would increase to 2 billion rials now.[208]

In a later letter of 1952, Arthur Richards replied to a letter stating that Iran improved the railroad from the Persian Gulf to Tehran- *a splendid piece of engineering compared with the main line of a modern American railroad.* Both the United States and United Kingdom brought in locomotives, improved roads, and improved the highways.[209] In fact, the Kerun Valley would be one of the greatest agricultural potentials for resettlement of Iran's farms and workers from the urban areas. It would cost about $238 million over a 15 year period.[210] On track, Iran began having agreements with Oman as the largest supplier, Pakistan, India and Russia, supplied dates

---

[206] AmEmbassy Tehran to Department of State, 21 August 1952, RG 59 988.52[988.72]/8-2152.
[207] Tehran to Department of State October 1952 RG 59 888.2553 AIOC/10-52
[208] Tehran to Department of State October 1952 RG 59 888.2553 AIOC/10-52

[209] Richards to Alton 25 September 1952 RG 59 988.512/9-252
[210] Tehran to Secretary of State, 27 November 1952, RG 59, 888.2614/11-2752

to Iran. These supplies of dates were then delivered to the United States and the United States paid Iran handsomely as a joint benefit for the dates.[211] In December of 1952, the Ford Foundation visited Iran and committed to provide Iran with $200,000 to $300,000 dollars each year for the next several years. These funds would help deliver private projects for the improvement of Iran's infrastructure. Some of the facilities would include vocational educational facilities.[212] During the next year, Iran had roughly 650 million to 700 million rials in expenses, causing a big deficit. But, the new surplus of tax collections and custom revenues, and tobacco monopoly profits would decrease their surplus. Also, due to the lack of funds, the 1951 Opium crop was not used as much and only produced 1,400 to 1,600 cases of 160 pounds each since the 1951 production. Despite the low prices, the area of opium plantations still decreased. There was law that opium was prohibited to be sold in Iran and to anyone in the country except Government agents, but on the black market more than 3,000 cases were smuggled to delivery. In 1952, there were about 1,750 cases of opium and an additional 1,200 cases making a total of 4,315 cases from August 1950, the initial production.[213] This trade strengthened the American and Iranian political economies.

A Poor Economic Summary

In 1953, the problems associated with the Mossedegh government and the conflicts with the Shah were becoming apparent. The Shah kept Mossedegh only until he was weak enough to remove later in the year. The plans to remove Mossedegh from his plenary power position, limiting the Shah's power and his nationalization policies hurt his diplomatic relationships. The nationalization of the Iranian telephone company occurred in the early part of 1953 with a budget of 500 million rials.[214] This new law became part of the Ministry of Posts, Telegraph, and

---

[211] Tehran to Department of State 21 June 1952, RG 59, 888.2614/6-2152.
[212] Tehran to Department of State 3 December 1952 RG 59, 888.571/12-352
[213] Enclosure No. 1 to Dispatch no. 989. 8 March 1952 RG 59. 888.571/12-352

Telephones. This ministry managed this new law and the domestic telegraph rates of five rials for the first ten words of Persian, etc.[215] The imports and exports had been rising for Iran. In May 1953, *the US plan to lend Iran Govt $40 million causing "panic" in exchange rates.* If there were loans backing up a currency, then the rate of rials per dollar went up and the worries of people brought the rate up to 100 rials per $1.00. Also, the United States was negotiating with the NIOC for oil purchases, but NIOC did not want to negotiate with the United States. There was a Japanese company that seemed to conclude an optimistic contract.[216] The Iranian economy during this time period was influenced by the inflationary fiscal policies. Due to the pending settlement of the oil dispute as of April 1953, there was growing skepticism that the government would not be able to politically and economically stabilize the nation. There were many internal political differences, but the crop production was going well with 80 percent of the terrain agricultural. Due to the nationalization scheme of Iran, Iran limited imports and had stigmatized the domestic industry and the employment of workers. There were many opportunities for investment in Iran, but private investment and foreign capital was restricted due to the government's policies. The State Department says, "Lacking an oil settlement with the British, there is no reason to believe the government will be able to discontinue its heavy inflationary borrowing from the Bank Melli." Consequently, there would be a rise in prices.[217]

During this year, the Iranian government as stated before, increased production of sugar and produced more than 55,024 tons of it. They bought and constructed part of the railway and a sugar factory. They raised the growers' share from 1,500 to 2,000 rials per hectare and began giving a higher quantity to growers. They employed a reasonable number of technical students.

---

[214] AmEmbassy Tehran to Department of State, Washington. 2 February 1953, RG 59, 988.30/2-253.
[215] Tehran to Department of State, 27 March 1952, RG 59, 988.24/3-1952.
[216] Tehran to Department of State, May 1953, RG 59, 888.00FA/5-52
[217] CERP to Department of State, 17 April 1953, RG 59, 888.00/4-1753.

Iran purchased nine to ten processing sugar plants. The imports and exports in the summer of 1953 decreased.[218] They were 38.6 percent less than the period in 1951. The trade with USSR also decreased significantly and imports were 29.2 percent lower in these months. Further, exports to the Soviets were 51.8 percent lower. For some odd reason though, it was in these three months before Mossedegh's overthrow that trade with the United states and Germany increased while trade with the United Kingdom decreased. The increase of exports was 122.48 percent while Germany went up with an increase of 82 percent.[219] The business conditions also improved during these months. It was also agreed during the time period that there would be an agreement of a technical assistance program. In 1953, Iran received $20 million for the program. This was known as the Point IV program and the contribution to the government was much less due to the oil dispute. The Point IV program allowed for the stability of rates, importation of goods into Iran, and a procurement of sugar through the United States. The problem with the Point IV program was that the funds were too restricted and were lacking since the United States' interest of economic development in Iran since 1950. The objective was to raise the standard of living before oil nationalization and increase resistance to the Soviets and Communist influences.[220]

In May of 1953, the Shah issued a decree turning over to the government the Crown estates and paying 60 million rials annually for the Imperial social welfare organization.[221] The economic plans under the administration were very rigid and dictator-like and reforms did not even stand a chance. Since there were no prospects of oil, the government chose to enter into private enterprises.[222] In July 1953, expenses mounted and Iran was spending 300 million rials per month, having a 150 million rials deficit from the NIOC. The government wanted to meet the

---

[218] Plan Organization in the years 1330-31. Sugar Factories of Iran, Inc. 17 April 1953, 888.00/4-1753.
[219] Tehran to Department of State, 17 April 1953, RG 59, 888.00/4-1753.
[220] Tehran to Department of State, 17 April 1953, RG 59, 888.00/4-1753.
[221] AmEmbassy Tehran to Department of State, 11 May 1953, RG 59, 888.16/6-553
[222] Department of Army to Department of State, 1953 July, RG 59, 888.00/7-53.

total budget deficit of 3 billion rials through tax collection, but it could not meet that as well. Bank Melli disavowed the utilization of Iranian gold reserves, but Iran needed money to pay its bills. The economy was so poor that now it is 130 rials per dollar.[223] Before the overthrow in August 1953, an agreement was signed between Bank Melli Iran and National Bank of Israel to promote an Iran and Israeli trade. This agreement remained secret for two months and was settled through a biannual payment of $500,000.[224]

Part 2: Section 6: Military Developments
First Revolution

The political dimensions of the First revolution were to limit Soviet influence through the elimination of the Tudeh party from politics in Iran. America wanted to enter into Iranian affairs, give citizens a better standard of living, and invite investment. They felt politically that if Iran was so dependent on the United States it would eliminate Soviet influence and the United States would win the Cold War, which they did. Economic factors showed the politics of oil diplomacy, the economic meaning of limiting communist influences and gaining influence in the oil business of Iran. The United States wanted to get rich and powerful, and they helped Iran achieve the wealth and the power the United States had in the Pre-Revolution. The United States began making profits from investments, monopolies, and trade. The Soviet Union, along with the British, had less and less of an advantage in Iran's exploitation. The United States used opium, the Export-Import Program, and the consortium agreement to gain power. Oil was power, and to control or at least influence Iran's oil was to get that power the United States needed in the Middle East politically, economically, and to be shown, militarily. The goal of the military

---

[223] AmEmbassy Tehran to Department of State, 24 July 1953, RG 59 888.00/7-2453.
[224] Department of Army to Department of State, 1953, August, RG 59 788.00(w)/8-53.

development in Iran was to create a regional security mechanism that would deter the Soviet Union from invading and potentially creating World War III. It was also an arrangement where the United States could point their nuclear weapons at close range in Iran at the Soviet Union. Though power and money were gained, the United States wanted to be able to defend themselves and U.S. military bases were established to protect Iran and gain a military advantage over USSR and win the Cold War. The United States wanted to be the regional security dominator in the Middle East and Iran wanted American domination of Iran so that it could be the sole Middle Eastern state with military strength.

In August 1951, the U.S. government was looking into renewing their MDAP contracts. The advocacy for Iran was intended to preserve the country's status as an independent nation and the MDAP would assist in helping them improve their country and be free. The U.S. government said, *we are giving military equipment and advice so that Iran will be able to give internal world and to resist aggression from across her borders.* The government further went on to say that Iran was important to the United States and worthy of their efforts because *it is a country of vast oil resources.* Russia wanted Iran for three reasons 1) its natural resources, 2) protection of their southern oil regions, and 3) to have power in the Middle East and improve their strategic position in South Asia, the Mediterranean, and Africa. The United States was not in a position to have Iran fall through the cracks because their loss would weaken the United States' influence in that region.[225]

The other possible ways the United States could lose Iran was if economic conditions became too paramount that the United States couldn't control its might, and if *oil revenues ended.* The deteriorating conditions would be enough to cause the communists to seize power in

---

[225] Enclosure to dispatch No. 231 18 August 1951 RG 59 788.5 MAP/8-2851.

Iran. If Azerbaijan was established, then Russia would use its ally Azerbaijan to attack Iran *Korean-style*. Azerbaijan favored Russia more than Iran. The third possibility of losing Iran was an *outright invasion launched by Russia. This would probably come as part of World War III.*[226]

Therefore, the purpose of military aid was to enable Iran to resist potential military threats by the Soviet Union and to preserve its internal order. Americans realized that without aid, Iran would not withstand a Soviet invasion.[227] At this time a private received $.40 cents a month, a sergeant about $100.00 a month, and a ration was bread and rice which cost about $100 along with one uniform. The situation was devastating for the Iranian Army. The army's program was outdated and the manufacture of Iranian equipment was slow and long. The training of the Iranian Army focused on basic training from the 1920s with inadequate equipment, vehicles, and weapons. At the time the army of Iran consisted of 4,500 men with only 12 plans for combat. The Navy was about 2,500 men with two ships in the Gulf. The conscript was illiterate and untrained and did not possess the skills to fight effectively. In fact, *ninety percent of the Iranian spend all their time being alive, leaving them no time for abstract ideas such as duty.* [228]

It was quite a good decision that Iran accepted the U.S. military aid because its military force was a security force dealing with internal uprising. It was not an army for the defense or offense of Iran. The conscript however did not understand the point of building up Iranian military and having Americans arms. *Are they supposed to help us fight the British-* one soldier questioned. They actually wanted help from USSR. The educated elite felt that Iran's acceptance

---

[226] Enclosure to dispatch No. 231 18 August 1951 RG 59 788.5 MAP/8-2851.

[227] Enclosure to dispatch No. 231 18 August 1951 RG 59 788.5 MAP/8-2851.

[228] Enclosure to dispatch No. 231 18 August 1951 RG 59 788.5 MAP/8-2851.

of aid would lead to terrible consequences. But, the commoner felt this was a great success- that the Iranian army would be facilitated with money and facilities. The acceptance of aid led to a rise in the rial and this agreement allowed Iran to sell their oil to any country. No strings were attached to the military aid grant. The United States would furnish more than arms and money to Iran; it also provided trucks, tires, and pharmaceutical supplies. Some circles like the elite felt inclined to support the United States while many still remained confused. In many political circles however, the agreement was known as a triumph.[229] The goal was to make the Iranian military force so strong *that they will be capable of maintaining internal security and international communism will realize that it has no hope of defeating* them.[230] Iran became the first country to obtain U.S. economic interests in Iran during those years of the Cold War. In a December correspondence, General Zimmerman reported that Iran would be able to maintain itself internally for a short time without U.S. military aid, but the suspension of aid would appear as if the United States had *abandoned Iran to Communists.* The suspension of military aid would provide a lower morale, deterioration of military equipment, and a decrease in the armed forces of Iran. But the Secretary of State, accepting Zimmerman's advice said that the United States couldn't hide the difficulty that would occur if it "sold" Iran to the Communists, and that future U.S. missions- if withdrawn- would be difficult to re-establish. Essentially, the U.S. military would be *extremely handicapped.*[231] In fact, Iran could not support itself financially, give money to its people and support a large military establishment. The State Department noted, "*At the same time, they need more military assistance or the country could not adequately resist the Russians.*" The U.S. Embassy in Tehran also relayed the Shah's urgent desire for military

---

[229] Tehran 1235 23 May 1952 RG 59 788.5 MAP/5-2352
[230] Tehran to State Department 12 July 1951 RG 59 788.5 MAP/7-1251.
[231] Tehran to Secretary of State 19 December 1951 RG 59 788.5/11-1951.

assistance and how *Iran plays on the eastern fleet of the Middle East.* It was later given to U.S. Congress for approval.[232]

By 1952, military aid started to pour in and the morale of the Iranian government and soldiers began to improve. In fact, *Mosadeq has repeatedly told me Iran would fight to last man if soil invaded.* Mossedegh admitted that Russia was his only fear of threat to Iran's security and the purpose of the country's involvement with the United States and the United Nations was to limit Russia's aggression.[233] All in all, all agreements with Iran must be clear because some English words cannot correctly be translated into Persian words.[234] Iran was known to surrender its ambitions in favor of U.N. principles. It supported the U.N.'s idea of collective security, and despite Russian threats, it did not fall prey to Communist influences and only asked Britain and the United States for aid. Military personnel of Iran were quite pleased on how U.S. military aid spurred the rapid progress of the War Ministry.[235] But one newspaper reported that American aid had also destroyed a country, because a country like Iran with conditions stipulated for aid had to relinquish their national independence and be enslaved to U.S. policy. The Iranian government needed to oppose the United States and ask American advisors to leave the country. *The paper sounds pretty communist if you know what I mean.* The Soviets actually threaten Iran because their economic and military policies align with the west, and they will surrender their foreign policies to those of the west.[236] In February the country experiences a high level of export sales and the possible sale of Iranian oil to Poland, Germany, Japan, and Hungary. These agreements would export more than 500,000 tons of oil at a 50 percent reduction in sale prices. But despite

---

[232] Tehran to Secretary of State 19 December 1951 RG 59 788.5/11-1951.

[233] Tehran to Secretary of State 6 January 1952 RG 59 788.5/1-652.
[234] Rountree to Merchant 14 January 1952 RG 59 788.5/1-1452.
[235] Tehran to Secretary of State 5 January 1952 RG 59 788.5/1-752.
[236] Tehran to Secretary of State 5 January 1952 RG 59 788.5/1-752

these economic successes, Iran was still facing problems militarily, especially with deficiencies in storing their equipment, and a delay in Iranian military supplies. But the world looks nicer because nine Iranian students returned from the United States from U.S. Army training courses. The MSP program however, was suspended so those already there would be allowed to finish their studies, and those en route would also be allowed to finish, but those scheduled to depart would be forced to remain in Iran.[237]

Military production was low and production costs were high. So Iran was creating an arsenal department similar to the U.S. Ordinance Corps to maintain the arms of Iran. But the lack of equipment was caused by lack of maintenance, an unorganized command organization and haphazard coordination of supply and maintenance. But new American weapons in Iran provided employment of additional army personnel.[238] The weapons continued to come in, though in February, aid ceased because Mossedegh did not prescribe to the collective security law where Iran cannot remain neutral. But another political circle stated that Mossedegh's refusal was political. Though it weakened the Iranian army, it also weakened the Shah's position as Commander in Chief. The U.S. embassy stated, *any simpleton can realize that Mosadeq's government is being supported by the Americans.* But no one understands why he is turning down U.S. military aid. The United States wanted to give it and wanted another authority to accept it, despite Mossedegh's refusal. Iran was eliminated from the important Middle East Defense Plan and further it would only receive weapons for internal defense.[239]

But, this limitation of aid and withdrawal from the Defense Plan was a severe blow to United States interests. The United States wanted to turn Iran into a strategic location, but by being there, they were insulting Iranians and people began blaming Mossedegh for his pro-

---

[237] Tehran 900 8 February 1952 RG 59 788.5/2-852.
[238] Tehran 900 8 February 1952 RG 59 788.5/2-852.
[239] Annex I Tehran 900 5 March 1952 788.5/3-552.

American policies. If Mossedegh had not completely rejected American influence, then he wanted to have American imperialism. In fact, American advisors did not help gain Iran oil, and they continued to roam freely. But, despite their refusals, President Truman still wanted to give aid to them because American aid would prevent a coup d'état from Communist Russia. He said in a report in 1952 that Iran needed a defense system against Communist pressure.[240] The current military mission cost Iran about $40,000 monthly, so financially without U.S. aid, Iran couldn't do much. Newspaper reports of May 1952, discussed U.S. military aid and Soviet influence on the Iranians. The papers were advocating freedom and that *we cannot agree that our army under complete American control. We are free as USSR to do what we can to improve our defensive security.*[241] America replied that military and technical assistance was not underwriting Iran's oil position and the dispute with Britain; "for every American dollar which Persia receives is a direct incentive to continued Persian intransigence."[242]

By July 1952 the American military had decided to leave American officers in Iran until both governments came to an agreement. Mossedegh wanted Iran to be a neutral state and felt that neutrality was not what the United States wanted. So Mossedegh was looking for a new friend and felt that strengthening the relationship between the USSR and Iran would consolidate the efforts of both governments - leading to a happy existence for both governments.[243] The United States wanted to counter this and felt that if they provided $35 million worth of jets to Iran, then perhaps current Iranian policies could be somewhat modified to suit U.S. interests. The strategy was to visit the Shah and propose new equipment, not stating what the equipment was. If

---

[240] Annex I Tehran 900 5 March 1952 788.5/3-552.

[241] Tehran to Secretary of State 29 April 1952, RG 59 788.5/4-2952.

[242] AmEmbassy London to Department of State 1 May 1952 RG 59 788.5/5-152;Tehran to Secretary of State 26 May 1952 RG 59 788.5/5-2652.

[243] Tehran to State Department 4 July 1952 RG 59 788.5/7-452.

the Shah asked for jets, the Americans would know nothing about the offer, but kept the offer of jets veiled and used as a final tactic between the Shah and America.[244]

The Iranians felt crowded by the influx of American policies. They felt that if America had simply helped the Iranian people to prevent communism, then Iranians would welcome the Americans, but the Americans have interfered in all matters of internal affairs of Iran, leaving no room for freedom and no friendship with the Soviets. When Iran needed help, then Iran pulled themselves out of foreign affairs and allowed the British to bend the knees of the Iranians once again. Furthermore, *the Americans are dead set on continuing their errors in Iran.* They had spent thousands of dollars advertising Mossedegh, but spent nothing for the Iranian people and continued to help the aristocrats of Iran too. The final interpretation from the Iranian public was this: *If the American policy is aimed at throwing Iran into the lap of the communists, then they can't do better than increase their support of Mosadeq. What does America stand to gain if Iran fell prey to Communism?* The concern was that Americans were only concerned with not giving up Iran to the communists, and nothing else. Even the military spies got medals in Iran, but the honest, hardworking officers got nothing.[245]

But they do get the $25 million military aid approved by Congress, supposedly.[246] Despite the neutral status of Iran, Iran was doing terrible financially and had to accept the military aid to run its nation. But, the military missions needed to improve and Americans not getting involved and their ridiculously high salaries of $30,000 per year were not helping the case either.[247] In order to compensate, the Mutual Defense Assistance Program planned to send

---

[244] Tehran to Secretary of State 18 July 1952 RG 59 788.5/7-1852.
[245] Tehran to Secretary of State 18 July 1952 RG 59 788.5/7-1852
[246] Tehran to Secretary of State 18 July 1952 RG 59 788.5/7-1852

[247] Tehran to Secretary of State 18 July 1952 RG 59 788.5/7-1852

military services and training aids to Iran in exchange for sending a number of police officers from Iran to the United States.[248] In late December of 1952 the U.S. government sent a neophyte Ambassador Henderson to assess the deteriorating conditions of Iran. While there, Ambassador Henderson made new offers, but before he could, Mossedegh requested picket boats for Iranian exports. Also, the United States agreed to offer more training to the Iranian Navy and provided six *40* foot utility boats for the Coast Guard and any anti-smuggling equipment. This would strengthen the Iranian Navy and Coast Guard at sea and provide greater defense for the Middle East.[249] *I do not know what is the Middle East and how far its boundaries extend,* replied Nuri Al-Said, minister of defense of Iraq. The defense of the Middle East and whoever controlled Iran would control the Middle East and win the Cold War.[250]

As the situation worsened in Iran in late 1952 and beginning of 1953, the MDAP still functioned with new arrivals of military vehicles for Iran's army. The secret plans of America were no secret anymore as different newspapers continued to publish statements such as "Americans build airports in Iran for bombers to attack USSR" and an overwhelming amount of articles spoke of military equipment in Iran and the construction of airports in provinces of Khusistan, Fars, and Baluchistan, Iran. The Iranian press felt that the United States was destroying national elements of Iran by creating aggressive military bases all across the country to bomb the Soviet Union. The press however did not report on the significant amount of ambulances, trucks, and parts. The U.S. Air Force tried to protect Iran by inventing some kind of spray against the Russians- this spray was located in Iran.[251]

---

[248] Tehran to Secretary of State 18 July 1952 RG 59 788.5/7-1852

[249] Secretary to Secret Service Information 8 December 1952 RG 59 788.5/12-852
[250] Secretary of Defense to Secretary of State 18 December 1952 RG 59 788.5/12-1852
[251] Despatch 137 8 July 1952 RG 59 788.5/7-852

PART 3

SECOND REVOLUTION

1953-1959

Part 3: Section 7 Political Developments
Second Revolution (1953-1959)

The Second Revolution began immediately after the overthrow of Prime Minister

Mossedegh in August, 1953. The United States were on their way of winning the Regional Cold

War with the Soviet Union. The Second Revolution is a story of an imposed leader who began

his tribute as the best thing for Iran and finished the Second Revolution with being a most

unpopular leader. He was imposed by the United States. Iran again was enslaved to a foreign

imperialist power, just a different name and era. The Second Revolution is also a story about the

maintenance of strength the United States had to do for six years. In order for the United States to attain hegemony in the Middle East, disintegrate the bi-polarity of the Soviet Union, and win the regional Cold War in 1959 at the end of the second revolution, Iran had to align its foreign policies with the United States politically, economically and militarily. In return, the U.S. had to maintain their power or be potentially overtaken by the lucrative influential offers of the Soviet Union. The offers of the U.S.S.R. would have destroyed American influence in Iran and the Middle East, the United States would have lost the Regional Cold War and also foreshadowed to lose the global Cold War. At the end of the second revolution, the United States won the regional Cold War and shifted the power balance onto American shoulders. Political Scientists and Historians like Fatemi knew that whoever wins the Middle East in the 1950s would win the Cold War. The U.S. won the Middle East in 1959; the Soviet Union began to decline in the 1960s compared to the United States and it officially collapsed in 1991. The key to their failure was losing the Middle East. The key to the Middle East was Iran. In result, the goal was to maintain American hegemony and to align Iranian foreign policy with the United States.

After the uprising that supported the Shah, pro-Shah forces overthrew the elected Prime Minister Dr. Mossedegh and established a new Majlis. General Zahedi, the Shah, and Americans were at the helm of the victory. America was pleased. In the First Revolution, America's goal was to politically demobilize any Soviet influence in Iran. This occurred by weakening the powerful Tudeh party and its communist influence. Communism was the technology that the Soviets used to try to win Iran, control the Middle East, and win the Cold War. In history, it is shown that the two superpowers: USSR and the United States were equal and in fierce competition. After the United States won the regional Cold War in the 1950s, it set the Soviets off guard and led to the turmoil in 1991. In this section, the political dimensions clarify that there was no more *giving in* to the Iranians; it was the Iranians that depended on America's foreign policy. America's foreign policy was to gain hegemony in the Middle East and Iran, now fully in the grasp of America could not turn or move, but only comply to the United States. The United State's goal was power. The economic goal of the Second Revolution was also to prevent communism, but it was to now gain profit from trade, monopolies, foreign investments, opium, sugar, etc. The goal was to give aid so Iran could make money for both themselves and the U.S. economy. In one instance, the United States gave $500 million total and 20 percent of their aids were gifts. The military component of this time period was finalizing and stamping the regional defense arrangement. It was to build up Iran's army capable to defend, have Iran be a lead participant in the defense arrangements against the Soviet Union, and it was to further the United States' military missions and training. The goal was to consolidate the regime under America and prevent World War III first threatened by the Soviets in the Second Revolution.

Aftermath of Mossedegh

In the aftermath, General Zahedi was the new prime minister and the Shah became the newly enforceable President/Monarch of Iran. The political landscape changed after Mossedegh left. By October 1953, there were no major developments in the domestic arena of Iran. Nothing was happening on the Mossedegh trial and the Senate and Majlis hadn't convened yet. The political elements still did not fully align themselves with Zahedi. The reports coming were to keep the majlis and not enter relations with Britain. In October 1953, Hoover went to Iran to ensure that the country did not enter into an oil diplomacy with Britain. Iran wanted to settle the oil question based on the nationalization law. On October 26, the Shah celebrated his birthday and gave crown properties to 1,600 peasants. There are ongoing negotiations between Turkey and Iran.[252] In January 1954, the government was still having problems trying to get off the

---

[252] Tehran to Department of State, 28 October 1953, RG 59, 788.00(W)/10-2853

ground. There are hundreds of candidates seeking elections.[253] The two biggest political priorities have been the elections and oil. In a radio address by General Zahedi on February 17, 1954, General Zahedia stressed "your participation in the conduct of the affairs of the country." He laid out ten measures that would bring success to the nation. His ten measures were: establishment of security throughout the country to prevent chaos, maintenance of the principles of security and justice, adoption of an attitude considered mannerly to foreign comrades, mechanization of agriculture, building of new roads, exploitation of natural resources, *the setting up of sugar, sugar cane* and textile factories, import of sufficient number of trucks for transport, repairs of railways, and the construction of the Karaj Dam.[254]

The biggest security mechanism that occurred in 1954 was the trial and subsequent verdict of Mossedegh's trial. In May 1954, Mossedegh was tried, convicted, and sentenced to three years of solitary confinement. General Riahis received hard labor for many years. Mossedegh said that he would appeal to the Supreme Court. The new Majlis was working to rescind all of Mossedegh's law decrees and repeal land reform law. After Mossedegh's fall, Iran began to receive international contracts from China and Japan. Both countries' ministers came to Iran to discuss a trade agreement. This trade agreement would give Japan 25 percent of crude oil and Japan was pleading for some "free" crude oil on an exchange basis. China was seeking the same. Tanaka, the Japanese oil company, told Iran that oil companies in Japan would want about 2,500,000 of crude oil every year. There were also agreements to receive one hundred Italian railway tank cars in exchange for Iranian oil with an additional two hundred tank cars coming soon.[255]

---

[253] Tehran to Department of State, 6 January 1954, RG 59, 788.00 (W)/1-654
[254] Radio Address of General Zahedi, 17 February 1954, RG 59 788.00 (W)/2-1754
[255] Tehran-Department of State, 19 May 1954, RG 59, 788.00 (W)/5-1954

The first decision for the Shah and the Queen to visit the United States came after a conversation with Ambassador Henderson in July 1954. The purpose of this historic visit was to settle the oil dispute and make an agreement. The United States was very concerned about this visit because they did not want a repeat of the negative consequences that had occurred after the Shah's visit to America in 1951. The second objective of the visit to the United States was to discuss the defense arrangement for the Middle East. Dulles said, "If handled appropriately, [the visit] would be the advantage of the United States." However, the visit had some conditions. The conditions included the following: resolution of the oil settlement, the visit would only be official for three days and the rest of the tour would be unofficial, and the representatives of the Iranian government needed to be ready to discuss subjects raised by the Shah. The date of arrival would be determined after some kind of oil resolution.[256]

The Central Committee of Tudeh Party of Iran explained that the Shah's trip to the United States was *an effort on the part of imperialist America…to turn Iran into an American military base.* This military base was to turn against democracy and be vindictive toward the Soviets. The intention of the United States was to gain control of the political and economic aspects of Iran. The Tudeh party was the communist party that the United States tried to suppress in order to stop the spread of communism and weaken the Soviets' position. But according to Tudeh, they went down into the actual needs of American intervention: political, economic, and military aspects. Though they were denounced as a vindictive organization, upon looking back at their views today it appears that they were correct. Furthermore, the Tudeh party renounced the Shah's role as the sole representative of the Iranian government and announced that any of agreements or *promises* would not be valid. They want peace and harbor hatred against Anglo-

---

[256] Memorandum for the President: John Foster Dulles, 3 July 1954, RG 59 788.00 (W)/7-354

Saxon policies and the American and Shah's efforts for foreigner influence.[257] The Tudeh party says:

> The Iranian nation most fervently expresses her allegiance to the International Democratic Peace-front under the auspices of the great Socialist Soviet Union and has long since resolved to support the aims of this gigantic front.[258]

The Tudeh Party was committed to preventing Iran from becoming an American military base against the USSR. They say, "the Iranian nation will never Soviet Russia, the world's stronghold of peace and democracy, but will turn against the aggressive forces of imperialism." Moreover, there were economic benefits that included an importation of unlimited goods, loans, American advisors, the planning of the Seven Year Plan and turning Iran into an American monopoly. It is interesting that the seven year development plan was an *anti-nation*. Many of the things the Tudeh party claimed occurred in Iran. The Tudeh party was against all forms of aid.[259]

In order to prepare for his departure to the United States, the Shah wrote a letter indicating his satisfaction with the U.S. government and the settlement of the oil dispute. He was particularly grateful for the American assistance and said he would 'Look forward an era of economic and social development which will improve the lot of my People, as well as further consolidate the security of the Middle East'. In the end, the Shah stated that "My people reciprocate to the full the friendship of your noble Nation."[260] The Shah of Iran was also confident of the knowledge of the military on August 21 1954, but wanted to begin studying economics to improve his basic knowledge. This message was given to Ambassador Henderson

---

[257] Tudeh Party, 3 July 1954, RG 59 7-354
[258] Tudeh Party, 3 July 1954, RG 59 7-354
[259] Tudeh Party, 3 July 1954, RG 59 7-354

[260] The Shah to Eisenhower, 8 August 1954, General Records of the Department of State, Record Group 59, 1950-1954, 788.11/8-854, National Archives, Washington DC (hereafter cited as RG 59, with filing information).

who informed the Shah of many self-educating economics books in the United States. The

economic advisors in the United States were also to consult with him.[261]

The Shah wanted to leave Tehran on November 22, 1954 and visit Switzerland,

Germany, and New York. Around December 15, he was planning to spend five days in

Washington, fly to California, go to Florida and from there take a car trip to New York.[262] In

light of this planning, Prince Ali Reza Pahlavi, the Shah's young brother wanted to go to the

USSR to hunt in the Greater Pamir Mountains. He wanted to go and track this wounded animal.

The Soviet government would grant the request since they knew how keen he was on hunting,

but it would lead to a political problem later with the Soviets.[263] After the oil agreement, the

Shah also planned to remove Prime Minister Zahedi from his position. Though Zahedi is honest,

the Shah has discovered a huge communist group in the government and army and speculates

that Zahedi may be involved as well.[264] The Shah's development plans are to construct a dam,

build houses for workers, give more land to peasants, reactivate the oil industry in the south,

raise the standard of living and "give everyone a free and an honorable life- everyone who is

interested in the existence and independence of this country." [265] While in Washington, the Shah

wanted to chat with the high ranking officers of the government and members of the Security

Council. He wanted to discuss Iranian security as well as the future of Iranian politics and

economics. The Shah also was not afraid to leave immediately after the ratification of the oil

agreement. The Senate cannot put any bill toward the Shah until many months later. He felt that

after the oil settlement was achieved that he needed the greatest minds to draft the laws. He

---

[261] Tehran to the Secretary of State, 25 August 1954, General Records of the Department of State, Record Group 59, 1950-1954, 788.11/8-2554, National Archives, Washington, DC (hereafter cited as RG 59, with filing information).

[262] Tehran to Secretary of State, 15 October 1954, RG 59, 788.11/10-1554
[263] Tehran to Department of State, 15 September 1954, RG 59, 788.11/9-1554
[264] Iran Foreign Office to Dayton Mak, 24 September 1954, General Records of the Department of State, Record Number 59, 1950-1954 788.13/9-2454 (hereafter filed as RG 59).
[265] Unclassified Document Desp.544: 24 September 1954, RG 59, 788.13/9-2454

wanted to go to the United States to "become better acquainted with U.S. leaders and people." The Shah further noted that if the opposition did succeed (because there was a huge opposition present), then he would seek the Regency council and take care of the situation when he returned, but he did not think that the Majlis or the Senate would succeed in doing so.[266] The cost of the visit would be $5,000.00 to Washington from New York. [267]

President Dwight Eisenhower responds to the Shah on October 26, 1954:

Imperial Majesty
Mohammad Reza Shah Pahlavi
Shahinshah of Iran

The people of the United States join me on this anniversary of Your Majesty's birth, in sending facilitations and sincere wishes to Your Majesty and to the people of Iran.[268]

Dwight D. Eisenhower

On October 28, 1954, Prince Ali Pahlavi stopped hunting to return to Iran and attend the Shah's birthday. On his return, the single-engine plane disappeared in the Elburz Mountains.[269] The Iranian Air force and U.S. Air Force of five American planes both began searching for the Prince. At first they thought to find the Shah's brother north of the Elurz Mountains, but parachutists found no trace there.[270] The celebrations for the Shah's birthday were cancelled. On November 2, 1954, they found the wreckage of Prince Ali's plane and identified his pilot, another passenger, and the Prince himself dead.[271] The Shah was devastated.

On November 15, 1954, the Shah determined that Queen Soraya, a male and female servant, two military aides, and Zahedi would attend them on their visit. He told the U.S.

---

266 Department of Navy to Shah, 25 October 1954, RG 59, 788.11/10-2554
267 Department of State 2 November 1954, RG 59, 788.11/11-254
268 Eisenhower to Shah of Iran, 25 October 1954, RG 59 788.11/10-2554
269 Tehran to Secretary of State, 28 October 1954, RG 59, 788.11/10-2854
270 Tehran to Secretary of State, 29 October 1954, RG 59, 788.11/10-2954
271 Tehran to Secretary of State, 2 November 1954, RG 59, 788.11/11-254

government that his military aides would carry weapons and he requested to have Secret Service men accompany him. But no one knew who was going to pay the bill. A chartered plane from Tehran to New York would cost $15,000.00. At this rate, he might as well charter a commercial plane, rather than a KLM chartered jet. The United States requested that he considered Pan American Airways to find a cheaper flight.[272] Thereafter, President Eisenhower requested a personal letter to be delivered in the Diplomatic Pouch to Queen Soraya who would be a happy acquaintance to Mrs. Eisenhower. President Eisenhower said, "As I believe you already know, we are planning to have you and the Queen for luncheon with us while you are in Washington. I hope you will find your American visit both enjoyable and restful."[273] Vice President Nixon and his wife were planning to receive the Shah at Washington MATs Airport (now known as Dulles International). After meeting with dignitaries from December 13 to December 15, the Shah left on December 16 on a plane to California. The total cost of the entire trip including ten round trip first class tickets, accommodations, food, etc would cost $20, 136.00.[274] Before the Shah's departure to the United States, the Shah found out that the Italians offered 200.000 tons of crude oil (the exchange of Iranian oil to Italy) to Israel at a greatly reduced price. Italy was not accepting sterling for the crude oil and the export goods of Italy were valued in terms of the crude prices.[275]

---

[272] Tehran to Secretary of State, 15 November 1954, RG 59, 788.11/11-1554

[273] Eisenhower to Shah, 19 November 1954, RG 59 788.11-1954

[274] Dulles to Embassy Tehran, 24 November 1954, RG 59 788.11/11-2454; The Shah's and Queens Schedule to the United States 8 December 1954, RG 9, 788.11/12-854

[275] Rome to the Secretary of State, 2 December 1954, General Records of the Department of State, Record Number 59, 888.2553/12-254 (hereafter filed as RG 50); Rome to Secretary of State, 4 December 1954, RG 59, 888.2553/12-454

Nationalism in the Second Revolution

According to State Department files and the Iranian population, the government of Iran did nothing. It was in fact known as the *Quiet Period* in Iran's history. It was a period to make the defense system of the Middle East complete. There was ongoing corruption with economic aid embezzlement by both Iranians and Americans. The population began to criticize the Shah and blame America. Iran began negotiating with the Soviets. The United States, afraid that it would lose hegemony, $8 billion dollars annually from oil and opium, began giving more aid. Supposedly, there was speculation that exchange of aid or some letters of Mossedegh's was to be exposed. One report said Hoover Jr. was the mastermind behind Mossedegh's topple from power. The United States faced the loss of hegemony if aid ceases. The relationship began creating tension and a lot of criticism against both countries. The aid coming in paid for the Shah's expenses while students were complaining to LBJ that education in Iran needs to improve. The population began requesting the United States to intervene in local politics, while the Shah's indecisive, insecure, and lavish lifestyle became exposed. Iran made more than $500 million dollars in oil revenues, did not set up diplomatic immunity for U.S. soldiers and provided $15 million to Iran so it could lead a monopoly and proceeds would benefit the United States. Eisenhower was backing Iran and went to Iran for support, giving more money. The more money Iran got, the more money the United States made in oil revenues.

The Shah's Nationalism

Since his youth, the Shah wanted to constrain the ideological atmosphere for a modern outlook. After Mossedegh, the Shah was able to compress political conflicts and fight against Iranian nationalism- a conflict. Nationalism was either a unified change in internal affairs, accepting Iran as an independent state, or something that was more positive. The Shah stated that the nationalism he wanted to breed was: *a policy of maximum political and economic independence consistent with the interest of one's country.*[276] He felt nationalism should be of self-interest preaching positivism, no imperialism, and provided a need assessment based on indigenous nationalism. All other kinds of nationalism would hurt the country and move it in the wrong direction. Democracy for the Shah was political, economic, administrative, and social. It was not just political rights, it also included political and economic rights. Further, economic rights or progress equaled material prosperity, where the role of the state was still involved in capitalism and the rights of workers, and employees were all protected. He said that *every man, woman and child in this nation is entitled to a decent minimum of these five things: food, clothing, housing, medical care and education.*[277] The only way to achieve such a state was through an international cooperation agreement where the pool of oil resources would be heavily guarded. The main concern was for the Shah to be independent in the new alliance, allow Iranian imports to enter into the Soviet Union and share the Aras and Atrak rivers to irrigate the unknown 200,000 acres of land. With the Shah meeting land reform laws, the economy and Iranian foreign exchange dropping because of lack of aid, the Shah's divorce of Queen Soraya and economic tensions at the end of the revolution, the Shah had to make changes.[278]

Eisenhower's Foreign Policy

Throughout this research, I was puzzled about the relationship between the Shah and President Eisenhower. Why did President Eisenhower continue to give foreign aid and assistance to Iran over the years? Was there something else happening?

---

[276] R. Sanghvi. *Aryamehr: The Shah of Iran.* (New York: Stein and Day Publishers, 1968), 223

[277] R. Sanghvi. *Aryamehr: The Shah of Iran.* (New York: Stein and Day Publishers, 1968), 230.

[278] R. Sanghvi. *Aryamehr: The Shah of Iran.* (New York: Stein and Day Publishers, 1968), 252-169.

Five Star General and President, Dwight D. Eisenhower had four concerns for developing his American foreign policy. His first concern was isolationism. He felt that foreign allies could set their own path, cooperate in peace through the United Nations, and control the atom bomb and economic aid. He felt that economic aid to underdeveloped countries was paramount because it would raise living standards and reduce social violence leading to their only resort of communism. It was indeed economic aid that was the weapon against communism and the Soviets. The point four program initiated with Iran was to prevent the country from falling into communism. The root of America's foreign policy during the second revolution was a greater world of peace with mutual understanding, alleviating difficulties and providing education training.[279] The goal was to have 675,000 barrels of oil a day flow toward the west. The United States wanted a protective wall in the northern tier of the Middle East and trade that was going east to foster foreign investment.[280] The foreign investment that Eisenhower was interested in was the investment similar in Saudi Arabia: setting up an oil consortium agreement. Like Aramco, Eisenhower wanted oil companies to pay Iran and deduct these foreign payments from their federal income tax returns.[281] The whole point of the foreign policy was military and what the United States could do to win this power struggle. It is interesting that staff members employed by Eisenhower were economic conservatives who did not want the passive president to spend money, however, like Dulles, they always agreed with the President.[282] This policy was what Robert Schulzinger called the *American Petroleum policy of the Middle East...*

---

[279] Allan Taylor. *What Eisenhower thinks.* (New York: Thomas Crowell Company, 1952), 142-153.
[280] Blanche Cook *Declassified Eisenhower (New York: Double-Day & Company, 1981).*
[281] Robert Divine *Eisenhower and the Cold War* (Oxford: Oxford University Press, 1981) 71-79
[282] David Capitanchik *The Eisenhower presidency and American Foreign Policy (London: Routledge and Kegan Paul, 1969),*39-45

Hegemony in the Middle East

The political dimensions surrounding the developments of this time period looked primarily at the maintenance of United States power and hegemony in the Middle East. Once Iran was dependent on America's foreign policy, it was time for the United States to exploit the resources accumulated over the First Revolution and spread their hegemony to the Middle East and win this Cold War. The first several months prior to 1955 were about the settlement of the oil consortium agreement and measures to prevent communism from spreading.[283] The United States began providing $127.1 million in loans and grants to Iran and this framework helped organize and provide military training to the Iranian government and its soldiers. The new proposals were to expand military assistance and provide developmental assistance to Iran's army.[284] These proposals were very modest from the Shah and ARMISH could meet them, but the thing to understand was the Baghdad Pact. This pact could be weak and ineffective if it didn't have U.S. political support. The United States participated in the pact for a time, but it did not want to because it did not want to form an imperialist identity which was also what the Shah did not want. The Baghdad Pact included several countries whose purpose was to maintain a regional defense network. This network would build up arms and an effective military. The Pact would be responsible for creating economic development and cooperation. The United States wanted to emphasize economic development and de-emphasize the military while Great Britain wanted to invest more on military and less on economics. The Soviet Union was a staunch enemy against the Baghdad Pact and was threatening to attack soft spots of the Northern Tier.[285]

In the Second Revolution, Iran had time to invest its resources into its industries. The industries were sugar, textiles, and cement. Only a few years prior, Iran was dependent on the

---

[283] AmEmbassy Tehran to Department of State 19 January 1955 RG 59 788.5 MSP/1-1955.
[284] AmEmbassy Tehran to Department of State 19 January 1955 RG 59 788.5 MSP/1-1955.
[285] Enclosure Desp. 641 Tehran 19 January 1955 RG 59 788.5 MSP/1-1955.

Soviet Union for sugar as they headed the sugar monopoly of the world. But then there were three major sugar plants worth more than $2 million dollars in investments. This joint investment by the United States and Iran gave America profit over sugar sales as Iran became the leading sugar monopoly of the world.[286] The natural water resources program took off and completed a 350 year old project to divert the water from the Kuhrang River into the Zayaendeh River. The others have been mainly other water resource projects. The educational project began building and completing training schools, elementary schools, etc- all provided by the United States. Interestingly enough, students involved in a foreign exchange program received an increase in stipend and an increase in participation.[287] This increase developed from the Iranian government suspending foreign exchange money to about 18 students in Europe.[288] It was because four to five students were group leaders at the demonstration in front of the Iranian Embassy in Paris in1955. In many newspapers, students contend that the government of Iran provided no foreign exchange subsidy for Iranians to buy foreign currency at low rates for two years. This uproar condemned the Iranian government's monarchy, advocated for a National Republic of Iran, and appealed to the United States to not pay us off, but help the students and rejection of full communism without collaboration with Russia. It further told the Iranian government how incorrect the relationship with Britain was and that all moral alliances should be suggested by the United States. The students felt the United States was the best advisor on Iranian foreign policy. The students disliked the corruption and condemned the Tudeh party. These are the reasons the students demonstrated against the Iranian Embassy in Paris. But the stipends had been reinstated.[289]

---

[286] Enclosure Desp. 1003 19 January 1955 RG 59, 788.5 MSP/1-1955.
[287] Enclosure Desp. 1003 19 January 1955 RG 59, 788.5 MSP/1-1955.

[288] Enclosure Desp.392 15 February 1955 RG 59, 788.5 MSP/2-1555.
[289] AmEmbassy Tehran to Department of State 18 May 1955 RG 59 788.13/5-1855.

The other matter of prime concern was the inculcation of the defense line agreement that Dulles believed would make Iran complete. After the completion of its border security, Iran needed to work on its internal affairs as many tribes of Iran still did not follow the law of the government. Iran needed to be consolidated. The road construction, the completion of railroads, and the Iranian Airways flights, were all military oriented, not economic. There was not much traffic. People did not use the railroad a lot and the flights were empty, only carrying mail and other products necessary for Iran. The schools and the level of instruction were also improving with enthusiastic students ready to read.[290] But despite these achievements, an Iranian businessman claimed that *there are deep rooted and persistent problem of corruption in Government*- this had been the forefront of the political developments in Iran.[291] But the overthrow was in fact appropriate because it decentralized the communist party and maintained internal security. The oil revenues of 1955, American loans and grants, and the successful economic development program had all been improving Iran. Iran was coming along and the Shah's commitment to political acceptance and military aid was paramount.[292] This period of 1955 was known as the *quietest periods of recent Iranian history.* There were many unanswered questions and no coordination in government.[293] In order to stave off the crisis, there would be two bills presented; one was on pure food and the other one was on drugs and began enforcing developments at the University of Tehran classroom to ensure productivity.[294] In these developments, Iran pledged that *they are the main bulwark against communism and the main architects of a stable, free world.[295]* Even in Baghdad, the strength of America and the comment

---

[290] Department of State to AmEmbassy Tehran 7 June 1955 RG 59 788.00/6-755.
[291] AmEmbassy Tehran to Department of State 7 June 1955 RG 59 788.00/6-755.
[292] Baxter to Allen 11 June 1955 RG 59 788.00/6-1155.
[293] Tehran to Secretary of State 11 June 1955 RG 59 788.00/6-1155.
[294] AmEmbassy Tehran to Secretary of State 19 June 1955 RG 59 788.00/6-1955.
[295] AmEmbassy Tehran to Secretary of State 19 June 1955 RG 59 788.00/6-1955

of having all men free were espoused by them. Iraq and Turkey were the first proponents of the Baghdad Pact and though Iran hesitated, they also joined and pulling Iraq to the Arab world would be a good move because it would help eliminate communism and strengthen hegemony.[296] In the United States the Shah's taxes were waived.[297] The Shah was encouraging other members to join the defense pact with King Saud of Saudi Arabia, joining the Iranian view. The Saudi king felt religiously that he was against communism, but politically, joining the Soviet bloc may not be so bad. He planned to visit Iran. But, Israel didn't join the pact because it had to accept giving aid to Palestinian refugees.[298]

Though the United States and the Shah both admit that the Iranian population supported the Shah, they were not really investigating their internal affairs. On July 22, 1955, during the anniversary of the return of power of Mossedegh, there were publications issued by a committee in Azerbaijan supporting Mossedegh and urging Iran to condemn the west's seizing Iranian oil. Once the economy was stabilizing, the Shah wanted to benefit from its politics. The Shah was looking at Turkey's position in NATO and the Middle Eastern pacts and observing how they dealt with the Russians, thinking of joining the profitable venture as well. The United States now had the power of threatening to cut aid from Iran if Iran chose to do so.[299] Besides the food shortages and attempts to deal with it, Iran entered into an agreement with the Afghan government over a river dispute.[300]

Knowing that the United States was on its way to winning the regional Cold War, the Soviet Union wanted to try their best to detract Iran's attention away from the United States and

---

[296] AmEmbassy Tehran to Secretary of State 19 June 1955 RG 59 788.00/6-1955.

[297] Foreign Distributors Division to Iranian Embassy 29 April 1955 RG 59 788.11/4-2955.
[298] Tehran to Secretary of State 23 August 1955 RG 59 788.00/8-2355.
[299] Tehran to Secretary of State 23 August 1955 RG 59 788.00/8-2355.

[300] Tehran to Secretary of State 13 October 1955 RG 59 788.00 (W)/10-1355.

made lucrative offers. One such offer was to drop support of the Tudeh party in Iran by coming to Moscow and signing an agreement of equality of rights between the two nations. This agreement would weaken the regional defense bloc that was against the Soviet Union. The United States had reinforced their armed forces against this meeting and tried to circumvent the anti-U.S. literature being circulated in the Iranian press.[301] This literature was also being supported by the Soviet Union who used their power and money to encourage these groups to publish these propaganda pieces.[302]

Politically, the primary figure in Iran was the Shah. But the government was able to reveal his stubbornness, his indecision, and hiring those who are loyal, not necessarily qualified. The people felt that the United States would prevent a loss of Iranian dependence to the Soviet Union and to the United Kingdom. For prestige, the Iranian government looked for the Americans. For advice, they turned to the United Kingdom. But by ignoring United States' advice, they could in turn join the Soviet bloc and India and resist settlements with Pakistan, Afghanistan, and Iraq- something that the United States did not want. From the pool of resources that the Shah accumulated, his major expenses were building up his army. At the end of 1955, the United States did not think that these American funds would be used against Pakistan or Afghanistan but felt that the *Shah is likely to continue to press for United States military aid and to accomplish that whatever is forthcoming is insufficient.* His comparison was with Turkey.[303] But the United States felt that the Iranian Army was built up to a degree that it could maintain itself internally against any threat. Iran was now not part of the defense arrangement and was waiting to see what the United States would offer *him* if Iran joined. He wanted a modern force

---

[301] Tehran to Secretary of State 13 October 1955 RG 59 788.00 (W)/10-1355.

[302] Tehran to Secretary of State 13 October 1955 RG 59 788.00 (W)/10-1355.

[303] Tehran to Department of State, 27 December 1955, RG 59, 788.13/12-2755.

with material, training personnel, and a huge budget in effect. It was quite contradictory that the politically involved Iranians including the military wanted the Shah to develop Iran economically, not militarily. Perhaps the Shah resisted because of the 1927 Iran-Soviet Treaty that forbid both countries to launch propaganda against each other. But, this agreement did not stop the Soviets from their propaganda attacks. If Iran joined the defense arrangement with the United Kingdom or the United States, the Soviet Union would charge violation of the treaty.[304]

The reason the Shah was so adamant about the build up of the army and though he had no warfare experience, he knew that in 1941 when the army failed the Anglo-Soviet invasion, he did not want to leave that murky mark, he wanted to give the Iranian Army a better reputation and increase its international prestige. In order for this to happen, he needed political support and money. The reason the United Kingdom was still involved was that the United States was not ready to abandon them and wanted them to have economic influence. Iran's foreign policy was under United States' surveillance and Iran were heavy on development. Iranians felt that by increasing the economic and social status of Iran to the world that it could combat imperialists. They tried to gain independence from the United Kingdom in 1906, the Soviets, and now the United States. The only way to secure a national sovereign state was through national pride and unity and by *exploiting East-West tension.* They could benefit from the richest country getting them their freedom. Through America's support of Iran's foreign and domestic policies, the United States could get Iran to a modern stage of independence and the United States could attain hegemony through this relationship.[305]

In the beginning of 1956 Senator Emani attacked Prime Minister Ala who replaced General Zahedi and his government. He tried his best to remain quiet, but he described the

---

[304] Tehran to Department of State, 27 December 1955, RG 59, 788.13/12-2755.
[305] Tehran to Department of State, 27 December 1955, RG 59, 788.13/12-2755.

situation in Iran as *incorrigible.* The new government under the Shah promised better reforms and idealistic solutions with an internal tranquility and a balanced budget. He said, "The treasury is empty. There is no confidence…of the administration. And the costs are skyrocketing and officials use fake statistics to tell us that it has dropped."[306] There was a lot of corruption in the different ministries and ministers came to him asking why such corruption existed in their departments. He further stated that there wasn't any internal security because more than 36 violent deaths occurred. He said, "You use over 50 percent of the budget for these forces, and yet crime is increasing."[307] But the *Jamshid Alam* replied that dealing with corruption would take over a generation, but Iran needed to have a plan to deal with economic development. The paper was pleased on the freedoms that Iran had achieved. *The Amini-Nuri* said there was no advantage in joining the Baghdad Pact, that the minister of industries received a portion of the profit. The government was getting too big and there was a lot of bureaucracy.[308] The intellectual class represented one of the three largest classes in Iran along with landlords and Mullahs. The intellectual class favored political and social progress and at this stage, these intellectuals were not happy with the government. The communists looked to the intellectuals for conversion and school teachers were those who represented the best of the intellectuals. Senator Sadiq says, *there can be no real progress in this country, no breaking away from the threat of communism, unless the needs of the intellectuals are met.[309]* The landlords and mullahs were not the ones to understand these difficulties. Iran must involve this class or it would revolt against Iran.[310]

---

[306] American Embassy to Department of State, 12 January 1956, RG 59, 788.21/1-1256.
[307] American Embassy to Department of State, 12 January 1956, RG 59, 788.21/1-1256.

[308] American Embassy to Department of State, 18 January 1956, RG 59, 788.21/1-1856.
[309] American Embassy Tehran to Department of State 20 December 1955, RG 59, 788.00/12-2055.
[310] American Consulate to Department of State, 6 January 1956, RG 59, 788.00/1-656.

The Iranian government was not doing well under an incapacitated leadership. The Shah lost support of the higher classes, his land reform laws were dangerous and Senator Emami asked the people of Iran: *Why you people do not make it your first task, for our good, for the Shah's good, and for your own good, to cajole and persuade him to abandon this foolish and tragic venture…* He went on to state that the political situation of Iran was worsening and the Arab-Israeli tension was intensifying. He told the United States that *your policy in the Middle East bends like a sheet of rubber whenever one of those fools makes a stupid move. No one knows where you stand.* In the matter of the Middle East, Senator Emami blamed the Egyptians for breaking up everything and says they are seen as *cultural barbarians.* He further stated that the United States was spoiling the Saudi King with money and resources for oil but they could get more in Iran, so why keep the relationship.[311]

The other news of this time was that the Saudi Arabian Embassy published propaganda against England, the negotiations with the Afghans still continued and Pakistan sat with Iranian officials in Tehran to discuss the demarcation of their common land: Baluchistan.[312] In February 1956, the United States offered $20 million in aid and the Soviet Union continued its attacks of the Baghdad Pact after a year of its existence. The thing that scared the Soviets was ongoing developments. The living conditions continued to deteriorate in Iran.[313] In March of 1956, there were many escapees that leaving the USSR to find peace and solitude in Iran. These escapees were generally those who existed in exile and were free to choose as a free citizen in the Iranian economy or find resettlement places for them to live. In 1956 the biggest concern was though Iran was benefiting from the Shah and his western policies, the Shah began to lose his reputation and political strength because of his bad leadership. The American Embassy says, "Unless this

---

[311] Tehran to Department of State, 7 March 1956, RG 59, 788.00/3-756.
[312] American Embassy to Department of State 19 March 1955, 788.00/3-1956.
[313] American Embassy to Department of State 19 March 1955, 788.00/3-1956

trend is checked, it may lead to a situation where economic conditions cannot be substantially improved because of a lack of political stability." The American Embassy reported this to the State Department in April of 1956. His popularity was important for the United States to stay in Iran. The United States did not think too much of it at that time. People did not like him in the government because he was not favorable to prime ministers and he provided no direction for the government. The government in turn may spin off on its own....[314]

A Second Seven Year Plan

In March of 1956, Iran formed their second seven year plan with a peculiar idea to help Iranian history. The historical making would come from the people of Iran. It was to provide a better standard of living with access to food, clothing, housing, better health care and a better education. Due to the images now posed by the west, everyone was grappling with this issue that their lives should be like those of the west and people were demanding their basic rights and necessities. If the people got a better living, they could help in the economic progress of the country. This economic progress could lead to social progress and then to nationalism. The oil agreement with the west surrendered Iran's nationalistic principles and the people needed some kind of nationalism. But the second seven year plan could not survive if the Shah did not involve himself in Iranian politics. The American Embassy states, *"the Shah's political position will become weaker with the passage of time unless and until he is able to satisfy the people with substantial economic advancement financed by oil revenues.[315]* In May of 1956 the Shah opened the 19 Majlis and delivered a speech. In his speech he did not tackle the rights of women, land reform, the high cost of living or rents. There was nothing about American assistance, but his concern in his speech was with Turkey. He felt the seven year plan was very important to him

---

[314] American Embassy to Department of State 21 April 1956, RG 59, 788.00/4-2156.
[315] AmEmbassy Tehran to Department of State 26 March 1956, RG 59, 788.00/3-2656.

and everyone must work hard to make it happen. The Shah further stated that it was the oil

revenues that would increase the economy.[316] The Shah was committed to battling illiteracy and

opium cultivation and consumption. In 1956 the Shah also had a chance to make it to the Soviet

Union and the Shah defended Iran very well.[317] Another document however stated that the

people did not feel anything or make any popular comment against the Shah's visit. This

document painted a rosy picture of the situation. It reported no change or opinion on the Iranian

budget, collection of taxes, land taxes, and the reformation strategies of the Justice Ministry.[318]

The dislike of the Shah

The American Embassy reported that the population was actually sick of the Shah. They

were concerned about rising prices. Though the Shah was still favored, he was being met with a

lot of criticism. An example of this criticism is a *semi-affectionate criticism* that the Shah did not

have a strong personality, while others said he was a puppet of the Americans, and that he was an

American tool. The biggest criticism of the government labeled it the *Shah's office boys,* and all

blame should be targeted to the Shah. Many felt that the Shah was not experienced to rule the

nation and some felt he was a British puppet.[319] Also, in the news, the Shah rejected India's

protest of Kashmir being part of the Indian Union and supported a quick settlement for the

independence of Kashmir.[320] With all these problems, the population was becoming apolitical to

the point that they become active only when it was in their interests. The population did not favor

social reforms. The political dissatisfaction from the elite came from British influence and the

elections. The lower class was also unhappy because of price levels and lack of economic

---

[316] AmEmbassy Tehran to Department of State 8 June 1956, RG 59, 788.00/6-856.
[317] AmEmbassy Tehran to Department of State 8 June 1956, RG 59, 788.00/6-856.
[318] AmEmbassy Tehran to Department of State 8 June 1956, RG 59, 788.00/6-856
[319] AmEmbassy Tehran to Department of State 8 June 1956, RG 59, 788.00/6-856

[320] AmEmbassy Tehran to Department of State 8 June 1956, RG 59, 788.00/6-856

development. The common man on the street saw no improvement in his life and attributed the lack of improvement to the Shah.[321] Seldin Chapin says, "less and less does the average taxi driver, ditch-digger, or peasant picture the Shah as his friend and protector, his hope for deliverance from a system he doesn't like." The west and the Shah live off this wealth and paint a nice picture while the population was aggravated with the West and the Shah. He said that time was running out and that action needed to be taken now to restore population prestige of the Shah's image otherwise the Shah would lose everything…..[322] Another State Department document admitted that his administration was great, but unless the government changed its practices and established firm leadership, the political, economic, or administrative reforms would be costly to the Shah. There was however no government at this time that could provide such friendly services and the Shah used everything in his power to gain money, and his relations with the Soviets would definitely go down.[323]

Known as the Imperial Purple, in June 1956 the Shah decided not to talk about the rising costs of living like they didn't exist, though he was concerned about the religion of his workers. The religion they followed could neither be communist or Tudehist, but extreme poverty conditions tempted them to break their religious ideals for hope. Though they may not want to eat bread, they have to eat something.[324] The current economy was stagnant with no one shopping and factories dropping production.[325] People began believing that the elite were tools of the British and disliked the government. The morale of the Iranian military was down and it was inefficient. But the Shah was not much concerned because the people were anti-communist. The

---

[321] Chapin to American Embassies 8 June 1956, RG 59, 788.00/6-856.
[322] Chapin to American Embassies 8 June 1956, RG 59, 788.00/6-856.

[323] Dispatch No. 892 8 June 1956, RG 59, 788.00/6-856.
[324] American Embassy to Department of State, 8 June 1956, RG 59, 888.00/6-856.
[325] American Embassy to Department of State, 8 June 1956, RG 59, 888.00/6-856.

mullahs were actually causing some commotion in this mess and because of their power were beginning to embarrass the government because of the rising costs of living. In this 19 majlis, the Shah was pleased to state that the adherence to the Baghdad Pact and prohibition of cultivation of poppies were good things for Iranian politics.[326]

A threat to United States Hegemony

After returning from the Moscow visit, the United States was concerned about their hegemony. They found out that the Soviet Union presented very lucrative offers, but the monarch stated his allegiance to the United States and relations were paramount.[327] President Eisenhower through a correspondence of Selden Chapin, the American Ambassador, congratulated the Shah's effective negotiations with the Soviet Union. He commented that *Iran's* foreign policies began improving under the Shah. The Shah of Iran responded by asking for increased funds for expenditures for joining the Baghdad Pact. He reassured the president about ongoing efforts, but requested money. Chapin said, "This is a familiar theme which the Shah almost always brings up during his talk."[328] On the lighter side of things, Princess Shahnaz and the son of General Zahedi, Ardashir, were getting married. The political marriage was to stabilize the military support of the Shah.[329] Throughout the towering problems in Iran, the American Embassy in Tehran assessed an internal, stabilized and externally diplomatic nation. In August 1956 the American Embassy believed that the army's morale was improving and economic reforms were occurring due to the adherence to the Baghdad Pact. But the government

---

[326] American Embassy Tehran to Department of State 25 June 1956, RG 59, 788.00/6-2556.
[327] American Embassy Tehran to Department of State 25 June 1956, RG 59, 788.00/6-2556.

[328] American Embassy Tehran to Department of State 10 August 1956, RG 59, 788.11/8-1056.
[329] American Embassy Tehran to Department of State 21 November 1956 RG 59, 788.11/11-2156.

was not assessing their foreign aid and the American Embassy reported, "While this government can be expected to continue in office so long as it serves the purpose of the Shah, its usefulness may be decreasing."[330] But the Hossein Ala government since its inception in April of 1955 was better than Zahedi rule as prime minister. The government had become more honest, though corruption still occurred, but not at high rates like before. In this government, the challenge was to create reforms and ministers made an effort to create that norm. The creation of new roads, industries, and a better control of 60 percent of Iranian oil all dramatically improved Iran.[331] The Shah believed in social reforms addressing illiteracy, but the fiscal position of Iran was still yet to improve and the Ala government did not address this.

The Baghdad Pact

Foreign relations in 1956 boiled down to the Baghdad Pact. The Iranian population did not like the pact as it severed their complete independence and sovereignty, but agreed to support it if the United States provided more aid. The other option was that the United States would defend Iranian borders if they were not given more money. The Iranian Army was improving, but was still viewed as unpopular. The complete internal security projects were being launched and reduced the amount of riots in the cities. One such security endeavor was to cease conflict with a Kurdish tribe that was deemed to be uncooperative. In another report, a gentleman visiting the government of the Consortium was displeased with the local administration and the collection of taxes.[332] Honest people did not want to work because the government squeezed every penny from their purses for their own profits. Further, the people could not go to courts because these officials were part of the governmental administration. The people of Iran disliked and distrusted the government despite their favorable opinion of Ala. The Shah's cabinet was

---

[330] American Embassy Tehran to Department of State 13August 1956, RG 59, 788.12/8-1356.
[331] American Embassy Tehran to Department of State 13August 1956, RG 59, 788.12/8-1356.
[332] American Embassy Tehran to Department of State 13August 1956, RG 59, 788.12/8-1356.

labeled as incompetent. Prime Minister Ala said that he made a law in 1948 as Minister of Interior that he did not want students to meddle in politics. Just because there was no martial law, does not mean the public should engage in destructive affairs. He did not like disruption in the ministries and anything that was harmful to the nation even if it is many press holdings, he wanted to eliminate it. He said, *I would rather rule for day or two as strong Prime Minister than as weak one for two-three years.* He was against corrupt ministers.[333]

In August 1956, a proposal was sent to Iran to purchase all Iranian caviar sold from a local fisheries agency. These wholesale products were completely bought out by the Americans who limited all access to Iranian caviar and Iranian trade.[334] As the Iranian, Turkish, Pakistani, and American relationships improved, the relations with the Soviet Union continued to deteriorate and the capture of installations across the border for NIOC was not another added benefit.[335] With the abolishing of Martial law, Iran formed a new Office of Security that would encompass a secret police trained and organized by the CIA. The agency was called SAVAK.[336] In light of the ongoing reaffirmations of religion, there was a rise of Ayatollahs, and a new Ayatollah who interprets religion and prescribes religious practices was forming. He is Ayatollah Haji Aqa Hosein.[337]

The previous section briefly discussed how the State Department was buying opium from Iran to help the pharmaceutical industries of Iran. The purchase of this opium allowed Iran to buy sugar and become a sugar monopoly. The country was relatively stable, so Iran banned the cultivation and production of opium. The U.S. government was appalled and told Iran it would get opium from Afghanistan, but needed Iran to produce it, not necessarily cultivate it. The

---

[333] American Embassy Tehran to Department of State 13August 1956, RG 59, 788.12/8-1356
[334] Tehran to Secretary of State 1 August 1956, RG 59, 788.00 (W)/8-156.
[335] Tehran to Secretary of State 5 August 1956, RG 59, 788.00 (W)/8-556.
[336] Tehran to Secretary of State 6 August 1956, RG 59, 788.00/8-656.
[337] Tehran to Secretary of State 6 August 1956, RG 59, 788.00/8-656.

United States promised to pay Iran for the production costs. A U.N. Narcotics committee allowed Afghanistan to export opium since Iran objected to it. The American government also embarrassed the Iranian government saying the production would not provide a loss of revenue since it is money they always seek.[338] Also, Iran planned to settle the Baluchistan dispute with Pakistan and resolve some water disputes it had with Afghanistan. In December 1956 there were no new developments, only a cultural agreement signed by New Delhi and Iran.[339]

The top news that the United States planned to provide a $52 million aid package in 1957 was met with criticism because the aid was not used properly. The Soviets were appalled by this aid and invited a group of journalists to go to the USSR for three weeks to give them information against the Shah. Such information showed how politically unstable Iran was and how all classes of the government were displeased with him.[340] The Shah's close associates were not religious and many middle classes were atheist, so communism wouldn't work and the Tudeh party was disappearing. Iran became a secular nation without religion. The goal of the United States then should've been to politically stabilize Iran and the Shah was the only person who could lead that effort.[341] A confidential file was delivered to the Honorable John Hollister of Iran requesting $45 million in aid that would politically stabilize the country. The letter said that the aid package would be their full utilization. Another $25 million was requested to help the regional projects of Iran and support cooperative programs and local currency.[342] Dulles further agreed, believing that such aid for the cooperative programs would indeed help strengthen the communication and living standards of Iran. These projects would also work to establish the northern tier defense systems and no delay in this matter should occur. Dulles said, *Iran, along with the Baghdad Pact*

---

[338] Tehran to Secretary of State 6 August 1956, RG 59, 788.00/8-656.
[339] Tehran to Secretary of State 6 August 1956, RG 59, 788.00/8-656.
[340] Tehran to Secretary of State, 27 December 1956, RG 59, 788.00/12-2756.
[341] Tehran to Secretary of State, 27 December 1956, RG 59, 788.00/12-2756.
[342] State Department to Hollister, 7 December 1956, RG 59, 788.5/12-756.

neighbor, constitute one of the best political nests the United States has in the area at this time.

He emphasized Iran's importance to maintain their interests in this world.[343]

Paul Jones, the editor of the Sentinel Tribune of Ohio wrote a letter to Herbert Hoover Jr. Assistant Secretary of State requesting Hoover to comment on how he planned the overthrow of Mohammed Mossadegh in Iran.[344] In an article of that paper, the Speaker of the House suggests:

> The United States is learning maybe too late- to concentrate more on economic
> and political defense and less on military defense. At the end of the war, the
> United States controlled 17 percent of the oil reserves in the Near East. Now, we
> control 85 percent.[345]

The article states that Herbert Hoover Jr., the outgoing assistant secretary of state *planned the overthrow of Mohammed Mossadegh in Iran. The British formerly got most of the Iranian oil. Now they get only a small amount while the United States get half.[346]* The State Department replied saying that Hoover's involvement in the overthrow- though he was the CIA agent in charge of Iran- was false, and in fact Hoover was in California at a meeting. Hoover had nothing to do with the overthrow of Mossedegh. The State Department further continued that Mossedegh refused to settle the dispute of oil and the cessation of oil revenues was becoming very apparent. The reason the United States got involved, so they say, was to stop communism from spreading in a nation that was wrought with chaos and no money.[347]

U.S. Hegemony could suffer

In February of 1957, the Soviets continued their tempting offers to Iran, but the United States had to get involved in the stability of the nation. The Shah was acting as both monarch and prime minister and though he was pro-west and anti-communist, he was very indecisive. He still

---

[343] Dulles to Tehran, 11 December 1956, RG 59, 788.5 MSP/12-1156.
[344] Paul Jones to Herbert Hoover Jr. 29 January 1957, RG 59, 788.5/1-2957.
[345] The Daily Sentinel, 26 January 1957, RG 59, 788.5/1-2657.
[346] The Daily Sentinel, 26 January 1957, RG 59, 788.5/1-2657.

[347] State Department to McCordock, 14 February 1957, RG 59, 788.00/2-1457.

needed to reminders of the United States' support. The Shah was adamant that he would not be deceived by the Soviets.[348] During this year, the Shah expanded his economy by gaining support from other Middle Eastern nations. He first approached Saudi Arabia. The Shah and the public were pleased with Eisenhower's new Middle Eastern policy of defense of borders through atomic bombings of USSR. But Iran was concerned that the bombings would start World War III. The atomic bombs would definitely be a deterrent, but local mini-wars in Iran were not suitable and the Soviet Union must understand that.[349] The loss of faith and trust continued in Iran as they believed that Iran was a corrupt nation not ready to treat them with respect. The public further did not like America's presence in Iran. The Iranian public did not understand the negotiations between Great Britain, the United States, and Iran, is thought the country should hate the west like they hated the regime. Another startling fact is that the people of Iran believed the Shah had large sums of illegal money, but he did not. The United States had to bring a new kind of democracy to Iran.[350] The time was long overdue and no communist could then be elected . The dislike of America increased in the cities. All the disappointments and bad things in life were attributed to the United States. People believed that the United States opposed free elections and wanted the Shah to run the country in fear of the communists gaining power. It was stated that the disappointments and all bad attributes slowly occurring in cities came about because of communist propaganda. But nothing could be done except to support the Shah. The American Embassy said that the Tehran government needed to do something about the armed bandits reported in the newspapers. The Shah issued notices to deal with the bandits, but the government had not yet.[351]

---

[348] Tehran to State Department, 28 February, 1957, RG 59, 788.11/2-2857
[349] American Embassy to Secretary of State, 28 February, 1957, RG 59, 788.11/2-2857.
[350] American Embassy to Secretary of State, 28 February, 1957, RG 59, 788.11/2-2857.
[351] American Embassy to Secretary of State, 28 February, 1957, RG 59, 788.11/2-2857.

In early April, the Shah appointed a new prime minister, Eqbal, to steer the political situation into a new era. He formed a new political party that was more conservative and tricky than the Alam party, which was composed of intelligent and very unintelligent people.[352] Lately, a mullah was creating trouble against the government in 1955 to 1956. This mullah of Shiraz city died as the representative of a new political religious brotherhood. The mullahs are against the government, but interestingly enough, they support and admire America.[353] When the Shah returned to comfort recent earthquake victims, he sensed a situation quite different than when he took power in August 1953. Quickly, he decided to take some constitutional power from the Prime Minister. He consolidated his rule to include a much more harsh form of dictatorship, involving matters of the state, parliament, and administration. He feared losing his throne.[354] The new prime minister quietly told many circles that he was displeased with the Shah's policies, but remained in office until his position and the Office of Prime Minister became of little importance to the state and to the dictatorship of the Shah. He was waiting for that position to be *tossed aside as being of no further use to the Throne.* The Shah needed to change his attitude and not ruin the reputation of being an able politician, but *the identity of the following prime minister was unimportant as long as the Shah continues his current role.* Personally, the Shah lost much popularity in Iran and the American Embassy believed that *he will have become an active symbol of evil in the eyes of the politically-conscious Iranians…..*[355]

The population thought that the Shah would lose his power and only hold power over the officer corps of the Shah's army before he was empowered to do so. But, the officer corps was also becoming dissatisfied with the political situation. The Embassy says, "There is always the

---

[352] AmEmbassy Tehran to Department of State, 17 July 1957, RG 59, 788.11/2-1757.
[353] American Consulate Isfahan to Department of State, 9 July, 1957, RG 59, 788.00/7-957.
[354] AmEmbassy Tehran to Department of State, 20 July 1957, RG 59, 788.11/7-2057.
[355] Amembassy Tehran to Department of State, 20 July 1957, RG 59, 788.11/7-2057.

possibility of the removal of the Shah from the political scene either by accident-*the Shah's love of piloting his own plane or driving in sports cars is well known*-or that of another assassination attempt.....[356]

The reason that the Shah wanted to take power away from the prime minister was not only because he could not delegate, but that Eqbal represented honesty and honesty through reforms for personal freedom and security. The Shah was not interested in reforms because they were not profitable. Though many conjecture that there was no progress in Iran, Iran actually surpassed its standard of living for the masses and a standard of justice and security, but it was weak in its management of its resources, not its wealth. The Shah was also jealous of Eqbal's popularity. Due to the terrible social structure of Iranian society, it was hard for U.S. policies to be implemented at the grassroots level. The idea of a community was not fully refined in Iranian society. At these times, people only think survival, not of others.[357]

The problem that was happening was a disconnect from information. The American Embassy reported their early findings of a potential upheaval in Iranian politics, while the State Department painted a rosy picture of the Shah and Iran. They also requested the press not to write anything against Iran, as the Shah and his government admired the U.S. government. For example, the Department of State's Public Affairs officers would report that there were no decreases in the Shah's popularity and the population looked *quite favorably* on the Shah. Also the Shah's men noted no problems in security and little changes in opinions of attitudes and development.[358] In fact, in a small meeting in Europe, the Iranian Ambassador listened to the Shah when the Shah said that there was no support for him in Iran. But he had to maintain material U.S. Aid. He wanted good reports even though false to go to the State Department. Dr.

---

[356] Amembassy Tehran to Department of State, 20 July 1957, RG 59, 788.11/7-2057.
[357] Ruter to Wolf, 29 July 1957, RG 59, 788.11/7-2957.
[358] American Embassy to Tehran, 9 August 1957, RG 59, 788.00/8-957.

Amini said that Chapin told the United States about the great friendship and found the State Department generous in its understanding of Iran and its issues. The Shah wanted to let the United States know how Iran was progressing in its agreements like the one with Italy on oil, its developments and its international success. The United States had no objections to this agreement with Italy, only that Italy could move after America's interest once Iran was dependent on Italy too.[359]

Under Eqbal, the financial situation got worse. Eqbal, according to Iran's leading educators from Columbia, Sadiq, was concerned about Eqbal and his conduct of foreign affairs. Sadiq was also concerned about the oil agreement with oil tycoon Matti in Italy and was negative about the Shah's regime. He was very favorable to the west. Sadiq saw the Shah getting a *closer and closer control over all facets of the Iranian government.*[360] Though the Shah ran this nation better than his father, he had two main problems. He did not have honest, smart, good people working for him. He felt he owed his throne and life to the officers of the Army and though many top level officers were corrupt, he won't do anything to them. If he followed this course, he would become unpopular at an early stage in his rule. Sadiq says, *If unchecked, this trend will eventually mean revolution or assassination.* The Shah thought that 95 percent of the people supported him, but they did not and Sadiq speculated that the Shah may not be in Iran after six years. Six years covers the years from 1956 to1962.[361] The Shah was a smart man. Nobody really knew what was going on in Iran. South Korea President Lt. Gen. Kim Chung Yui just agreed with diplomatic relations with Korea and Iran.[362] After this negotiation, Iran had funds to purchase two Douglas DC-3 airplanes from Scandinavian Air and Transocean Air and bought

---

[359] Department of State to Amini, 20 August 1957, RG 59, 788.00/8-2057.
[360] AmEmbassy Tehran to Department of State, 15 August 1957, RG 59, 788.00/8-1557.
[361] AmEmbassy Tehran to Department of State, 15 August 1957, RG 59, 788.00/8-1557.

[362] AmEmbassy to Department of State, 1 June 1957, RG 59, 788.00 (W)/6-157.

some Fighter Jet planes too.[363] Immediately Soviet Ambassador Pegov, a member of the

Supreme Soviets went to Moscow for a meeting. In a meeting between Americans and the Shah,

the Shah had little concern and was quite ignorant of how unpopular he was, but told him that it

took 12 years of power to garner the immense power he had in July of 1957.[364]

While the Shah continued his consolidation of his power, he had a negotiation with the

Oil Kings of the Persian Gulf, but the United States came in and denounced Iran for continuing

these oil negotiations. For the first time since 1954, the Shah heavily criticized the United States

for breaking the agreement with the oil kings. The "foreigners" interfered in Iranian foreign

policy… After this statement was issued, the Shah told the Embassy he did not want the United

States to know about these harsh words. He wanted to tell them of the ongoing friendship with

the United States and that Iran was pursuing an independent sovereign policy.[365] Eqbal's long

time friend and supporter was an editor of a small newspaper. The small newspaper published a

childhood photo of the Shah on a horse. The caption showed that the Iranian press insulted the

Shah. It read, *He who sits on horseback with a tilted hat is neither fit to run nor rule a country….*[366]

In an earlier discussion, it was stated how the United States contributed more than 20

percent of gifts to the Shah. One such gift was a Steuben glass sent to the Shah via the

Ambassador. But Dulles reported that these gifts should not be reported as a gift from the

President or the U.S. government.[367] Iran also used to influence the affairs of Syria and lessen

their trouble. Iran advocated for the United States to fully participate in the British Petroleum

consortium agreement so the United States could make more money and send it to Iran.[368] In

---

[363] AmEmbassy to Department of State, 1 June 1957, RG 59, 788.00 (W)/6-157.

[364] AmEmbassy to Department of State, 1 June 1957, RG 59, 788.00 (W)/6-157.

[365] AmEmbassy Tehran to Department of State, 1 August 1957, RG 59, 788.00/8-157.

[366] AmEmbassy Tehran to Department of State, 1 August 1957, RG 59, 788.00/8-157
[367] AmEmbassy Tehran to Department of State, 26 September 1957, RG 59, 788.11/9-2657.

September 1957, the Shah became very disturbed about such Soviet statements that uttered *Iran would be knocked out by conventional weapons and missiles in event hostilities.* NATO and Iran began to re-path Iran's defense policies and establish more American bases in Iran. The Shah took advantage of this threat and requested Americans to provide funds to build up a larger army, missiles, and a build up of any additional modern equipment.[369] On October 21, 1957, shortly before the Shah's birthday, his daughter Princess Shahnaz and Zahedi's son, Ardeshir were married and showered with immense gold coins.[370] Syria began thinking of the events of 1953 when the coup created broken relations with them. However Syria still wanted to remain friends with Iran, but they were suspicious of the United States. There were tariff reductions between the USSR and Iran and a trade agreement that Iran accepted to trade with the Soviets.[371]

On October 26, 1957, the Shah celebrated his birthday. He remarked that the economy of Iran was good, the rail link with Turkey enabled Iran to trade with Turkey, agricultural markets were on the rise, the oil agreement was a great achievement and Iran was receiving many oil contracts, too many to consider. There was however, a proposed transit agreement with the Soviet Union. The Shah planned trips to visit Jordan, Syria, and Lebanon. The reputation of Eqbal declined. Iran made a Soviet Air agreement. Both Britain and Iran were reaching an agreement with the Shah on the Persian Gulf and they decided for no sovereignty plans for Bahrein, no establishment of an Iranian consulate in Kuwait or interest of Iran to take over Kuwait and no interest thereafter. Though the Shah said, no negotiation, the British still forwarded his comments for a negotiation.[372] In December 1957, the cold weather in Iran left

---

[368] AmEmbassy Tehran to Department of State, 3 September 1957, RG 59, 788.00 (W)/9-357.
[369] AmEmbassy Tehran to Department of State, 21 September 1957, RG 59, 788.00 (W)/9-2157.
[370] AmEmbassy Tehran to Department of State, 21 October 1957, RG 59, 788.11/10-2157.
[371] AmEmbassy Tehran to Department of State, 25 October 1957, RG 59, 788.00 (W)10-2557.
[372] AmEmbassy Tehran to Department of State, 25 October 1957, RG 59, 788.00 (W)10-2557.

20,000 people homeless in earthquakes and killed more than 1,400 with bodies still remaining to be found.[373]

In 1958, Eqbal finalized his new party. The new party was called Mellat and included 58 deputies and 16 senators. It was formed on the Shah's orders. Many parties included another freedom party broke away from the main two parties. The Mellat party was heavily supported because the politicians liked him more than the Shah. The senators however did not care and would run as independents even though the Shah said that no one could be elected if not part of the national parties.[374] In a visit to Italy, the Foreign Minister discussed the Shah's willingness to endeavor in cultural and economic relations with Italy and sent naval cadets to schools in Italy. There was an ongoing battle on the Shattal Arab River between Iran and Iraq and though Iran wanted to remain friends with Iraq, Iraq continued its differences. A new union among Egypt and Syria and Jordan and Iraq were formed.[375] These were maneuvers by the Soviets to weaken the hegemony of the United States and have Middle Eastern states form against the Iran and west pact so that communism and Soviet hegemony could spread.

In February 1958, Dulles agreed with President Eisenhower's decision to allow the Shah to visit Washington in June despite his visits to Japan, China, and Brazil.[376] From the Tehran Embassy, Charles Stelle said that if the Shah continued to face disappointment in U.S. military and financial assistance, Iran would abandon ties with the west and cede its membership in the Baghdad Pact. But though the Shah may be anti-communist and pro-west internally, he did not hesitate to accept the offers the Soviet Union was preparing. If the Shah withdrew from the Baghdad Defense Pact, the following consequences are likely to occur: 1) the Shah and Iran

---

[373] AmEmbassy Tehran to Department of State, 28 December 1957, RG 59, 788.00 (W) 12-2857.
[374] AmEmbassy Tehran to Department of State, 28 February 1958, RG 59, 888.00/2-2857.
[375] AmEmbassy Tehran to Department of State, 10 February 1958, RG 59, 788.00/2-1058.
[376] Department of State to AmEmbassy Tehran, 27 February 1958, RG 59, 788.00/2-2758.

would no longer feel being paid off to do acts of the U.S. and the UK., 2) the American doctrine would still apply in Iran with or without their participation in the Baghdad Pact, 3)Iran will be independent in developing their own foreign policies. 4) Iran will receive Soviet offers and potentially empower communism in Iran. Stelle says he will *take a plunge which he inwardly fears might be fatal to himself and to Iran.*[377] Though the Shah feels that the country can be sustained by oil revenues, basic development should not be slowed and that access to more loans would be easier. A large part of Iran's budget goes to the army and military expenditures. The Shah further wants a grant to cover its budget deficit-*but the reasons he wants such assistance is primarily for the same reasons that he wants more military assistance-to expand his Army and keep it happy; and aid is still the number one item in the Shah's program.*[378] He also became aware that the people were dissatisfied with him and he needed to strengthen the army or potentially lose his throne. He partly blamed himself for not establishing effective leadership around him, so he now turned to the Army and SAVAK. The Shah however, does not know the full truth, and if he did know that he was working hard for the betterment of a nation and thrived in the world as the best leader who made the most progress in a short time, he would feel disgusted. Though he made his own foreign policy, he was not weak, but shy. The Shah does need the support of the United States and western democracies, but on his own terms. He was annoyed by western inference into his affairs of state.[379]

In April, 1958, a new tension arose in the politics of Iran. A Kirkuk Kurdish lawyer spoke for the Kurds who desired their own entity. They had their own language and culture. Taking pieces away from Turkey and Iraq, they wanted their own kingdom and autonomy within

---

[377] Department of State to AmEmbassy Tehran, 27 February 1958, RG 59, 788.00/2-2758.

[378] AmEmbassy Tehran to Department of State, 20 July 1957, RG 59, 788.11/7-2057.
[379] AmEmbassy Tehran to Department of State, 20 July 1957, RG 59, 788.11/7-2057.

Iraq.[380] The recent marriage with Queen Soraya ended and Zahedi believed that his son would become the new heir to the throne since the Shah did not produce a male heir. There was another alliance being formed between Iran, Pakistan, Turkey and Afghanistan.[381] The pending visit by the Shah will include a request for more aid. There was an execution of a squad of communists belonging to the Tudeh party. Though the crimes were legally called treason, not murder. This justified the act of execution. A new company made a bid for the oil exploitation of Iran and the Shah was very pleased.[382] In an historic visit Iran flew to China for a five day visit. They discussed a proposed joint trade venture between the two countries. China pleaded for anti-communist policies and the Shah was pleased about the potential trade agreement.[383] The United States was concerned. In correspondence, Foreign Minister Hekmat reported about Iran's Foreign Policy for a *unilateral renunciation of nuclear weapons,* but Nehru India is pro-soviet. The other concern is that Iran needed a better judicial system.[384]

The fear was that the *same misfortunes that befell this area by interference of Americans will now befall this area by their withdrawal.* If the United States withdrew from Iran, it was clear that the Russians would come and craft a new foreign policy that would likely be against America. It is only the *US can save non-communists world from communists clutches.* Some of these topics were discussed at the meeting with Eisenhower. The new Middle Eastern Federation increased U.S. aid and the settlement of Bahrein were also to be discussed.[385] In July, Iran asked for $9 million for aid for the Iranian police. The State Department disagreed and felt that aid should be given to higher priority items, not matters of police for a police state like Iran. The

---

[380] American Consul, Kirkuk to Department of State, 10 April 1958, RG 59, 788.00/4-1058.
[381] AmEmbassy Tehran to Department of State, 5 April 1958, RG 59, 788.00/4-558.
[382] AmEmbassy Tehran to Department of State, 5 April 1958, RG 59, 788.00/4-558.
[383] Department of State- Office of Chinese Affairs to Department of State, 13 May 1958, RG 59, 788.11/5-1358.
[384] Am Embassy Tehran to Department of State, 6 June 1958, RG 59, 788.00 (W)/6-658.
[385] Am Embassy Tehran to Department of State, 6 June 1958, RG 59, 788.00 (W)/6-658.

Iranian police may enter into riots or inadvertently use training against the United States. The Iranian police was the authority to maintain internal law, so the Iranian government directly funded them, not an outside source. If Iran had shown some success, the opinion may have been different, but that was not the case. The biggest threat across Iran's borders was the Soviet Union. They could not meet this threat successfully and progress while maintaining internal order. Before further training, aid, and a mission to the United States, the United States felt that training and aid given to date should be analyzed to see if it helped the Iranian state.[386]

President Dwight Eisenhower thinks in July, 22, 1958 that the relationship with Iran needed to be maintained. President Eisenhower reaffirmed, *It is needless for me to say how deeply I appreciate the assurances given me, by an ally whose friendship and assistance we so highly value.* He realized that the Iranian armed forces needed to be strengthened with more economic aid. Eisenhower said also that Iran needed a *stronger army,* and *is the shield of the Middle East.* Iraq and the change of its regime made America vulnerable. The attention is over to them and Iran's empowerment is needed to defend America against Iraq.[387] Gordon Taylor, the second secretary of the American Embassy in Tehran, was looking into what Eisenhower promised. Iran was expecting about $50 million in 1959 and considered the deficit from the consortium and other expenditures would be another $70 to 90 million bringing a total of $120 to $170 million for one year in 1959. This does not include the amount needed for the Iranian armed forces. The government of Iran looked into more American assistance *in view of the President's message of July 20.*[388]

On September 18, 1958, Senator Lyndon B Johnson wrote a letter about the drinking water and state of affairs of education in Iran. He wrote with return correspondence to his

---

[386] Williams to Mosser, 28 July, 1958, RG 59, 788.5 MSP/7-2858.
[387] Eisenhower to Shah, 22 July 1958, RG 59, 788.00/7-2258.
[388] Gordon Taylor to Own Jones

secretary at the United States Senate, Office of the Democratic Leader, in Washington D.C. if you choose to reply at CA-4-3121-extension 5141:[389]

> I am enclosing a communication I have received from one of my constituents. I will appreciate you giving serious consideration to this problem based on its merits. Please let me have as prompt a reply as possible returning the enclosure, in order that I can inform the writer.[390]

In reply, William Macumber, Assistant Secretary of the State Department, wrote back to Senator Johnson that the ongoing aid program was occurring and that the State Department could not investigate the complaint of one student. He advised the Senator to reply that the Shah had *many expressions of deep gratitude for US efforts in Iran.* He explained the aid's accomplishments listing a port that provided clean drinking water to a village. The majority of the aid was given to the Iranian government who improved agriculture, health, education, and developments of Iran. The assistant secretary believed the student was ignorant about these affairs or rather maybe the assistant secretary chose not to disclose information that could ruin their aid to Iran. He further wrote that the student was ignorant about the fall of Mossedegh when the treasury was empty and the country considered inadequate. It was America who gave Iran economic assistance and the opportunity to meet its foreign and domestic obligations.[391]

The complaint of the student was that the aid was not being used properly and that education and other developmental projects were still weak.....

The History of the Cessation of Communism

In this era of political developments, it was widely discussed that 1953 to 1959 was a period for American sustenance of their hegemony and the cessation of communism in Iran. Doris Graber of the *Political Science Quarterly,* wrote that the right to intervene for the cessation

---

[389] Johnson to Department of State, 18 September 1958, RG 59, 788.5 MSP/ 9-1858.
[390] Johnson to Department of State, 18 September 1958, RG 59, 788.5 MSP/ 9-1858.
[391] Macumber to Johnson, 30 September 1958, RG 59, 788.5 MSP/9-3058.

of communism began in 1947 after Truman's declaration that: "totalitarian regimes imposed on free peoples, by direct or indirect aggression, undermine the foundations of international peace and hence the security of the United States"- *it must be the policy of the United States to support free peoples who are resisting attempted subjugation by armed minorities or by outside pressures.*[392] This statement allowed the United States to intervene into affairs of Iran and tell the Soviet Union that the United States would not let communism spread. The Truman Doctrine thus initiated its footsteps to take out communism, but only when and if it was justified in national terms or had a direct effect on the United States, as Dean Acheson later told Congress. It was in 1957 that President Eisenhower created his doctrine on foreign policy stating: *it was essential to American safety to keep the Middle East non-communist. The United States would give economic and military aid to Middle Eastern nations to lessen their susceptibility to communist blandishments. This aid was to include the employment of the armed forces of the United States to secure and protect the territorial integrity and political independence of such nations, requesting such aid, against overt armed aggression from any nation controlled by International Communism.* [393]

The Eisenhower doctrine was limited, but it was specifically designed to show the Soviet Union that the Middle East would be an area where communism would not spread. The military assistance Eisenhower provided was an overt armed aggression. The spread of communism was a threat and intervening with consent into other states that were pushed by the Soviet Union or a movement to create communism was a necessary fixture for involvement.[394] Hence, Iran became

---

[392] Doris Graber *The Truman and Eisenhower Doctrines in the Light of the Doctrine of Non-Intervention.* (Political Science Quarterly: Academy of Political Science, 1958) 321

[393] Doris Graber *The Truman and Eisenhower Doctrines in the Light of the Doctrine of Non-Intervention.* (Political Science Quarterly: Academy of Political Science, 1958) 322

[394] Doris Graber *The Truman and Eisenhower Doctrines in the Light of the Doctrine of Non-Intervention.* (Political Science Quarterly: Academy of Political Science, 1958) 322

an area where the Soviet Union would expect American resistance. The United States would not stand by and passively watch as the Soviet Union engulfed the Middle East and potentially won the Cold War to spread their communism. But due to the lack of clarity of the doctrine, the United States could come in to any country they chose to stop the spread of communism. Graber describes that: "this country should not permit itself to be dragged into Middle Eastern conflicts any time a country waves the red flag of communism to get American aid."[395]

In the summer of 1958, the Shah needed money to balance the budget in 1959. He needed $107 million with another $20 million for other expenditures. The Shah said the United States refused to provide anti-aircraft missiles and to train some of his troops. The Shah told Turkey that if aid was not coming, t he would have to seek other ways to protect Turkey and the north.[396] Turkey was concerned that this other option would be with the Soviet Union that could potentially weaken the security of Iran and ruin the political situation of Turkey in the long run. The Ambassador from Pakistan said the Shah would wait a week and the United States should give him some aid to shut him up.[397]

In a letter written to the Shah, it said that the U.S. government was particularly concerned with Iran signing a treaty with the Soviet Union. The State Department was concerned with the future security of Iran. They stated, "It is my profound conviction that the principal objective of the Soviet Union in Iran remains unchanged and that objective is inconsistent with Iran's independence and integrity and with the security and stability of Your Majesty's regime." The letter further states it is history that demonstrated that the Soviet Union has used these nonaggressive agreements to *lull prospective victims and make them less alert to their danger. I*

---

[395] Doris Graber *The Truman and Eisenhower Doctrines in the Light of the Doctrine of Non-Intervention.* (Political Science Quarterly: Academy of Political Science, 1958) 332
[396] Tehran to Mouser, 29 January 1959, RG 59, 788.00 (W)/1-2959.
[397] Tehran to Mouser, 29 January 1959, RG 59, 788.00 (W)/1-2959.

refer, for example to Latvia, Lithunia, Esthonia, Finland, Poland, and the Nationalist Government of China. [398]

There was increased tension in Iran. There was an increased criticism of the regime that was rampant in the poor classes of Iran. The State Department says, "much speculation in non-official circles that anniversary overthrow Mosadeq would see disorders or coup d'état, though this anxiety not shared by security officials." On the anniversary of the overthrow, there were riots. The government rented a population from outside towns to line up in the streets and cheer for the Shah as he drove by and promised more developments. Though others showed up, it was not a day in support of the regime.[399]

The Climax of American Hegemony in the Middle East

In 1959, the climax of American Hegemony began in the Middle East. It was in this very year that the United States was extremely close of losing Iran and losing their hegemony in the Middle East. If the U.S. lost their hegemony, they would have lost the regional Cold War and the global Cold War. Eleven months later, the reverse occurred and they won the regional Cold War. As 1959 began, the cheerless Iranian faces embraced the United States and the United States did not underwrite the $107 million needed for Iran. The Secretary of State, John Foster Dulles, was also unhappy and cancelled his visit to Karachi. Iraq experienced a fall of Arif and General Qassim took over. Qassim was viewed to probably have communist influence- the U.S. State Department said. There was a coup in 1959 that might seem more favorable to the Iran regime. Ayub Khan takes over as the new leader of Pakistan. Also in 1959 the Pope was seriously ill and the Shah did not make his way over there.[400] The Assistant Secretary of Defense, Jack Irwin, II, wrote a letter to the State Department requesting the Shah to have exclusive jurisdiction to the

---

[398] State Department to Shah, 29 January 1959, RG 59, 788.00 (W)/1-2959.
[399] Am Embassy Tehran to State Department, RG 59, 788.00 (W)/8-2258.
[400] AmEmbassy Tehran to State Department, RG 59, 788.00 (W)/1-1759

U.S. military. This would allow the U.S. military to commit crimes and receive no punishment. The State Department responded that it would be difficult for the Shah to implement a grand task, and also, the current punishment for soldiers who violated law were little to nothing.[401] Turkey and Pakistan signed a bilateral agreement. Between Ankara and Karachi, the feeling of an Iranian agreement was also imperative. The feeling of this agreement was to involve the United States as they sought their regional interests.[402]

The State Department wrote a letter to the President stating that they were *concerned that Shah might conclude agreement with USSR would be highly detrimental Iranian security and to free world interstate.*[403] Since America did not meet the Shah's demands, the execution of this treaty was quite possible. The statement said that America should remain unalarmed and unconcerned that the Shah was proposing to do this, so that he could carry out his bluff. It would be good to capture him when and if he came back to the United States. The letter said, "there is also possibility that Shah might naively have non-aggression treaty with the Soviet Union-would give him some added security.[404] Ankara says that the Shah acted *in this way fifty percent because he has been disappointed with USA aid and USA political guarantee and fifty percent because of this fear of Russians, and especially of USSR propaganda among Kurds and among other sectors Iranian population.* [405]The Shah further felt that he had no protection with the British. The Foreign Minister feared the Soviets and the prime minister was against signing the treaty with the Soviet Union, and was not pleased with America. This position will have a bad effect on the United States. Turkey was also upset about the Iranian developments. The Iranians told the Turks that the Soviet Union would protect Iran for their independence and integrity and

---

[401] State Department to John Irwin, 16 January 1959, RG 59, 711.551/1-1659.
[402] AmEmbassy Tehran to Department of State, 29 January 1959, RG 59, 788.5/1-2959.
[403] Department of State (President) to Am Embassy Tehran, 30 January 1959, RG 59, 788.5 MSP/1-3059.
[404] Department of State (President) to Am Embassy Tehran, 30 January 1959, RG 59, 788.5 MSP/1-3059.
[405] Ankara to Secretary of State to Secretary of State, 30 January 1959, RG 59, 788.5/1-3059.

to cease all propaganda of the Kurds. Also, no Russian soldier would come to Iran and Iran won't be a base for the Russians. Iran would not sign a bilateral aggression treaty with the United States. This was the climax of the hegemony race between the Soviet Union and the United States.[406] America thought they lost the Cold War, because the shield was going over to the communists.

Hosein Eshraqi, a member of the Consul of Iran in San Francisco and brother of former Mayor of Isaphan explained that the corruption in Iran was from top to bottom. Franklin Crawford said, "He blames the Shah for not making any effort to rid the country of this age-old curse."[407] The Ambassador of Iran expressed why the American press asserted that the Shah was in peril. An article in the *New York Times* by Sulzberger talked about the Iranian tribes no longer influencing domestic policy. The *US News and World Reports* also were not favorable of Iran. The Ambassador was confused why the U.S. press was beginning to write negatively about Iran. Now the country had immense speculation of America and Iranian public support of America and its policies began to dwindle. The Ambassador reported that it should be the interest of the United States to offset these articles by showing strengths of stability and progress in Iran. He did not want to tell the press what to write, rather what was correct to write about Iranian affairs.[408] America was asking missionaries to go to Iran and educate students about proper farming and training. There were many missions set up in Iran and doctors were ample. The American-educated students returning to Iran have nothing better to do but government jobs, which were a waste of their talent. The conclusions became clear that without the support of the United States and United Kingdom, *the Iranian regime would quickly collapse.*[409] If popular support was

---

[406] London to Secretary of State, 31 January, 1959, RG 59, 788.5/1-3159.
[407] American Consulate Isfahan to Department of State, 21 May 1959, RG 59, 788.5/5-2159.
[408] Ambassador of Iran to Department of State, 5 May 1959, RG 59, 788.00/5-559.
[409] Stelle to Department of State, 5 May 1959, RG 59, 788.00/5-559.

withdrawn from the Shah, the Shah would be evicted in hours. The Shah was afraid and critical of the Western press. However he trusts the Western Ambassadors. For the sake of Iran, the Ambassadors told the Shah to take evasive maneuvers of his current policies. This reminder came again every six months. This reminder was a threat that he could lose the government, the army, and his throne. If he took this action, he would also blame western ambassadors for the unpopularity of his regime, and get more aid for the West without reforms.[410]

The Shah of Iran wrote a letter to President Eisenhower about the exploratory conversations with the Soviets. The Shah wanted to maintain his presence in the Baghdad Pact and in the treaty of mutual defense. The treaty of non-aggression between the Soviet Union and Iran was to eliminate the tension between both nations. Iran would not accept Russian bases or do economic or military bilateral aid with the United States. The Shah said, *it might be possible to bring about a détente in our relations with the USSR whilst maintaining our position in the Baghdad Pact.* However, no consensus has been made yet on the terms.[411] It was later agreed that the United States and United Kingdom would intervene in the Soviet-Iran negotiations and provide a lucrative offer to secure the United States' interest in Iran. The soviet negotiators in fact pushed hard for the Soviet-Iranian pact, but the Iranians wanted to stay in BP and did not want a US bilateral agreement.[412] Many people in Iran felt that the British still controlled Iran, that Iran never became independent. Mirashrafi, an ex Majlis deputy and supporter of the Shah during the Mossedegh regime told the United States to use some people in Iran and have them back America's political support. The United States made a mistake supporting a monarch that could lead to war between it and the USSR.[413]

---

[410] Stelle to Department of State, 5 May 1959, RG 59, 788.00/5-559.

[411] Shah of Iran to President Eisenhower, 11 February 1959, RG 59, 788.00/2-1159.
[412] Tehran to Secretary of State, 7 February 1959, RG 59, 788.00/2-759.
[413] American Consulate, Isafahan, to Department of State, 15 June, 1959, RG 59 788.00/6-1559.

Also, in Iran, no money or development was happening to the southeastern part. The southeastern part of Iran is known as Baluchis, a poorly organized and quite impoverished tribe. They became a province in Pakistan. These tribes could however give trouble by forming Baluchi nationalist propaganda. The other tribal concern to Iran was the largest tribe of Iran, the Kurds who numbered 900,000 in 1959 and their issues were becoming international.[414] Pakistan's Ayub Khan discussed that the Shah was good person and became friends with him. Ayub Khan also favored the U.S. General in command structure. The reason Ayub Khan supported U.S. structure was to get more aid. He also said that Pakistan did not need help with its armed forces, but needed better weapons and arms to arm the armed forces. In this affair, Turkey, Iran, and Pakistan were much closer and could exchange men for the use of the BP command if they chose to do so. Ayub was not afraid of losing aid from America, rather stood at his posture thinking his country was at its height. He was discussing foreign policy options in Rawalapindi with his advisors. Also in August the Soviets resumed their heavy propaganda attacks against Iran and the United States.[415]

There were rumors that this *propaganda war* would end. Such propaganda included a so called freedom that the U.S. Military entailed while exploiting the oil resources of Iran. Nehru planed to come to Iran for a visit.[416] On August 20, it will be the 6 anniversary of the overthrow of Mossedegh and the Shah gave uplifting speeches of a better economy than 1953. Also Eisenhower engaged in talks with Soviet's Khruschchev. No one knows what will happen to Iran. Eisenhower will have difficulties telling allies how he will concede to the Soviets. Eisenhower wants peace and feels he can attain this peace by calling a truce with the Soviet

---

[414] American Consulate, Isafahan, to Department of State, 15 June, 1959, RG 59 788.00/6-1559.

[415] Karachi to Secretary of State, 27 July 1959, RG 59, 788.00/7-2759.
[416] Am Embassy to Department of Army, 20 August 1959, RG 59, 788.00/8-2059.

Union in 1959. If Eisenhower does so, Vice-President Nixon will have a promising election and bid for the President of the United States over Rockefeller. The Algeria state was causing tension between France's De Gaulle and the United States. France wanted the United States to sanction Algeria and use the atom bomb for the continuation of the Cold War. But Algeria was costing their reputation, but the United States declined to do so. France had to stand up or else be pushed down by Soviets and the Americans.[417]

In November of 1959, the relationship between Iran and Pakistan strengthened. They both exchanged their deep and sincere friendship between Iran and Pakistan. The Iranian people were very happy about Pakistan's government and their kind views, but were deeply upset by the Soviet propaganda. The Pakistan Foreign Ministry said, "Pakistan people will show same reaction to Soviet propaganda against Iran as being shown by Iranians." Both nations unified against any type of foreign aggression. Iran for many centuries also had defended the Sheikdoms of the Persian Gulf from foreign invasion. But Bahrein is not part of the Persian Gulf territory, and is Iranian.[418] But despite the friendship of Ayub and the Shah, Radio Moscow called both of them servants of imperialism. The radio broadcast said that both nations were plotting against Iraq and Afghanistan and Iran was spending its money on useless military equipment while India, empowered by the Soviets, built its military.[419] The Shah responded that he did not spend that much on military expenses. It was very small compared to other countries, but this small military as he imagined would not stop them from defending their borders.[420] Pakistan President Ayub Khan flew to Turkey along with Iranian officials to sign a treaty of commerce, trade, and

---

[417] Am Embassy to Department of Army, 20 August 1959, RG 59, 788.00/8-2059.

[418] Am Embassy to Department of Army, 20 August 1959, RG 59, 788.00/8-2059.

[419] Am Embassy to Department of Army, 12 November 1959, RG 59, 788.00/11-1259.

[420] Am Embassy to Department of Army, 12 November 1959, RG 59, 788.00/11-1259.

residence. This treaty was among the CENTO Muslim leaders. This meeting of the top three

Muslim leaders was to unify their purpose and Iran stood as the political center for CENTO

peace missions. President Khan was also very pleased with the developments in Iran. Ayub told

the Shah not to be disappointed if he does not get everything he wants.[421] President Eisenhower

planned to visit Iran and to *extend substantial aid underdeveloped countries to strengthen

defenses against foreign aggression.*[422] In late 1959, the Shah married again and the State

Department considered that some modern gadget like a tape recorder would be a good wedding

gift.[423] The wedding was scheduled for December 21, 1959, and the Shah will officially be

crowned Emperor since he will bear a son. Once a son is born, then a King becomes Emperor.[424]

President Eisenhower said:

> On behalf of the American people, Mrs. Eisenhower and I wish to extend our
> warmest congratulations to your Imperial Majesty on the occasion of your
> impending marriage. We wish you both every happiness and success in the future
> as you guide the destiny of your great nation.[425]

The Shah also visited Israel and spoke about the important shrines in Jerusalem.[426] On

December 28, 1959, the honorable Shah of Iran was concerned over the Lippman articles. It was

these articles that could remove the United States from Iran and the Shah wanted to consolidate

his rule before the United States pulled out. But these new articles convinced him that he should

pursue a new foreign policy and consider Soviet offers. These articles pointed how the foreign

policy was inconsistent with Iran and affirmed the friendly visit of President Eisenhower.[427]

---

[421] Am Embassy to Department of Army, 12 November 1959, RG 59, 788.00/11-1259.
[422] Am Embassy to Department of Army, 12 November 1959, RG 59, 788.00/11-1259.
[423] Am Embassy to Secretary of State, 10 November 1959, RG 59, 788.00/11-1059.
[424] Am Embassy to Secretary of State, 10 November 1959, RG 59, 788.00/11-1059.

[425] Paris to Secretary of State, 19 December 1959, RG 59, 788.11/12-1959.
[426] Jerusalem Palestine to Department of State, 6 November 1959, RG 59, 788.11/11-659.
[427] Tehran to Secretary of State, 28 December 1959, RG 59, 788.11/12-2859.

Second Revolution Conclusion

In the Pre & First Revolution, the political developments of Iran were focused on their desires. Iran wanted independence and the Shah wanted unlimited power, respect, and money. The Shah and Americans cut a deal that they would provide ample economic and military aid to Iran in exchange for the single commodity that strengthened the US to win the Cold War: oil. The result was bringing more than 600,000 barrels of oil to the west. After the collapse of the Mossedegh regime, the Shah and the international oil companies sat together to discuss how each of them would remain profitable. Iran and the United States became very happy at the conclusion of the deal. It was Eisenhower's policy to provide economic aid to underdeveloped countries, but this aid was not a peace gesture or a kind-hearted gift from the United States, this aid had strings attached. The United States would fund certain economic industries like sugar, opium, and certain departments that would be profitable to them. In the later years of the Second Revolution, the United States was making more than $9 billion annually with just a small percentage of oil.

Iran was making money, but the Shah did not spend much of the money on Iran, but rather his luxury life, sports cars, palaces, etc. Iran wanted to be an independent military nation strengthened in the 1950s. They wanted to be part of the regional defense system, a nation that could defeat communism, and a state sovereign in its will to receive aid for its infrastructure. Iran received more than $1 billion up and until 1959 in both economic and military aid, but the money was not being spent on its economic projects. It was going heavily into military investments and the Shah's personal ventures. Though the United States knew and placed certain caps on the aid being submitted, they were also making money from their investments and their economic strategies in Iran. Like Eisenhower stated, economic aid to Iran was the tool to defeat communism. The Shah was money and power hungry. Whatever was the best offer, either the Soviets or the Americans, he would have taken. If the Soviets in fact met the terms of the Shah, the Shah would have ended his alliance with the United States and taken the Soviet money for more aid and military equipment.

It was towards the later half of the Second Revolution that people began realizing how quiet their economy and infrastructure really was because nobody was doing anything to improve the country. The infrastructure problems were overpowering. Iranians began criticizing the Shah and the honest, yet corrupt government. And the people did not know what to do but revolt against the man who promised them freedom and hope. Though the United States considered Iran a valuable place and the Shah promoted his optimistic and less nationalistic strategies, nothing was happening. All the aid came in and was going to the Shah, not the country. The country was losing money in its treasury, its economics, and military. The United States began to wonder if the Tudeh party would come, so they sent more aid and troops to suppress the Tudeh party since it was economics that was the key to win the Cold War. Despite the many apparent visual difficulties and strong signs of a potential coup in 1959 followed by the replacement of the leadership in government, the Shah knew he was about to be removed and would not be the one to lead the country. But no one did anything for fear that person would be executed too. The U.S. Embassy in Tehran, political circles, and Iranians expected that the reputation of the Shah deteriorated so much that it was over, yet he stayed on for another twenty years. The question remains, why?

Part 3: Section 8 Economic Developments
Second Revolution

The Economic Aftermath

In the year of the overthrow of Mossedegh, the economic aftermath was mainly to prevent the spread of communism. The prevention of communism was established through

Eisenhower economic foreign policy. It was economic aid according to Eisenhower that would potentially hurt Communism and the spread of Soviet influence in Iran. In a letter dated August 26, 1953, General Zahedi, Prime Minister of Iran, requested President Eisenhower an *orderly country in which they can enjoy higher standards of living*. Zahedi called for a better economic character and urged the United States to help Iran in this critical time period of Iran's history. He wanted to improve his domestic and international relations. He stated, "I am sure that I voice the feelings of the great majority of the people of Iran when I state that Iran desires to contribute its share to the maintenance of peace and to the promotion of international goodwill."[428]

President Dwight Eisenhower replied to his letter,

"The American people continue to be deeply interested in the independence of Iran and the well-being of the Iranian people." He was pleased about how happy the Iranians were of the aid package and that Iran wanted to maintain friendly relations with the United States. He asked his Ambassador to help Iran with the U.S. aid programs in Iran and his firm commitment to Iranian affairs. The aid being discussed here was the huge aid package Iran received in August right before the overthrow. It was this aid that led to a huge decline in the exchange rates as no one demanded imports. President Eisenhower concluded, "Your request will receive our sympathetic consideration and I can assure you that we stand ready to assist you in achieving the aspirations for your country which you have outlined."[429] Richard Gailey, an editor, wrote to Mr. Adams about the congratulatory message from the President to the Shah. He wrote:

> *Dear Mr. Adams,*
> *I consider very unwise President's Eisenhower's congratulations to the Shah of Iran. That nation is very much in a tumult and if a sudden shift in power*

---

[428] Zahedi to Eisenhower, 26 August 1953, RG 59, 888.00/8-2653.
[429] Eisenhower to Zahedi, 26 August 1953, RG 59, 888.00/8-2653.

*should take place the powers-that-be, considering themselves scorned, might turn from the West. **Let's be more cautious.**[430]*

There were also negotiations encouraging trade between USSR and Iran over copper ores and other strategic items. When Zahedi took over, he found the treasury to be empty and the government in debt to Bank Melli for more than 17.7 million rials. The common person on the street knew that Iran badly needed aid. There were foreign exchange obligations and Bank Melli was making $8 million a month and the exchange demanded Iran for $120 million dollars was 96 rials per 1 dollar.[431] It was a mess. In September Eisenhower gave $45 million emergency aid funds to Iran. This request was to "restore a measure of unity and establish a foundation for greater economic development." The goal was to increase stability in Iran and develop a healthy Iran.[432]

Under Zahedi trade negotiations between the Soviet Union and Iran continued. The USSR exported rails, copper, nickel, and telephone cables while Iran imported carpets, opium, and refined sulfur.[433]

In October 1953, C. Edward Wells had a conversation with media operations. He wanted to bluntly inform them why Iran needed economic aid. The first reason was that every country needs help from outside countries. Iran did not have the international capacity to develop its technical skills, its capital, and did not have the know how to exploit their own resources. The borrowing of capital could improve living conditions, provide training to develop technical skills, and provide capital to deal with economic frustrations. The emergency aid grant was almost depleted and the question was how much more aid would reduce tension?[434] The $45

[430] Gailey to Adams, 28 August 1953, RG 59, 888.00/8-2853.
[431] AmEmbassy of Tehran to Department of State, 14 September 1953, RG 59, 888.00/9-1253.
[432] Murray Snyder to the White House Office- 5 September 1953, RG 59, 888.00/9-553.
[433] AmEmbassy Tehran to Department of State, 9 September 1953, RG 59, 888.00/9-953.
[434] C. Edward Wells to N Spencer Barnes, 16 October, 1953, RG 59, 888.00/10-1653.

million package was to stop the deterioration of the economy until April 1954.[435] It was in America's best interests as Wells describes, to help a country in need to prevent conditions from getting worse. The emergency aid was given directly to the Iranian government without any middle man. The money was used to help merchants put money back into the economy. The other reason was to get merchants to build roads and houses and hire men needed for that construction. There were about 18 million people in Iran and the money that was available would not meet the needs of the people.[436] The biggest question of all was: "Why did the United States decide to give emergency aid to Iran?"

The reason was that there has been a friendship maintained between Iran and the United States for many years. Wells reported, "Americans simply like to help the Iranians, in the same way any individual may want to help a friend." America did not want to interfere with Iran's internal politics, but wanted a strong state so that the Iranians would not be enslaved like the *Georgians.* It would not hurt America if Iran's situation went astray, but it would hurt America if other imperialist nations took over Iran and "it would finally become a serious danger to the American people."[437] The $45 million allocation consisted of $10 million to the minister of finance for the import of essential goods; $10 million for purchasing more rials; $6 million to purchase sugar; $6 million for additional sugar; and $6.7 million to be purchased for essential commodities.[438] In November 1953, there was an improvement of rials with $100,000 backing the rials now.[439] In December 1953, Iran and Turkey made a transit agreement for the construction of travel channels between Iran and Turkey.[440] At the end of 1953 expenditures still

---

[435] Mr. Warne to Spencer Barnes, 14 October,, 1953, RG 59, 888.00/10-1453.
[436] AmEmbassy Tehran to Department of State, 16 October, 1953, RG 59, 888.00/10-1653.
[437] AmEmbassy Tehran to Department of State, 16 October, 1953, RG 59, 888.00/10-1653.

[438] Turnage to Kirk, 30 October 1953 RG 59, 888.00/10-3053.
[439] Department of Army to Department of State, Nov 1953, RG 59, 888.00/11-53.
[440] Department of Army to Department of State, Dec 1953, RG 59, 888.00/12-53.

continued to exceed income. Import goods and the cost of living improved. Rains improved the agricultural condition of Iran, creating 5,000 more tons of tobacco and 70,000 tons of rice. Even salaries were maintained and revenues were being produced.[441]

In January 1954, America began influencing the oil regime of Iran and the British also tried to get themselves into the negotiation process. Meanwhile Iran and the Soviets began debating over their border problems and Japan bought 3,500 pounds of raw cotton from Iran in exchange for Japanese cotton.[442] Iran received another $25 million loan from Exim Bank and the minister of national economy drafted thirty-five articles of foreign investment, laws that would regulate foreign capital into Iran.[443] Also in February, the legendary Agha Khan wanted to finance the construction of a dam in the southern province of Iran. The Doroudzan dam would be called Agha Khan Dam because the famous tycoon and leader of the Ismaili Muslims was financing it. The money needed was 400 million rials to build the 753 million cubic meters of water and 2,000 kWh dam.[444]

An agreement finally came through between the British and Iran on February 16, 1954. The British signed a contract with Iran that provided 24 locomotives at a total cost of $2,773,747.20. The Iranian government initially paid only 80,160 pounds with the remainder to be paid in three installments from January 1, 1957 through January 1, 1959. The people from these provinces had been disconnected and wanted the railway system in place to connect to the other provinces both culturally and physically. Also, the railway would provide food to deficit areas from places with a food surplus. Iran could begin to pay for this if an oil settlement was early and if these development projects could take reform.[445]

---

[441] AmEmbassy Tehran to Department of State, 27 November 1953, RG 59, 888.00/11-2753
[442] Department of Army to Department of State, January 1954, RG 59, 888.00/1-54.
[443] Department of Army to Department of State, Feb 1954, RG 59, 888.00/2-54
[444] AmEmbassy Tehran to Department of State, 11 February 1954, RG 59, 888.2.11/2-1054
[445] AmEmbassy Tehran to Department of State, 20 February 1954, RG 59, 988.512/2-1854.

The agreement reached among the British and Americans created a consortium agreement. The Iranians received a larger share, British Petroleum, the second largest and various American companies from 4 to 8 percent. In November of 1954, a payment of $2.05 million would be paid to Iran.[446]

On February 28 1954, an agreement was signed between Iran and the United States giving Iran an additional $6 million in aid. The development funds also stabilized the rates and plan to propose for rate unification. A large amount of development was needed in Iran.[447] The treasury was gaining momentum but liabilities and assets were less than 15 billion rials. The only way to improve the country's financial position was through the following ways:

1) Increase in public revenues and reorganization of administration agencies. 2) Discontinuance of borrowing from Bank Melli and no more withdrawal of excess bank notes. 3) Effective American assistance to meet budgetary deficit. 4) Stabilization of exchange rates. 5) Prohibition against unproductive expenditures. 6) Stimulation of increased production of essential consumer goods. 7) Payment of salary increases to civil servants. 8) Establishment of balanced budget. 9) Reorganization of the fiscal agencies and regulation of accounts of the various ministries. 10) Establishment of stability in public administration. [448]

The goal was to have more aid and less Soviet influence. Foreign aid was also a killer against communism in Iran. Trade with the Soviets increased and existing quota arrangements would expire on March 31. There had not been new quota arrangements. The cost of living declined at a very small percentage.[449] In order to afford to purchase the imports and provide an operating budget to Iran, the United States gave another $9 million in aid grant to Iran in May 1954 until August 20, 1954.[450] In foreign exchange reports, Iran is making more than $350,000 per working day and $9 million a year now.[451] The Iranian State Railways' plan is to purchase

---

[446] AmEmbassy Tehran to Department of State, 20 February 1954, RG 59, 988.512/2-1854
[447] Department of the Army to Department of State, 4 March 1954, RG 59, 888.00/3-454
[448] Department of the Army to Department of State, 4 March 1954, RG 59, 888.00/3-454
[449] Department of Army to Department of State, 30 March 1954, RG 59, 788.00(W)/3-3054.
[450] Department of Army to Department of State, 12 May 1954, RG 59, 788.00 (W)/5-1254.

10,000 tons of rails from France and England at a cost of $25 million with 10 percent down.[452]

There were some 22,000 total rails needed for urgent repair.[453] Using the currency provided by

U.S. aid funds, the government of Iran purchased 10,000 tons of Formosan sugar, planning to

import 30,000 tons of it and to export more to other clients.[454] Also, Sir George Binfey, the

director of United Steel Ltd. signed a contract to purchase 104,500 metric tons of steel rails and

accessories and 500 switches at around $10 million. In exchange the British would give Iran

24,000 to 27,000 rails under a pre-1951 contract price of $80.00 a ton.[455]

 The Bank Melli removed 32 million rials of bank notes and released a $1 million note cover

with a $7 million note cover. Now Bank Melli has more than $12,258,000 in reserves. Iran

Airways signed a one year agreement with Swiss Air for commercial service between the two

countries. In fact Iran earned more than $32 million in the foreign exchange averaging $10.2

million a month. [456]

On June 1 1954, Mr. Warne, the U.S. director of operations and missions had a meeting

with the prime minister of Iran, his son, and the foreign minister about Iran's commitment to

various economic programs and how they could continue to stabilize payment to these

institutions. The Prime Minister, General Zahedi, replied that purchases made for the

government were made after careful study and review of the expectations required of Iran. The

proper considerations were made to price, quality, and credit. There would be no commissions to

---

[451] Department of Army to Department of State, 12 May 1954, RG 59, 788.00 (W)/5-1254.
[452] Department of Army to Department of State, 12 May 1954, RG 59, 788.00 (W)/5-1254.

[453] Department of Army to Department of State, 12 May 1954, RG 59, 788.00 (W)/5-1254.

[454] Department of Army to Department of State, 12 May 1954, RG 59, 788.00 (W)/5-1254.

[455] Department of Army to Department of State, 30 June 1954, RG 59, 788.00 (W)/6-3054.

[456] Department of Army to Department of State, 2 June 1954, RG 59, 788.00 (W)/6-254.

the seller. The prime minister gave the example that if Iran purchased $1 million worth of automobiles, the Iranian representative of the seller should not get $250,000.00. Zahedi said, "Commissions of this kind promoted corruption; the firms receiving them were naturally tempted to offer shares to Iranian purchasing officials as bribes."[457]

The reason Warne and his colleague were so interested in the economic situation of Iran was because 1) Iran was receiving a hefty payment from the United States; and 2) the United States remained as the chief supplier of Iranian imports bringing in 22.2 percent of Iranian import trade. Germany was Iran's best customer buying 15.2 percent of Iran's exports and the United States bought 14.9 percent of Iran's export goods. In the German consortium agreement, Germany offered $60 million in credit to Iran, France offered 5 million francs and Japan remained active in purchasing Iranian cotton and goods. In the last quarter of 1953, financial problems still continued and there was a rapid mobilization of U.S. aid funds to support the government's budget. The decrease of the exchange rate came from the rise of imports, removal of certain restrictions, and another $19 million in U.S. aid.[458] Many business circles were impressed with Iran's maintenance of the 96 rials per dollar and price on all foreign goods increased. American aid provided salaries. Interestingly enough, October was a month of retail prices on the rise. For goods over $3,000 foreign exchange rests are important, but if we remain below $3,000, then the bank can liquidate. In order to replenish all pharmaceutical goods, Iran received 50 million from Bank Melli and $800,000 from U.S. aid funds. The Export Development Bank was giving credit to help finance purchases from producers.[459]

The gentleman in charge of the oil solution in Iran, a representative from the United States and son of President Herbert Hoover, was Herbert Hoover Jr. Hoover began his

---

[457] Memorandum of conversation 7 June 1954, RG 59, 888.00/6-754.
[458] Memorandum of conversation 7 June 1954, RG 59, 888.00/6-754
[459] Memorandum of conversation 7 June 1954, RG 59, 888.00/6-754

negotiations with Iran discovering that since nationalization of oil, Iran had many losses. Japan rolled up its tankers near Abadan and took thousands of tons of oil which was the last shipment of oil to the Japanese Ido Mitsu Co. under the AIOC. A rumor came in that the House of Commons wanted to establish relations with Iran.

In July 1954, the Shah of Iran and the Queen wanted to go to the United States. Dulles felt this visit would be a keen advantage, because the visit would discuss Iran's future defense arrangements and confirm an oil settlement. The visit would be official for three days. The oil settlement was the main concern.[460] Unfortunately, before July ended, Ann Arbor Motor Sales and Service contacted the State Department requesting payment in the amount of $48.36 from Mr. M. Pahlavi, the Shah's brother, who was charged the amount for repairs on his 1953 Cadillac. That amount had never been paid.[461] The visit and tour would cost around $9,000 and the oil settlement was the main concern.[462] Another economic agreement had been reached between the Soviets and Iran on the purchase of the Pahlavi Bandar property that supplied Russian oil products. This property would be purchased for $3,300.00. In 1954 while there was a shortage of wheat, Iran exported 100,000 tons of it.[463] In the U.S. consortium agreement, the Soviet Union was pushing for the Turkish-Pakistan pact so that they would not enter into the consortium agreement. Furthermore, this pact would enhance a nuclear and economic relationship fostered by the Soviet Union. The consortium agreement was America's effort to get control of Iran's economy, *that this enslavement directly related to US plans for aligning Iran with Turkey and Pakistan, and that military bases for US use being made ready in Iran...* The oil consortium agreement was to get control of Iran's economy and weaken the Soviets. It was to

---

[460] Byroad to Secretary Dulles 30 June 1954, RG 59, 788.11/6-3054.
[461] Ann Arbor Motor Sales to M. Pahlavi, 26 July 1954, 788.11/7-2654.
[462] Byroad to Secretary Dulles 30 June 1954, RG 59, 788.11/6-3054.

[463] Department of Army to Department of State, 7 July 1954, RG 59, 788.11/7-754

remove all communist and potential Soviet influence from Iran. The Iranian press resented the United States' interference in Iran's internal affairs. The Soviets further responded that the United States' interference in Iran's internal affairs was a "sponsored military bloc in the Near and Middle East."[464] Iranian National Airways transported its first pilgrims under contract with the Saudi Arabian government. In the oil settlement, Chief Negotiator Amini stated that the negotiations were over; it was just the compensation that needed to be made. There were several broadcasts in the Soviet Union about Iran's alliance with the United States and against the USSR.[465]

The Oil Consortium Agreement

The moment in Iran's history, August 5, 1954 marked the day that oil negotiations were over. Ali Amani, chairman of the Iranian negotiating team and Howard Page of the United States issued a statement that the Iranian government and the consortium committee had reached an agreement to "restore flow Iran's oil to world markets." The compensation to the AIOC and the conversion of Iran's currency from sterling to dollars would take place. This consortium agreement would operate in the Netherlands and Ian. The operation of the oil fields would be managed by the consortium. Iran would receive in fixed payment and taxes from the crude oil sales an amount of 50 percent and take 12.5 percent of total exports of crude oil. These fixed sums would be paid to Iranian refinery operations. The agreement period was for twenty-five years with extensions. It is quite intriguing that twenty-five years from 1954 was 1979 when the revolution occurred in Iran. Iran's total income for the first couple of years would be 150 million pounds and production would be 500 million barrels.[466] The press "reported extensively

---

[464] Department of Army to Department of State, 14 July 1954, RG 59, 788.11/7-1454

[465] Department of Army to Department of State, 28 July 1954, RG 59, 788.11/7-2854

[466] Department of Army to Department of State, 11 August 1954, RG 59, 788.11/8-1154.

congratulatory messages exchanged between Shah and President Eisenhower, Prime Minister

Zahedi and Foreign Minister Entezah with Secretary Dulles." Now, the *number of papers*

declared the next main policy issue before Iran would be participation in regional defense

arrangements. Other local items of interest were question of cont US financial aid to assist in

Iran's budgetary difficulties. [467]

In September 1954 the previous $9 million in aid ran out by August 20, so the U.S.

government issued $10 million of aid grants to meet its urgent foreign exchange and budgetary

requirements and another $800,000 of dollar exchanges were made available for financing

imports from the United States.[468] In October 1954, the oil agreement had gone to the Senate for

approval and the agreement would be effective promptly on January 1, 1955. The loans provided

to Iran had some terms and conditions. First, the Export-Import Bank funds were to be used for

development purposes only to generate more money and reduce the cost of projects. These

development projects were to be used for the benefit of America only and it would be considered

inappropriate to generate funds not tied to U.S. sources.[469] These loans would range from a $35

million loan for development purposes; $12 million loan for budgetary surplus and another $25

million loan for aid. This loan arrangement was preferably sought before March 21. [470]

Petroleum developments concluded a passage of the oil bill by the Senate on October 28,

which the Shah signed the very next day. It was the biggest story in the Tehran press. Now,

"Iranian oil after more than once again began flow in volume to world markets as the consortium

members immediately began loading."[471] In November 1954, Iran only moved 25,000 tons of

sugar to the USSR with 100,000 tons of rice sitting in Iran. The Shah began warning university

---

[467] Department of Army to Department of State, 11 August 1954, RG 59, 788.11/8-1154.
[468] Department of Army to Department of State, September 1954, RG 59, 788/.11/9-54
[469] Tehran to Secretary of State, 24 October 1954, RG 59, 888.00/10-2454.
[470] Tehran to Secretary of State, 17 September 1954, RG 59, 888.00/9-1754.
[471] Department of Army to Secretary of State, 5 November 1954, RG 59, 788.00/11-554

professors against teaching ideas not supported by the government. A report has it that the Shah would purge university professors in place during the time of Mossedegh. In the local press communists were saying that the uprising was caused by the instigation of foreign elements and that western powers were at the height of this uprising, because the communists wanted to tarnish all relations between the United States and Iran.[472] The Export-Import bank received applications for assistance in financing the Karaj Dam for a total of 18 million dollars and other development projects for $35 million, totaling $53 million. This is very close to the commitment of $85 million to Iran so the difference would be provided through FOA funds.[473] The Export-Import Bank replied to the applications that "the United States-Iran relations are one plateau which can be described as friendly and mutually responsive." In the Shah's visit the next month, the Shah would leave to Iran the ability to make oil income themselves, but potentially risked the oil income going to the Soviets. The Export-Import Bank also supported the defense arrangements of Iran. [474]

In December of 1954, another agreement concluded between Iran and India over the exchange of goods. This five year negotiation treaty of commerce and navigation was signed on December 15, 1954. India was very anxious to see their textiles, tea, and spices go to Iran while Iran exchanged some goods to Iran.[475] The Shah left Iran en route to the United States. Many newspaper editorials state the visit would be fruitful and better than the darkest days of Iranian history.[476] There were many rumors of course, that the USSR had carried over with the Tudeh party to convince the Iranian government while the Shah was gone to join the Turkish Pakistani

---

[472] Department of Army to Secretary of State, 19 November 1954, RG 59, 788.00/11-1954

[473] Glendinning to Department of Treasury, 2 November 1954, RG 59, 788.00/11-254
[474] Broade to Kitche, 2 November 1954, RG 59, 788.00/11-254.
[475] Department of Army to Department of State, 3 December 1954, RG 59, 788.00/12-354
[476] Department of Army to Department of State, 3 December 1954, RG 59, 788.00/12-354

Pact or any other Middle Eastern arrangement. Many Iranians felt that Soviet interest in Iran was because of the Tudeh party and that they wanted the Tudeh party to take over the government. In December the government gave the Majlis a bill authorizing $150 million dollars and 10 million pounds from the United States and Britain.[477] The following companies expressed interest in being admitted to the Iranian oil consortium agreement: American Independent Oil Co. in San Francisco, California, Cities Service Company in New York, Anderson-Pritchard Oil Corp. in Oklahoma City, Louis Jubel in New York, and the Northwestern Refining Co. in Saint Paul, Minnesota.[478] In a newspaper clipping, the Anglo Iranian Oil Co. changed its name to the British Petroleum Co. Limited, or BP. In a statement by Sir William Fraser, he suggested that company capital be increased to 120 million pounds. The reason for the name change was that BP had represented AIOC since 1921.[479]

In a later letter, Jackson Rothbone, president of the Standard Oil Co. of New Jersey wrote a letter about the Monroe Doctrine. He was pleased that Eisenhower was to follow the Monroe principles of "an era of good feeling." *US News and World Reports* stated Eisenhower's political philosophies were also of good feeling. He wanted to know when the settlement of oil would be available to the public *so that I might compare the politico-economic principles advocated in my proposal.* [480]

The Shah's economic dependence on the United States

Economically, the United States wanted their foot in the door to strengthen their influence and lessen communist influence and frankly, like historian James Bill reports in his book *the Eagle and the Lion,* Iranian oil would be made available to the west and proposals for

---

[477] Department of Army to Department of State, 3 December 1954, RG 59, 788.00/12-354
[478] Department of State to London, 9 December 1954, RG 59, 888.2553/12-954.
[479] London newspaper clipping, 17 December 1954, RG 59, 888.2553/12-1754
[480] Tunstill to Rothbone, 31 December 1954, RG 59, 888.00/12-3154.

negotiating an oil settlement occurred because the United States wanted to enter into the oil business of Iran. If the United States could economically strengthen Iran, then it could benefit from Iran's exports, monopolies, and foreign investments. At this point, the United States had given millions of dollars to Iran so that they could influence domestic policy. This influence led to the overthrow of Mossedegh and quite handsome percentages of oil export sales to American companies. The United States used Mossedegh's influence to take oil away from the British and align their policies with Great Britain. The Iranians felt they were being paid off as they received more than $567 million in economic aid up to 1960.[481] Historians like A. Saikal assume that if it were not for Pro-Shah forces, Mossedegh would still be in power. But Pro-Shah forces that swept the Shah back into power made one big mistake: *the Shah's regime became dependent on the United States for its immediate survival and continuity*[482]. The Shah constrained Iran's policy options and aligned them with the west. Iran's foreign policy and economic development became exploited to the world. Iran's dependency created two advantages for the United States: 1) it made Iran very vulnerable to pressures; and 2) the economic and military leverage gave the Shah the opportunity to consolidate his rule, suppress internal opposition and external threats.[483] The Shah and the United States wanted to strengthen their commitments for a politically stronger Iran and a hegemonic United States, defeating the Soviet Union and winning the Cold War.

The Shah of Persia was fairly well educated in Switzerland. He was eloquent in his political and military policies, but he was weak in his economic policies. His weakness was not attributed to his lack of interest, but rather his lack of training. He had an economic vision: to grow Iran to become the most powerful industrial nation in the Middle East and the world. But he needed money. In November of 1949 he visited the United States requesting supplies and

---

[481] James Bill *The Eagle and the Lion* (New Haven: Yale University Press, 1988).
[482] A. Saikal. *The Rise and Fall of the Shah. (Princeton: Princeton University Press, 1980), 46.*
[483] A. Saikal. *The Rise and Fall of the Shah. (Princeton: Princeton University Press, 1980), 46.*

funds. At that time the United States was not interested in the foreign economies of the world.[484] The United States was following a path of isolationism. But later with the Eisenhower doctrine, the United States revised their ideas and felt it was imperative to assist underdeveloped nations, especially the ones in the Middle East. They felt only economic aid could stop communism and also empower America's wealth. The Shah was a modest young person who represented the monarchs of Northern Europe. He felt his constitutional powers were between Sweden and England. The Shah compared the internal situation of Iran with 17th Century England, when the ruler of the kingdom would revolutionize his kingdom. .[485] He would also intervene in domestic policies, discharging employees of the government, and conducting ministerial duties. The chaos in Iran perpetuated the growth of Russian communism and the Tudeh party. The Shah faced the situation as if he was in Sweden- not doing anything about it. His throne will come to an end if he does not do something. [486]

The Shah was not pleased that the American public accused him of corruption.. The Shah stated, "I do not pretend that we are perfect. In the 3,000 years of our history, we have contributed as much- if not more- than any other nation to the world. Give me ten years of peace and friendly relations with the great powers within the United Nations Charter and my country will be able to establish the fundamental basis for the economic prosperity which would follow with rapid steps."[487] The Shah further stated that he welcomed more foreign investment. Meanwhile a bill was pending to be passed guaranteeing such an event. The Shah hoped that the *economic rehabilitation of Persia would be achieved with the assistance of the United States....*[488]

---

[484] Profile-Shah of Iran 10 February 1957 RG 59 788.00/2-1057.
[485] Profile-Shah of Iran 10 February 1957 RG 59 788.00/2-1057.
[486] Profile-Shah of Iran 10 February 1957 RG 59 788.00/2-1057.

[487] Page 2 of Enclosure 10 February 1957 RG 59 788.00/2-1057
[488] Page 2 of Enclosure 10 February 1957 RG 59 788.00/2-1057

Considering the "economic rehabilitation" of Persia, there had been quite deep pressure for a rate change in the foreign exchange for Iran, but the United States did not want to change the rate due to the failing economy. The failing economy had produced several articles in a bill to raise the real estate and income taxes for Iranians. Iranians were not pleased.[489] An example of the opinions voiced by the Iranians came from two arrested Mullahs from Tabriz who were preaching anti-government and anti-US remarks in their sermons. One Mullah denounced the government order of the abolition of the veil and raising the legal age of a girl to be married from nine to sixteen. Also, he was not pleased with American propaganda and misinterpreted the Quran stating that politics were allowed in religious sermons. It was not right for Americans to be social or interfering in the society of Iran.[490] Another Mullah claimed that the current government would not support the Shah, and believed government offices were poor and ineffective.[491] Despite these propaganda remarks about how deprived these religious figures were, the unemployment rate at the time was zero and pay for construction and unskilled workers had risen. States like Azerbaijan negotiated with Iran to purchase dried fruit from Tabriz, using an initial loan application made to Bank Melli. Another crop that was looking well to export was wheat. So, there were no problems in Tabriz, but there were rising costs all across Iran.[492]

The Shah requested Iranian economists and American experts to investigate why the country was not making much money from oil. He knew he was being cheated from the AIOC years before, but after the consortium agreement and many discussions, everything got back on track. The Shah admitted that it was he himself who worked for the nationalization of oil that

---

[489] Tehran to Secretary of State 24 January 1955, RG 59, 888.131/1-2455
[490] AMConsultate Tabriz to Department of State, 1 June 1955, RG 59, 788.00/6-155.
[491] AMConsultate Tabriz to Department of State, 1 June 1955, RG 59, 788.00/6-155.

[492] AMConsultate Tabriz to Department of State, 1 June 1955, RG 59, 788.00/6-155.

would end British and Soviet rule of their oil, though the nationalization of oil was accused of

Mossedegh.[493] He stated that Mossedegh was power hungry when he began fighting the British,

and that the Shah liked the British. He hoped to continue working on a new arrangement.

Essentially the Shah stated that Iran was producing at very low production rates, compared to the

high production in Saudi Arabia, Kuwait, Bahrein, and Iraq. Also, the communism situation in

Iran seemed to be under control, but the disintegration of the Tudeh party caused by the Iranian

government involved illegal acts of torture and unnecessary brutality sometimes directed against

completely innocent people.[494] It was up to America, Pakistan, and Iran to keep an eye on the

developments of Afghanistan and ensure that communism didn't happen there or else it would

infiltrate into Iran. The U.S. Embassy also stated that Iran and the United States were the players

of the world that could resolve the Kashmir issue. Nehru was a smart man whose policies were

not acceptable and the United States must do something. Iranians also advocated for U.S.

involvement in the Baghdad Pact. Iran and the other members of the Baghdad Pact could not

ensure a regional defense system without the tactics and support of the United States. The

interesting "leadership of the Shah" was then called interference into Iran's government affairs.[495]

The bad economy and bad future were attributed to the Shah. One such document from the U.S.

Embassy stated that Eltehaj manipulated the Shah. The U.S. Embassy would in fact pool all oil

revenues together, separate the military budget into an internal security and a foreign security

budget, and then ask the United States to pay for it. If the United States declined, then Iran would

cut back on their internal security- but it could not defend the country without the support of the

---

493 Enclosure No. 1 to Tehran 1 June 1955, RG 59, 788.00/6-155.
494 Enclosure No. 1 to Tehran 1 June 1955, RG 59, 788.00/6-155.

495 Enclosure No. 1 to Tehran 1 June 1955, RG 59, 788.00/6-155.

United States. In this person's opinion, he felt he would not ask the United States and would not grant Iran any money to balance the budget without knowing what the money would be used for.[496]

A new Seven Year Plan

In July 1955 a new seven year plan was approved and it included expenditures of $900 million including an extension of oil revenues, infrastructure projects and the construction of six airports.[497] Any surplus of the 12.5% of total crude oil production profits given to Iran would be provided to the NIOC to help the deficit and any needs of the government. Also, perhaps 10% of any surplus would be given to the Ministry of Finance. The plan also included borrowing from internal and foreign sources.[498] The Plan organization provided Bank Melli 3 million pounds sterling and another IMF approval for a second $8.75 million.[499] On April 8, 1956, the Majlis approved a new State Budget Bill providing the compulsory retirement for teachers and judges to be between 70 to 80 years of age. Our friend Sadiq disagreed with this bill because it showed a deficit of 4 billion rials, the income tax was unfair because it burdened the poor, and the bill did not include a better tax ratio. Others agreed, yet the bill was passed. One such senate member attributed communist infiltration in the university, and in the ministry of education to all be removed.. Another Senator said that the bill showed lavish expenses of the Senate and everyone who approved it would betray the founders of the Constitution. One Senator even went as far to call for the elimination of the Ministry of Foreign Affairs because *we don't have an independent foreign policy...*[500]

The United States provided Iran $1 million for the planning period in 1951, over $23 million in 1952, and another amount of more than $23 million in 1953 and in 1954, adding

---

[496] Enclosure No. 1 to Tehran 1 June 1955, RG 59, 788.00/6-155.

[497] Department of Army to Department of State, 1 July 1955, RG 59, 788.00/7-155.

[498] Department of Army to Department of State, 1 July 1955, RG 59. 788.00/7-155.

[499] Tehran to Secretary of State, 5 November 1955, RG 59, 888.131/11-555.

[500] Enclosure No. 1 to Tehran, 8 April 1956, RG 59, 888.00/4-856.

everything up provided more than $131,737,000.00. An amount of $60 million was given to Iran in emergency assistance for their own budgetary purposes. They followed the advice of USOM who told them about the currency conversion plan, importation of sugar, medicine, and a local currency.[501] The United States Missions also guided them to alleviate any pain or suffering in Iranian cities. Though preliminary work was done in the first two years, nothing had been done yet because no American surveys had arrived yet. The officials who were handling United States' aid funds were accused of misappropriating them. These officials were both Iranian and American. The common statement of it "is not a joke" was written on additional requests for foreign aid to balance the budget.[502] Many Iranians believed that the Point IV operations that had not been executed were due to *embezzlement and graft on the part of high Iranian officials, and possibly on the part of a few Americans.* This belief was also shared by radicals, students, landlords, politicians, and other officials. In fact, *the United States Government itself stated that aid funds had been embezzled by both Iranians and Americans and that large amounts of the aid funds were wasted in useless projects and equipment.[503]* This investigation persuaded Congress to reduce aid, and in effect people in the United States would not be very happy. The Americans however showed that it was some government officials who abused the aid, not Americans.[504]

In March 1956, the United States approved a $20 million aid package to Iran so that Iran could meet its budgetary needs.[505] Iran was facing tremendous failures in its accounting and only had $7.5 million in cash on hand. Iran was looking for consultants for management, auditing, accounting, and shipping.[506] In the exchange transactions, Bank Melli made more than $2.4

---

[501] Tehran to Secretary of State, 4 March 1956, RG 59, 788.5-MSP/3-456.
[502] Tehran to Secretary of State, 4 March 1956, RG 59, 788.5-MSP/3-456.

[503] Tehran to Secretary of State, 4 March 1956, RG 59, 788.5-MSP/3-456.

[504] Tehran to Secretary of State, 4 March 1956, RG 59, 788.5-MSP/3-456.

[505] Tehran to Secretary of State, 4 March 1956, RG 59, 788.5-MSP/3-456.

million in one week. The cotton exports had been doing very well. The Iran-Soviet Border talks were not at a standstill, but there had been no serious issues. Foreign Minister Ala made a political speech saying that Iran was not neutral, but that a decision needed to be made on regional defense. This decision would relate well with the independence of Iran, instead of moving Iran toward working with just foreign powers.[507] In April of 1956, the Shah visited Isfahan, Yazd, Kerman, and other places of Iran that were seriously damaged by the flood. The Shah offered only 3 million rials, or about $39, 500 for the victims of the tragedy. This fund was provided by Iranian Army Officers. [508]

The Shah told Iranians that he would ask for further economic assistance. He firmly believed that Iran would be making more money over the following five years, approximately $500 million in oil revenues. He believed he would receive $1 billion in oil revenues by 1968. At the time Iran had $210 million in annual oil revenues. He asked the United States to give an additional $250 million for the next five years, until his military was self sufficient, and economic and social programs were well-guarded.[509] In the later parts of 1956, the goods of wheat, cotton, sugar, and almonds were successful. [510]Even though the Shah hand-picked the Majlis, no one in the Majlis approved the World Bank loan to be issued to Iran said, Philip Clock, first secretary of the United States Embassy. [511]

In this period of economic turmoil and political problems, American aid came to the rescue *through one of the most difficult periods in her history.* Dulles stated to the American Embassy that *Iran is a significantly stable influence in the Middle East and is exercising strong*

---

[506] Department of Army to Secretary of State, 19 May 1956, RG 59, 788.00/5-1956.
[507] Department of Army to Secretary of State, 19 May 1956, RG 59, 788.00/5-1956.

[508] American Consul Isafahan to Department of State, 8 August 1956, RG 59, 788.11/8-856.
[509] Guy A Lee NEA to GE Mouser 23 June 1958, RG 59, 888.00/6-2358.
[510] American Consulate Meshed to American Consul 28 August 1956, RG 59, 888.20/8-2856.
[511] Desp. 460 Tehran to AmEmbassy London, 28 August 1956, RG 59, 788.5/8-2856.

and progressive leadership with the area. We believe that United States aid has assisted Iran in assuming and maintaining this constructive role.[512]

A statement was issued by a committee auditing the expenditures of the State Department. The chief of the sub-committee on the United States Aid Operations in Iran determined that problems of Iran be eliminated. Peter Hardy wrote to Secretary Dulles referring him to government operations, stating that both parties could correct the weaknesses of the report. [513]

The State Department Fights for more Iranian Aid

The goal of the United States was to keep Iran and its oil resources from the other side of the iron curtain because this would be an *important goal in the Cold War.* The United States was not concerned how the money was spent, but that the money was spent in a manner deemed fit for the United States. Those who objected or questioned the money spent were disciplined, and large sums of money continued to arrive in Iran. The State Department felt that this was erroneous, and the Mission and State Department were always worried about the expenditures. Furthermore, the commitment of funds was also described by the CIA as illegitimate for peace-time expenses, as an effort to fund the Cold War was not supported.[514] Also, Iran participated very nominally in the expenses of the program and U.S. dollars were Iran's main asset. The State Department also rejected the Committee's 1953 findings that Iran did contribute or make payments to this program benefiting them. The Committee said that the United States provided funds to stabilize the foreign exchange, give aid to alleviate budgetary concerns, and other types of aid.[515] The question is how did any of these programs looking at the disaster today contribute

---

[512] Dulles to AmEmbassy Tehran, 24 January, 1957, RG 59, 788.5 MSP/1-2457.
[513] Peter Hardy to Secretary Dulles, 7 February 1957, RG 59, 788.5 MSP/2-757.
[514] International Operations Sub-Committee Report on US Aid Operations In Iran, 7 February 1957, RG 59, 788.5 MSP/2-757.
[515] International Operations Sub-Committee Report on US Aid Operations In Iran, 7 February 1957, RG 59, 788.5

to Iran? For example, the United States provided $10 million in direct aid to Iran for industrial and improvement projects. The United States looked at these projects and knew they had to be implemented in Iran. However, it had been four years and these projects had not been implemented. The economic development of Iran had mainly been in oil and they manipulated the United States to get oil money. The State Department replied that the Comptroller General did not report any of the expenditures as illegal. In response, the Committee said the Comptroller General felt that giving U.S. Aid of $5 million over four years to Iranian students studying in the United States, and additional $2 million in subsidies to purchase foreign currency at low prices were unauthorized. The State Department replied that in March 1952, the Iranian government had to suspend the aid to 800 students in the United States and they had to decide to keep them there or send them home. Families and other local programs kept those students in the United States.[516]

Another interesting paradigm is that $12.7 million was given in the earlier part of 1951. But, the amount was so little that it was not able to finance the government's budget or development plan. It was given to someone's pocket. It was also during this period before the oil settlement that oil revenues fell and that $12.7 million was not used. These oil revenues also-despite American representation- were made available to the country. Hence, the Committee requested that before U.S. aid was approved, Iran should be able to pay the money back. The State Department acknowledged that this was true with past loans, but currently, Iran was not planning to pay back the loans.[517] The Committee ended their conclusions stating that:

MSP/2-757.

[516] International Operations Sub-Committee Report on US Aid Operations In Iran, 7 February 1957, RG 59, 788.5 MSP/2-757.

[517] International Operations Sub-Committee Report on US Aid Operations In Iran, 7 February 1957, RG 59, 788.5 MSP/2-757.

Iran's oil revenues are, and have been for some time, adequate to finance both the Government's operating budget and their ambitious development plan. Thus, their chronic budget deficits appear to be an outgrowth of financial management methods rather than lack of resources. [518]

The State Department again countered these statements stating the oil revenues were inadequate for the budget of Iran. They also replied to another statement stating that ICA did not remove any pertinent facts to the implementation of the program. The sub-committee felt that Congress had not been able to control the information on how the funds had been spent because of the removal of these facts. The sub-committee further stated that Iran's loans had also increased from a small amount of $30 million to more than $225.9 million and negotiations currently were underway for another $137 million, which did not include the $65 million oil settlement.[519] The International Operations Sub-Committee stated that every year this aid to Iran had been justified as a temporary measure and these presentations had always omitted information needed about the grants. Perhaps more information would have eliminated this mismanagement of funds. The State Department did not believe the same temporary measures applied to Iranian economy should be considered temporary or occur each year. The different levels of aid were due to the fluctuating economy changing with different forms of leadership, economic chaos, and communist infiltration. Iran's economic developments had made a big difference and could be said to have been supported by the United States. Dulles and Hardy would look into the issue.[520]

---

[518] International Operations Sub-Committee Report on US Aid Operations In Iran, 7 February 1957, RG 59, 788.5 MSP/2-757.

[519] International Operations Sub-Committee Report on US Aid Operations In Iran, 7 February 1957, RG 59, 788.5 MSP/2-757.

[520] International Operations Sub-Committee Report on US Aid Operations In Iran, 7 February 1957, RG 59, 788.5 MSP/2-757.

A transmission from Kabul came to the secretary of state stating that the Shah was negotiating with Ambassador Chapin to get extra money to build Afghan airports such as Kandahar International, which would increase their ties with the West and between Iran and Pakistan. The airport would also help ship cultivated opium into Iran for them to package it and ship it to the United States. The airport construction would also provide upgraded cement runways too.[521] The Speaker of the Majlis, Hekmat was overly concerned about statements from the State Department. He said,

> I am not an economist, but I really don't understand what you mean when you talk about Iran having all the money it needs for development projects- and the limiting factors now being labor, skills and materials. [522]

Hekmat was referring to the deficit of unemployment, local construction ceasing to exist, and mismanaged funds. Hekmat said, *"I will be the first to admit that our Government has shown bad judgment and poor management in expending your aid funds…"* [523]

Another way to stabilize the economy was through lower bank rates. With lower bank rates, the fiscal economy of Iran could improve with more borrowing and more spending of money in the economy. [524]Another way to stabilize the economy was that a local travel agency in Iran suggested the creation of a tourist office for the Bureau of Tourism of the USSR. This tourist office would handle the tourist traffic coming into Iran and the Soviet Union. The biggest arrangement shared among the two countries was skiing arrangements. There would also be different classes of travel. The tourist office felt that with tourist traffic, more money would flow into the economy.[525] Iran made new rules for not discriminating against imports coming from the

---

[521] Kabul to Secretary of State, 18 November 1957, RG 59, 788.5/11-1857.

[522] Hekmat to First & Second Secretary of Embassy, 7 March 1957, RG 59, 788.5/3-757.

[523] Hekmat to First & Second Secretary of Embassy, 7 March 1957, RG 59, 788.5/3-757.

[524] Hekmat to First & Second Secretary of Embassy, 7 March 1957, RG 59, 788.5/3-757.

[525] Tehran to Department of State, 29 May 1957, RG 59, 888.181/5-2957.

United States and its total deficit with the country was about $138.8 million. In this deficit trade agreement, Iran had to lower its foreign exchange to about $50 million to ease the deficit. [526]

The problem was that Americans needed to understand the psychology of Iranians. The understanding was very simple: they don't want to be bought out. Iranians felt that the Government of Iran made many concessions to the United States, but in return the United States had only given aid that didn't benefit them. After Iran joined the Baghdad Pact and an announcement was made that the United States would be giving more aid, and aid at first was given in portions not suitable for the average Iranian, then people began to wonder about America's involvement in Iran. These emotions began when the Soviet Union offered Iran $100 million and the Anglo-Americans offered aid for the Aswan Dam. In both circumstances, Iranians, who still claimed Afghanistan as their homeland, felt that Iran should get a better deal than Afghanistan. [527]

Owen Jones wrote to Iran about the surplus property and land-lease accounts. He stated that they requested the Iranian government pay $801,753.56 to the land-lease account and a past due balance of $2.1 million. The past due amount and unpaid balance was $18,033,636.91 at the time. [528]In November of 1957, the Shah was waiting on his $20 million aid from 58 funds. This money would meet the budget deficit that Iran had in the following year. He had to raise civilian and military salaries. That could not be postponed any longer. The U.S. Embassy had some difficulties in the beginning convincing the Iranian government that the debt owed to them had to be paid back. [529] As of December 31, 1954, Iran still owed $62, 772, 394.58. It was therefore

---

[526] Tehran to Department of State, 29 May 1957, RG 59, 888.181/5-2957.

[527] Tehran to Department of State, 29 May 1957, RG 59, 888.181/5-2957.

[528] Owen Jones to Iran, 30 September 1957, RG 59, 788.56/9-3057.
[529] Tehran to Secretary of State, 30 November, 1957, 788.5 MSP/11-3057.

important that the current debt of Iran be taken into account before more aid was given. He also hoped that the increased tax money would help in this regard, and oil revenues had to be increased because the government needed compensation.[530] The Shah was not too happy about receiving only $6.5 million for the construction of the airfields. This money would be insufficient in terms of barracks and ammunition. Another airfield was also needed besides QOM. Turkey had nine air force bases designed by Gulf engineers. He was hoping that the U.S. Air Force would be able to intervene and help with the design of the airfields in Iran. Looking at 1958, Iran can be proud of its economic success over those last few years. Iran would receive another hefty sum in 1958.[531] The income had arrived from taxation, oil revenues, and resources. Ambassador Chapin hoped that $76 million of new money would be arriving in the fiscal year of 1958. This aid package would mainly suit American experts.[532]

At the beginning of 1958 Iran was involved in a procurement exercise with the United States military on site. The Chief of the ARMISH/MAAG agreed to reimburse Iran a total allotment of $171, 160, 708.5 rials.[533] The ICA or International Cooperation Administration wrote to the Under Secretary of Economic Affairs Douglas Dillon that the military construction in Iran had to change from the previous method of the Department of Defense, employing Corps Engineers and financed through partly dollars and partially local currency. The ICA proposed that the construction projects should be completed in dollars and come out of the military assistance funds granted for Iran. The U.S. government could save $2 million to $3 million if they implemented this plan. Before, money was unaccounted for. Now the income provided to them would be limited to the dollars provided and any other would certainly be acquired

---

[530] Tehran to Secretary of State, 5 December 1957, 788.5 MSP/12-557.
[531] Tehran to Secretary of State, 30 November, 1957, RG 59, 788.5 MSP/11-3057.
[532] Tehran to Secretary of State, 5 December 1957, RG 59, 788.5 MSP/12-557.
[533] Tehran to Joint Embassy/Agriculture/USOM, 11 January 1958, RG 59, 788.5 MSP/1-1158.

themselves. If the United States accepted this proposal, they faced the problem of auditing and reporting the values of the military expenditures. If military construction was done primarily through rials, then how would they keep track of the investments and what would they report as an investment in 1959? The estimated completion date was June 30, 1958. There had been only $6.5million allocated for the military construction such as QOM airfield. So, the Department of Defense needed to send in more money according to section 501 for an immediate transfer. [534]

In response to the 1958 receipt of funds, the Shah negotiated with General Taylor to the point of blackmail requesting more aid. He stated to the United States that America was not ready to go to war with the Soviet Union. So it seemed perfectly clear that America needed to empower the allies of that area to prevent war against the United States. In fact, he was looking at the BP (British Petroleum) military planners for advice on Iranian's future policy. Furthermore, he began persuading BP that Iran was not only key, but the very purpose of the BP and their military strategy in Iran depended upon Iran's consideration of BP.[535] Iran's deficit at that time was approximately $100 million. The Foreign Minister now considered loans from the International Development Loan Fund and the Export-Import Bank. The Counselor of the Iranian Embassy came to U.S. officials requesting a general credit of $250 million for the next five years. The United States was unaware of such a claim. In fact, Mr. Williams was surprised by Mahdavi's request and that a counselor of the Embassy was demanding such high numbers from the United States. The credits from the Development Loan Fund (DLF) or the Export-Import bank were processed soon after receiving proposals for specific projects. The proposals were urgently requested to compensate for their limited funds. The United States also wanted the Department to obtain some kind of notification that Iran would remit payment of $40 million.

---

[534] ICA to Dillon, 13 January 1958, RG 59, 788.5 MSP/1-1358.
[535] Tehran to Secretary of State, 13 January 1958, RG 59, 788.5 MSP/1-1358.

Senator Kennedy, in fact, proposed that the amounts sought in DLF should be explored first and whereby DLF could give at least a credit of $75 million for projects in Iran. [536]

In an interview with Hekmat, he believed that although the budget situation was "fantastic" in 1958, there would be a rise of expenditures that Iran could not afford. He felt the impossibility of making more money, and the dangers of inflation were incoming, and both Iranians and Americans knew about rising expenditures.[537] The problem was that the expenditures were military ones. They were spending too much for just internal security or to prepare for a war that was never to be started. If the essential needs were met and Iran was just guarding borders and not making missions across the world like in Argentina, then Iran would have a surplus. Military expenditures were weakening the economy. Furthermore, Hekmat believed that along with the United States, the Shah was ignorant of the reasons Turkey had a stronger army than Iran. Even if Turkey did not have the best of weapons, they would be better than Iran having the best rifles and weapons. The problem was that Iran's conscript was indeed brave, but the officer corps was very disorganized and dysfunctional. A complete reconstruction of the policies of Iranian military was needed.[538] The final amount of credit was the $250 million, but it was an unspecified amount of time. There was discussion that the $30 million to $40 million dollar aid would also be given over many years.[539] Though the $40 million was to be used for military expenditures, the Shah was planning to use this acquired credit for the construction of a hotel in Tehran. This hotel would be important, placed in the Pahlavi Foundation, and attract future investment. The cost of this hotel was upwards of $10 million. [540]

---

[536] NEA: Berry, Kennedy, Williams to US Government, 30 January 1958, RG 59, 788.5 MSP/1-3058.
[537] AmEmbassy Tehran to Department of State, 14 January 1958, RG 59, 788.00/1-1458.
[538] AmEmbassy Tehran to Department of State, 14 January 1958, RG 59, 788.00/1-1458.

[539] Excerpt from minutes of Country Team Meeting 28 January 1958, RG 59, 788.5 MSP/1-2858.
[540] Tehran to Secretary of State, 23 April 1958, RG 59, 788.5 MSP/4-2358.

The tracking of the amount of aid requested from the United States was quite interesting. The United States did not see themselves giving so much money and in return did not know they were going to make so much money. It was a simple small token of kindness, helping the Zahedi government and the Shah get the country back on track. When Iran collapsed, they had no money in the treasury, tremendous amounts of political unrest, and no diplomacy with Britain. They could only turn to the United States. The original level of support or foreign aid the United States wanted to give was about $67 million for 12 months. They felt that after this aid package, Iran would have enough energy to spin off on its own. The original $67 million was later cut down to $45 million and added in the same year as another $15 million. Iran began making more than $ 5 million a month.[541] Bank Melli initially would publish monthly amounts to the government stating cash on hand, then with the amount of aid coming in and the maintenance of many monopolies, it became even more complicated. The efforts of the new government of Iran and the United States were unclear. . The existing fear of communism and the ignorance of the threat also continued as communists continued their demonstrations in Iran. The thing that was interesting was whether an initial amount of $23 million following Mossedegh's overthrow was justified and needed. It is not a large amount, but big for Iran. Iran's productivity was created on the premise that $8 billion annually was coming into the United States, so what do they do? The people were trying to find ways to put money in the economy. [542]In 1952, the United States gave 2.4 million and only $13 million in technical assistance in 1958. In November 1952, the United States appointed a leader, William Warne, from the Department of the Interior to manage the economy. The burden of proof was on the United States to convince Congress to give money to Iran. Iran had a lack of funds, but that was not enough for them. The chief role was to indeed

---

[541] United States Aid Operations in Iran, 7 February 1957, RG 59, 788.5 MSP/2-757.
[542] United States Aid Operations in Iran, 7 February 1957, RG 59, 788.5 MSP/2-757.

keep the country going during a period of insolvency brought about by the nationalization of the oil industry. The problems of the economy and the political unrest could lead to an outright communist attack, which the United States wanted to avoid. This was convincing to those guaranteeing the aid packages to Iran, as well as that Iran would settle the oil dispute, giving cheap oil to the United States. The development aid packages also helped local villages attain the basic necessities of life: shelter, water, and food. According to this technical assistance grant, Iran was to provide $80,000 a year to the United States and the United States would only provide services and equipment. The United States was not obligated to provide anything else. The only reason why oil was thought to be somewhat of a "tangible improvement" was that Iranians felt that oil and the economy was not improving despite their income. It was America's interest and negotiations that changed the viewpoints of some Iranians, though many still felt that there was a lot of money in Iran, but it was not being spent on them.[543]

Construction of Developmental Projects

Different cabinet ministers had been touring the provinces of Iran, such as a province called Fars, to give money to the villages. Another tour was headed by Prime Minister Eqbal to the eastern parts of Azerbaijan trying to improve schools, health facilities, and ensure proper communication methods.[544] An amount of 100 million rials was given to the University of Tabriz to remove any faults and complete the dorms.[545] All Foreign Exchange transactions in Iran have now been allotted to Bank Melli who implemented new measures for this bill. In July 1958, the Plan Organization announced that the Development Loan Fund would provide a credit of $40

---

[543] United States Aid Operations in Iran, 7 February 1957, RG 59, 788.5 MSP/2-757.

[544] American Consulate Isfahan to Department of State, 27 January 1958, RG 59, 788.13/1-2758.
[545] Am Embassy Tehran to Secretary of State, 11 October 1958, RG 59, 788.13/10-1158.

million to finance development projects in Iran.[546] Dillon wrote to the Secretary of State that economic development had been discussed and needed to be put on paper. The reason being was that the grant of $40 million needed to be allotted properly. These projects would persuade DLF of a satisfactory outcome and avoid any future deals. Also, the Shah was interested in establishing a university in Shiraz City equal to American standards. It would not be an American university, but an Iranian university developed with American support and organizations. Dillon reported from Karachi.[547] Later he was in New Delhi and reported that he met with Bell Atlantic, Macintosh and the Iranian Plan organization chaired by Ebtahaj. They sat together to discuss development projects in Iran. They worked out a deal together where both Bell and Macintosh would help in the road construction, port improvements, road progress, and engineering. At the time expenditures were $200 million and $150 million.[548] In a discussion with Senator Fulbright, the Shah advocated for more military needs, but Senator Fulbright indicated that *educational and economic development were more important than military forces.* While speaking with the Senator, Senator Fulbright learned that the requests were not new and the U.S. government would make a decision appropriate to the Shah.[549] The Shah also proposed that the U.S. government increased its production of oil to a 50% increase in Iran so that Iran could benefit from the production too. This would entail Iran meeting its developmental and military demands. It had a political connotation that if large oil production was met, then Nasser could not go higher, and if he did, he could cause imbalance of the market. However, the oil companies in the United States were private and the U.S. government could not tell them what to do. Some of them were going to Kuwait for more money in the consortium agreement. The fear

---

[546] Department of State to AmEmbassy Tehran, 3 July 1958, RG 59, 788.5 MSP/7-358.
[547] Tehran to Department of State, 1 October 1958, RG 59, 788.5 MSP/10-158.
[548] New Delhi to Secretary of State, 8 October 1958, RG 59, 788.5 MSP/10-858.
[549] New Delhi to Secretary of State, 8 October 1958, RG 59, 788.5 MSP/10-858.

was that if Egypt produced more oil than the United States and Iran *shared its oil economy,* then Egypt along with the Soviet Union could *be used for subversive purposes throughout Middle East.* [550]

The construction of American barracks in Sanandaj, Kordestan was ahead of schedule. This project was financed directly through America and would be completed in December 1960. This was a strategic location that already headquartered the Sixth Iranian Army Division. This project built 217 buildings and refurnished many more. The cost of this strategic location was about $11 million with overhead costs at 15%. They had about 200 employees working on this project.[551] The average worker received about 7 rials per hour, roughly a third of a cent and a daily intake of 56 rials was above average per day in Iran.[552]

Also, the Turkish Iranian railway plan was underway and would cost about $43 million. The balance of $38 million would remain a loan to the government of Iran. This showed the power of the Baghdad Pact and would better represent the regional interests of the other countries. In order to take this loan from DLF, it was suggested by Dulles at the ministerial meeting in Ankara in January 1958. None of the private firms in this project had a share. Delew, together with Gonduiling would consult on the railroad on the Turkish-Iranian line. It would construct 222 km long railways in Turkey from Mus to the Iranian border and include two harbors and ferry boats. The railway would pass through an area of wealth.[553] Since it was a joint project of the Baghdad Pact, it helped the economic and social relations of the member countries in the Pact. The total cost of the project, both in Turkish and Iranian, was roughly $90,350,006, of which $48,700,000 was foreign financing and $41, 650,000 were overhead costs. A sum of

---

[550] New Delhi to Secretary of State, 8 October 1958, RG 59, 788.5 MSP/10-858.

[551] Am Consulate Tabriz to Department of State, 11 June 1958, RG 59, 788.5 MSP/6-1158.
[552] Am Consulate Tabriz to Department of State, 11 June 1958, RG 59, 788.5 MSP/6-1158.
[553] Ministry of Foreign Affairs, 17 November 1958, RG 59, 788.5 MSP/11-1758.

$100,000 had been made available to the Turkish section for a total of $12, 070,000 by the United States to fund this railway project. [554]But the proposed loan for the reconstruction and development of this line went under scrutiny when the Under Secretary of Treasury wrote to State Department's Herbert Prochow, deputy under secretary, stating that Iran would be receiving a loan despite not remitting payment for the land lease obligations on their surplus property. They felt no future loans should be made to Iran unless the slate was clean. Even in 1949, a representative of the Iranian government told the U.S. government that no payment was required on credits made to Iran. If this was true, it needed to be investigated. [555]

In anticipation of 1959, Iran would receive a technical aid package of $5.8 million and $3 million in defense support. The Baghdad Pact bilateral agreements were also underway and soon to be completed due to the rising tension that the Soviets could potentially cause. The oil revenue distribution was changed to 15% of the plan organization, giving more money to Iran. [556]This new budget was balanced and the $19.3 million deficit decreased due to the increased oil revenues. The expenditures planned were $174 million with revenues to about $152 million. A deficit of $22 million would be covered through short term borrowing from Bank Melli. So the Shah wanted the value of his aid approved as he went before the Majlis to propose the difference between $35 million to 40 million for approval. The U.S. government said that there could be another $30 million dollars. In these days, Iraq and Afghanistan were under constant pressure and the Shah was deeply disturbed by these events.[557]

---

[554] Ministry of Foreign Affairs, 17 November 1958, RG 59, 788.5 MSP/11-1758.

[555] Department of State to Honorable Irwin, 19 November 1958, RG 59, 788.8 MSP/11-1958.
[556] Department of State to Officer in Charge of Iranian Affairs, 24 November, 1958, RG 59, 788.5 MSP/11-2458.
[557] Tehran to Secretary of State, 8 December 1958, RG 59, 788.5 MSP/12-858;Tehran to Secretary of State, 13 December 1959, RG 59, 788.5 MSP/12-1359.

The potential American Economic Meltdown

In February 28, 1959, Prince Colam Reza Pahlavi, the Shah's half brother, told the U.S. Embassy that: "We're very interested in avoiding, here in Iran, one of those …revolutions like the one which took place in Iraq."[558] He stated that they should follow a different course to prevent such revolution from occurring.[559] A new reform program was initiated by the Shah to tackle corruption in government life and social life. He passed a program that would reduce the number of government employees to lessen their business dealings. Six months later, this reform program ended without any success and questionable laws were coming into existence.[560] Due to the commercial exchange rate, Bank Melli was making $1.5 million a day and selling at 79.50 rials per dollar.[561] The United Kingdom and Iran signed an agreement that allocated a 10 million pound loan for five years at an interest rate of 4%.[562] The loan was to finance the imports and manufacturing of goods. In February the expenditures were $416.2 million and revenue was $401.1 million, hence no savings. There were continued Soviet propaganda attacks on Iran's regime. The Iranian government reassured the public that no such attack would happen. A new law was beginning to take form. This new law was an enforcement law that could save the Shah's regime. A $12 million bill was passed along the territorial sea of Iran against the United States' and the United Kingdom's objections to protect itself from Saudi infiltration. The Shah was planning to marry the daughter of the former King of Italy, Umberto. Many politicians believed that this marriage would be damaging to the Shah's regime in Iran. The deficit of $107 million was requested to be covered by U.S. aid. Iran's first oil tanker was coming to Iran. The vessel was ordered 2.5 years ago and another one would be completed in six months.[563]

---

[558] AmEmbassy Tehran to Department of State, 28 February 1959, RG 59, 788.00/2-2859
[559] AmEmbassy Tehran to Department of State, 28 February 1959, RG 59, 788.00/2-2859

[560] American Consulate Isafahan Iran to Department of State, 23 April 1959, RG 59, 788.00/4-2359.
[561] Consulate Isafahan Iran to Department of State, 23 April 1959, RG 59, 788.00/4-2359.
[562] Department of the Army to Department of State, 1 February 1959, RG 59, 788.00/2-159.

Iran was currently waiting on the bilateral agreements among the regional states. The Soviets also received information that there were American bases in Iran. They were telling the world about this news. The Soviets were saying: "Oppressed and dissatisfied people and relying on bilateral agreement to save this rotted and corrupt throne." They also stated that the foreign intruders would not save the regime, but rather create a hated dynasty. In order to combat the Soviet propaganda, the Shah created a national holiday on February 28th called Nation Day. More than 80,000 people participated in the ceremonies, though they were all from government agencies. [564]

In another correspondence, Foruqi told the U.S. embassy about the Shah's weakness. He was commenting on his upbringing, saying that it made him distrustful and in fact responsible for the murder of RazaMara and General Afshartus. The reason the Shah was so weak was because the Queen's relatives were all advising him and being poor advisors, they had weakened his position. After the death of his brother, he decided that he was to run the country directly. He was to prove himself to be ruler of the Shah. In a brief moment with the Shah's mother, *the Shah had banged his fist on a table and shouted: "I will be Reza Shah! I am Reza Shah!"*[565] At this time Prime Minister Ala was also very weak, but very honorable. The Shah had huge bank balances in the United States and the United Kingdom. He could not live on the income from the Ministry of Court. In order to maintain his family, he spent 8 million rials a year ($100,000 a year in 1959). The Shah gave each member of his family, mother, sisters and, brothers about 60,000 rials a month ($750.00 in 1959).[566] Princess Shams brought Queen Soraya to marry the

---

[563] Department of the Army to Department of State, 1 February 1959, RG 59, 788.00/2-159.

[564] Department of the Army to Department of State, 1 February 1959, RG 59, 788.00/2-159.

[565] Tehran to Secretary of State, 20 April 1959, RG 59, 788.5 MSP/4-2059.
[566] Tehran to Secretary of State, 20 April 1959, RG 59, 788.5 MSP/4-2059.

Shah. The Shah and the Queen was a great couple, but being Queen, she was bored and could not bear children. They separated and hated Princess Shahnaz. The Shah was still married to her, due to the possible scandal of divorce. The Shah was the only stabilizing person in Iran. Foruqi also advised the government of the United States that the giveaway land was sometimes not free, but sold in portions to peasants who paid 2000 rials a month to maintain ownership of their lands. [567]

The United States granted another aid request of $20 million dollars to ensure economic stability, bringing the grand total to a quarter billion dollars since 1951 and more than $48 million in 1959. Also, there would be military aid that strengthened the government. The Shah ran an efficient government, but he micro-managed people. Once General Zahedi stated, "Why doesn't the Shah leave us alone? I am a Division-General; I don't interfere in the command of a Lieutenant. It was a year ago that the Shah took all power into his hands, appointed Hossein Ala, a weak, yet honorable man as Prime Minister."[568] There was a proposed sum of $900,000 to go to the construction of field posts and planned deployment of Army units from the South to tactical positions in the North.[569] In late February, the USOM-MAAG reviewed the military budget. The Prime Minister planned to present a budget deficit of $23.9 million, total expenditures of $405.9 million, and total revenues of $382 million. This is a strategic move so that Congress will have enough time to approve another U.S. aid package. [570]

The Foreign Trade Bank of Iran received a request from Mr. Van Vlierden from Bank of America to purchase 550 shares of the new foreign trade bank deemed as Export Development Bank. If this request was approved, the small Bank of America would receive 20% of all capital

---

[567] Tehran to Secretary of State, 20 April 1959, RG 59, 788.5 MSP/4-2059.
[568] Tehran to Secretary of State, 20 April 1959, RG 59, 788.5 MSP/4-2059.

[569] Tehran to Secretary of State, 20 April 1959, RG 59, 788.5 MSP/4-2059.

[570] Tehran to Secretary of State, 14 February 1959, RG 59, 788.5 MSP/2-1459

share profits from the bank. This would also entail that the Banco Commerciale Italiano and the Deutsche Bank of Frankfurt would own 14.5 % of the profits. The goal was to have foreign interest get 49 % of the total capitalization and give the remaining 51 % to Iran. The former Bank Melli manager would run the new bank. Bank of America hired a western banking associate to help with the agreement. Senator Kennedy s also stated that the Federal Reserve Board asked about the State Department views and Kennedy stated that the State Department views were very much favorable. Mr. Van Vlierden felt there was significant economic progress in Iran, its financial practices were good, and the collection of taxes was outstanding. It was in fact the loan from the Development Loan Fund that established the new development bank of Iran.[571]

In September 23, 1959, Bank Melli insured a loss of $33 million in the foreign exchange bringing its value of gold down to $273 million. A total of $13.3 million was transferred to cover the new note, gold and foreign exchange, bringing the total value to $150 million since its notes were backed by loans.[572] On November 6, 1959, the Shah arrived in Amman, Jordan and many chiefs of the diplomatic mission greeted him. The Shah was concerned about Afghanistan talking in three minute intervals to the Embassy representative. The representative from Amman's U.S. Embassy said he visited Iran many times from Kabul and was close to Ambassador Shayesteh. He told the Jordan U.S. Embassy foreign officer that Afghanistan armed by the USSR was a great threat to Iran and Pakistan. The Shah inquired whether an attack would come to Iran from Afghanistan. The U.S. representative said it was more likely from USSR, and would target northwestern Iran.[573] In a 1956 policy with Afghanistan, the Shah asked if the United States could take responsibility of losing Afghanistan, take some kind of responsibility or reversal and

---

[571] Bank of America to Foreign Trade Bank of Iran, 21 May 1959, RG 59, 788.5 MSP/5-2159.
[572] AmEmbassy Tehran to Department of State, 31 October 1959, RG 59, 788.11/10-3159.
[573] Amman to Secretary of State, 6 November 1959, RG 59, 788.11/11-659.

reverse the $100 million Soviet credit offered to them and they could become closer allies. The representative agreed with the Shah's points, but admitted that blackmail was not U.S. policy. Former Finance Minister Malik in 1956 also stated that the United States outbid the Soviets and we didn't because Afghanistan was not a priority to us. The United States however planned to help the Afghans in civil aviation preventing Soviet influence, with a transit project, Helmand Valley development, at a cost of $6millon.[574] The U.S. government gave a wedding gift, a set of Steuben glassware to the new Queen of Iran, Fatima, from Paris. This gift was similar to the one given to Princess Shahnaz in 1957. The current gift was authorized by the American Ambassador, making no reference that the President or U.S. government funded it. But, the gift was on behalf of the President and Secretary. [575]

In a *Washington Post* column, George Dixon wrote that the U.S. government had given royal gifts to the fiancée of the Shah. He wrote:

> All us in this country can feel we have contributed to bride-to-be's ecstasy. Our gifts make up nearly 20 percent of Iran's whole budget. The Shah does not take criticism from us but he is not so touchy about taking arms and money. I have just obtained very latest figures on our giveaway Iran and they are staggering. Up to end 1958, we gave Iran $379,738,000 in military aid, and $329,639,000 in economic assistance. This year 1959 we have already given marrying monarch's country another $50,000,000-and more is programmed. That's our payers to sensitive ruler. He divorced his previous wives Fawzia and Soraya, because he said they had failed to give him a son. Odd, I am informed by medical men who do this kind handicapping, are considerably more than even against third one doing any better. If Farah Diba (Fatima) fails give his son I suppose he will look to us to help him start all over again. [576]

Despite this statement in the *Washington Post*, on December 15 1959 President Eisenhower gave a Paul Revere Silver bowl with the presidential seal engraved as another wedding gift to the Shah from the President. The gift arrived in a wooden crate weighing 63

---

[574] Amman to Secretary of State, 7 November 1959, RG 59, 788.11/11-759.
[575] Department of State to AmEmbassy Tehran, 17 November 1959, 788.11/11-1759
[576] Department of State to AmEmbassy Tehran, 7 December 1959, 788.11/12-759.

pounds on a Pan American Airways flight on December 17 at 10:00 AM, Flight No. 2. The Presidential party would also give congratulations and not issue a statement on another gift to the Shah. [577]

The Chief of Personnel noted that the Ministry allowed a new division called the Division of Economic and Technical Assistance so that all economic aid programs would be funneled through this division. All foreign governments dealing with the Ministry of Foreign Affairs and giving foreign aid had to deal with this division to keep track of investments- "in order that the ministry might be able to assess the political consequences of such aid." The re-organization cost 180 million rials. The salaries of government employees in the Ministry of Foreign Affairs were low, but increasing them would increase others, and Iran could not afford that. The Ministry of Foreign Affairs planned to send delegations to Argentina, Austria, Canada, and Indonesia. They created new consulates in Calcutta, Izmir, and San Francisco. [578]

In preparation for the visit by President Eisenhower, the Iran government drafted economic and social policies and emphasized another DLP loan of $130 million to cover the rest of the proposed second seven-year plan. If the Iranian government did not get this loan, they would not be able to maintain their development program as planned. These problems were discussed by both President Eisenhower and the Shah.[579] Iran felt the aim of economic and social development was an old aim of four years that seemed imperative for the "achievement of conditions to meet its responsibilities for the active security of the free world." The Government of Iran prepared a five-year financial plan that included all of Iran's expenditures and resources for the next five years. There were also steps preparing for Iran's inflation mechanisms. [580]The

---

[577] Department of State to AmEmbassy Tehran, 15 December 1959, RG 59, 788.11/12-1559.
[578] Department of State to AmEmbassy Tehran, 15 December 1959, RG 59, 788.11/12-1559.

[579] AmEmbassy Tehran to Department of State, 30 December 1959, RG 59, 788.11/12-3059.
[580] AmEmbassy Tehran to Department of State, 30 December 1959, RG 59, 788.11/12-3059

economic period of the Second Revolution prevented the spread of communism and economically stabilized America's influence in Iran. The main role of American stability in Iran was Eisenhower foreign policy that allowed numerous amounts of economic aid to be granted to Iran.

Part 3: Section 9 Military Developments
Second Revolution

The military developments in the second revolution were mainly to secure the Regional defense arrangement of the borders of Iran and to continue the influence of the U.S. military missions providing training and resources to the Iranian Armed Forces. Also, the developments included more ammunitions, jets and enormous amounts of military aid. The goal of the Shah was to be the supreme Middle Eastern military power and it became just that a few years later. Also, Iran wanted to prevent any attack on Iran and wanted to defend itself against the Soviet Union. The Soviet Union threatened WWIII and potential conventional attacks onto Iran. The United States did not want to engage into another war and further did not want the Soviet Union to militarily weaken Iran.

The Military Aftermath

After the overthrow of Mossedegh in August of 1953, Iran expected a rapid Tudeh Party coup d'état. But, the arrest of Mossedegh and the influx of the Pro-Shah forces prevailed against the opposition's forces. The people were very worried and felt that the ongoing rift between Mossedegh and Tudeh was the cause of Mossedegh's removal. Soon after removal, Major General Batmanqilich worked hard to maintain the morale of the officers of the military while Tudeh leaders were being arrested and leaflets destroyed. The Iranian Army decreased by 10,000. The biggest and perhaps the worst event that took place in the beginning of the Second Revolution was that the *atmosphere of the country towards the West changed with uprising anti-Shah acts.*[581] It was the Second Revolution that enabled the United States to win the Cold War

---

[581] Tehran to Department of State 13 January 1953 RG 59 788.5/1-1353.

and defeat the Soviet Union. By the end of 1953 Iran was entering into negotiations with Turkey, but foolishly had no strong military and defense system to maintain their position against the Soviet Union. There were also rumors that the defense systems of the Middle East were taking form in Iran and Pakistan. The goal was to transform Iran's into an arrangement that would become the official American source for military bases in the Middle East. U.S. military aid jumped right into the lap of the Shah and Iran in 1954. The United States invented wire services that increased aid for Iran and Pakistan so Pakistan could also benefit from helping the United States win the Cold War. Military bases in Pakistan, an ally of Iran and the West, were needed.[582]

In 1954 the concern was that Iran was building itself militarily, but weakening itself politically, as elections and parliamentary processes had yet to occur. The two biggest stories were elections and oil.[583]

The main reason for strengthening a controllable small army of Iran was to defend portions of the country from the Soviet Union and prevent the accumulation of atomic weapons and the acquisition of certain passes including deserts that would defeat the Soviet Union if invaded and also harbor the retreating Iranian army. Iranian soldiers were intelligent, hard-working, religious, and loyal people defending the honor of the state, therefore, there could be no speculation on the execution of missions against the Soviets. The Turkish-Pakistani defense systems could potentially also help defeat the Soviet Union.[584] In March of 1954 when the United States Military Mission went to the summer palace of the Shah in Babol, Iran, they spoke about about the defense system at some length. In the beautiful garden of the palace, the U.S. Mission and the Shah spoke from 12:00 noon to about 5:30 PM. Road conditions were terrible

---

[582] Secretary of State to Tehran 17 December 1953 RG 59 788.5/12-1753.
[583] Tehran to State Department 6 January 1954 RG 59 788.00(W) 1-654.
[584] Tehran to Secretary of State 18 March 1954 RG 59 788.5/3-1854.

and they had to transfer from a Chrysler, to a Jeep, to a dump truck, to a GMC, and finally to a horse to reach the airport and leave.[585]

The three points that the Soviet Union wanted from Iran and shared with Iran were: **a warm-water port, control of the oil fields, and the ability to cut off the Mediterranean Far East's lifeline to the sea.** If Iran achieved these three points, then the Soviet Union would be weakened and the United States would attain hegemony of the Middle East. The United States further acknowledged that they felt they needed to spend $1 billion in military aid and $1.5 billion in economic aid for Turkey to also help attain United States hegemony and victory of the Cold War.[586] The points further made were that fifty percent of the military was in Tehran and its distribution was inefficient. The military justice system, the redistribution of the army, and stability of assignment with no favoritism were all things that needed to be improved. The conscription system was also a problem because the majority of recruits were from the poor, uneducated class and their sole reason for joining was to have money. The conscription system needed to teach pride of their uniform, country, and service to the community as a respectable citizen. The morale of army officers was low and the living conditions poor. The health policies and sanitation policies were also neglected. There was no supervision of cleanliness and mess operations. All of that needed to be organized.[587]

The Shah went on to continue requesting vocational and technical training, schools, unit training, and many other educational matters to be provided by the U.S. Air Force, Navy and Army. The U.S. Mission determined that the five key points in approaching Iranian military

---

[585] Tehran to Department of State 30 March 1954 RG 59 788.5/3-3054
[586] Tehran to Department of State 30 March 1954 RG 59 788.5/3-3054

[587] Tehran to Department of State 30 March 1954 RG 59 788.5/3-3054

policy were: *giving arms, five battalions of 155 howitzers, US training in Iranian divisions, infantry support and additional tanks*[588].

The defense of Iran would run across the northern line to protect all potential passages to the Middle East. If the United States also wanted to protect Turkey, it had to supply Iran with adequate forces to do so. Iran's armed forces requested to be developed within economic means. The Shah felt that economic conditions and living conditions had to match with the military building of Iran. He was sure that Iranians would defend their homes and the uprising on August 19 in support of the Shah supposedly showed that the people were dedicated to uplifting Iran. Iran was in fact also getting jealous of Turkey receiving more aid and wanted to take away aid from the country, so Iran could become the *policeman of the Middle East*. The Shah was not concerned with the eastern part of Iran because Pakistan received $100 million and another $30 million from Turkey in military aid. The Pakistan Army was grander than Iran's army and would do its job to protect the eastern part of the Middle East. The defense of the Middle East lay in the west and northwest. The U.S. Mission said, *this is the hinge to the defense of the Middle East and once could not afford to fall back any distance.* Turkey was an option, but the Shah did not want Turkey to defend Iran. [589]

The United States and Great Britain agreed that Iranian military needed to be capable of maintaining the internal security of Iran. The U.S. government said *that it would be in the interest of Iran and of the whole free world for Iran to have armed forces which not only would be able effectively to assist in maintaining internal order but also would be capable of engaging in defensive action in case Iran should be attacked.*[590] The ideal army would be modest in size,

---

[588] Tehran to Department of State 30 March 1954 RG 59 788.5/3-3054

[589] Tehran to Department of State 30 March 1954 RG 59 788.5/3-3054

[590] Henderson to State Department 17 March 1954 RG 59 788.5/3-1754

not very illustrious, practical, and well-organized and would be able to subsist against the financial strains of the economy and advance into a country great in size and strength. This army needed to be developed slowly and in such a manner that would attribute profit to the United States. The United States would only contribute until it could be determined that Iran could defend itself. Iran also did not want Iraqis, Pakistanis, or Turks to defend Iran. Iran would take prime responsibility for defending its soil. The United States called for immediate action to develop the Iranian army. Once the army was developed, then it could enter into secret talks with nations to find out *we know something of our neighbor's plans-what areas they contemplate holding and to what they plan to retreat so that we can coordinate our movement with theirs.* The Shah wanted to understand the transport facilities and all modes of neighbor aggression. The Shah and Ala urged Admiral Wright to encourage the United States to build the most effective and inexpensive military *so that Iran could play an appropriate role in regional defense.* But this factor of regional defense should not remain in stone or else the United States would be committed in its entirety to Iran....[591]

In essence, the objectives mentioned above would provide defense of the Middle East from Soviet invasion. It was necessary for Iran to join the Turkish-Pakistan pact.[592] The funds available to the Shah would be determined by Congress each year and these factors looked at the political and economic developments of the Middle East and South Asia. Congress \determined each year if Iran utilized its natural resources to build its economy so that it would not be dependent on U.S. funds anymore. The mode of cooperation between the United States and Iran was also paramount in their decision-making and the level of determination to defend its independence and state. It also left the states of the Middle East and South Asia to enter into their

---

[591] Henderson to State Department 17 March 1954 RG 59 788.5/3-1754

[592] AmEmbassy Tehran to Department of State 7 April 1954 RG 59 788.5/4-754.

own defensive arrangements, though Iran felt that no defense arrangement could improve the security of its borders. In essence:

> It is quite possible that eventually the United States will be influenced by regional defense as well as by individual country defense considerations in deciding the kind and amount of military aid to be extended to the countries of the Middle East and South Asia.[593]

In July 1954, the Shah wanted to visit the United States with his wife to discuss the role of the defense of the Middle East. Ambassador Henderson told the Shah *the part we would expect Iran to play in Middle East Defense arrangements.* It was on the agenda of the Joint Chiefs of Staff, but there were other priorities. It became a present NSC policy that caused Iran to join the Middle East defense arrangements. The Shah however, indicated that he did not want to participate unless his defense forces were fully built.[594] The United States was on its way to achieving victory in the Cold War. Oil and suspended talks between the Iranians and Soviets raged in newspapers as NY Journal Oil editor, Wanda Jablonsky visited Iran to tell the world of the industry of oil in Iran.[595]

On August 25, 1954, the Shah told General McClure, chief of the U.S. Military Advisory group in Iran that Iran needed new ammunition, military transport factories, more tanks and anti-aircraft weapons, and an air program for Iran's new jets. The Shah also told the Secretary of State that he was informed on his military matters, but would like to gain an understanding of economics. He wanted to improve his knowledge on economics before he went to America. He was advised to consult some books and have Bray, an economic counselor teach the Shah economics.[596] The Shah wrote a letter to President Eisenhower in August of 1954 thanking him

---

[593] AmEmbassy Tehran to Department of State 7 April 1954 RG 59 788.5/4-754.

[594] Memorandum for the President 3 July 1954 RG 59 788.5/7-354.
[595] Confidential Department of the Army 13 January 1954 RG 59 788.00(W)5/1-1354.
[596] Tehran to Secretary of State 25 August 1954 RG 59 788.11/8-2554.

for a successful oil settlement and a grant of funds. He told the President: "I look forward to an era of economic and social developments which will improve the lot of my people, as well as further consolidate the security of the Middle East." He later thanked President Eisenhower for the American assistance. [597]

Before the United States prepared for the Shah's arrival, preparing to meet his medical needs, relaxation, and his concern over military support and defense organization, the State Department sent a telegram to the President that the oil settlement had created favorable opinion of the United States in Iran. Economic aid of $5 million and a loan of $83 million from the Export-Import Bank brought political and economic stability, and U.S. Military Aid improved U.S. armed forces providing internal security and methods to protect against external aggression.[598] The primary purpose of the Shah's visit to the United States was to see how Iran would play in the Northern Tier defense arrangement of Iran and the plans for regional security. The Shah wanted to join only on one condition: that the armed forces of Iran would be developed. The United States recommended, "We would welcome Iran's adherence to a regional defense arrangement of Turkey, Pakistan, Iraq and are prepared to help develop in the Iranian armed forces defensive delaying capabilities." It was when the army was fully developed that the United States determined Iran's role in the defense arrangement.[599] The goal was not to develop a regional defense arrangement in Iran that would hurt the economy, but the United States would request for more funds in 1956 to help subsidize the costs of maintaining the regional defense arrangement. The only assurance the United States needed was that "as oil revenue increases, the Shah will see to it there is enough set aside to support the armed forces without further reliance on foreign aid."[600]

---

[597] Shah of Iran to President Eisenhower 8 August 1954 RG 59 788.00/8-854
[598] Memorandum to the President 13 December 1954 RG 59 788.00/12-1354
[599] Memorandum to the President 13 December 1954 RG 59 788.00/12-1354

The powerful American Military Influence

President Eisenhower stated that their most important resource for ousting communism in the Middle East, especially in Iran, was economic aid. Though the plan was to provide economic aid to Third World developing countries, the main impetus was to suppress any or potential influences of Communism. It was economic aid, political developments, and military improvements in Iran that weakened the Soviet position in Iran. The Armed forces was how the Shah consolidated his rule and become influential in the affairs of the nation. In the past, the military was under the constitutional and traditional control of the ruler of the kingdom. Realizing how poor Iranian soldiers were in their tactics, the Shah made moves to expand and organize the military.[601] The United States provided military aid so that American influence in Iran could lead in American hegemony in the Middle East. America wanted to establish a regional defense system against and directed at the Soviets which would incapacitate their abilities to initiate war or propaganda of communism in Iran. This small American military mission began in 1942 and led to the development of a United States Military Mission committed to ending communism.[602] From 1953 to 1960, the U.S. military extended a lot of military aid for internal order and to handle any aggression from abroad. The military expanded the number of troops from 100,000 to 190,000, built a modern air force, and sent thousands overseas to America for military training.[603] The total military aid until 1960 was $535.4 million- the largest to any non-NATO country. At this time, there were also more than 10,000 Americans in Iran. ARMISH- the American Military Advisory group- advised the Minister of War about his military plans, administration, and training. It was GENMISH, another American military organ that helped improve the interior conditions of Iran. The Central Intelligence Agency helped

[600] Memorandum to the President 13 December 1954 RG 59 788.00/12-1354
[601] Amin Saikal. *The Rise and Fall of the Shah. (Princeton University Press: Princeton), 1980.* 53.
[602] Amin Saikal. *The Rise and Fall of the Shah. (Princeton University Press: Princeton), 1980.* 53.
[603] Amin Saikal. *The Rise and Fall of the Shah. (Princeton University Press: Princeton), 1980.* 54.

establish SAVAK, the intelligence division of Iran. SAVAK was also assisted by MOSSAD, the Israeli Intelligence Agency. Throughout this time, the Soviets were displeased with the Shah, but the Shah garnered enough military strength to off-set the victory of the Soviet Union that hurt their ambition in winning the Cold War many decades later.[604]

In early 1955, discussions began on how Iran was going to become so superbly powerful that it could deteriorate Soviet influence in Iran. The discussion began with the Foreign Operations Administration, the Defense Department and the State Department. In this meeting, officials discussed many scenarios and potential solutions to the military problem in Iran. They came up with an answer: provide an "intensive program of training designed to improve military efficiency and enhance the military capabilities of its existing forces." The Shah in fact stressed that all efforts would now be turned completely toward the training offered.[605]

Military Aid battled against Communism

The Defense Department was to provide the training from January 1955 to June 1955, covering all parts of the military. In order to potentially fully train these able men, the Defense Department placed a price tag of $4,065,000 to train Iranian soldiers in which $1,500,000 would be used for local means. Some of the most basic requirements needed were rifles, classrooms, and a training center. [606] It is further a known fact that the structure of Iran's Air Force was very weak and it was only the U.S. military assistance that alleviated the efforts, assigned better staff, improved operations at the Military University of Iran, improved training facilities, etc. Military studies reported how inefficient and ineffective the military structure tended to be. In other organs of the military structure, there was also need of improvement. The Defense Department

---

[604] Amin Saikal. *The Rise and Fall of the Shah. (Princeton University Press: Princeton), 1980.* 54-55.

[605] Department of State to Staspons, 27 January 1955, RG 59, 788.5 MSP/1-2755.

[606] Department of State to Staspons, 27 January 1955, RG 59, 788.5 MSP/1-2755.

relates: all *three types of effort are necessary in the chain of defense which should be strong along the border of the USSR.* [607] It wasn't until 1955 that Iran received more than $206 million in military aid. The aid was broken down into defense arrangements, defense forces support, roads, installations, barracks, etc. Before the Shah left in 1955, the United States offered him an additional $15 million to build up his army and another $4 million in training missions. [608] The grant for training missions also provided funding for training facilities, classrooms, training aids, clothing, and defense site construction. The money provided would be ample to achieve their success in training and developing Iran's military.[609] The Foreign Operations Administration wrote to Under Secretary of State Herbert Hoover that the funds approved were a step to improve the Iranian training effort. The $3.5 million was taken from the $20,500,000 MDAP funds that were previously promised to Egypt and asked the Iranian government to donate $565,000 to also help the program. These amounts were not to be specified to the Shah as he left from his visit to the United States.[610]

The construction of facilities was imperative to store ammunition in Iran. A State Department report stated that *"it is essential to the effective defense of the country for the IIA to have stores of war reserve ammunition located in the three key areas."* The total cost of the three facilities was $320,000.00. Also, despots were also established to keep the strength of the Iranian Army.[611]

---

[607] Department of State to Staspons, 27 January 1955, RG 59, 788.5 MSP/1-2755.

[608] Assistant Secretary to Acting Secretary, 2 February 1955, RG 59, 788.5 MSP/2-255.
[609] Tehran to Secretary of State, 8 February 1955, RG 59, 788.5-MSP/2-855.
[610] Foreign Operation Administration to Herbert Hoover Jr, 5 February 1955, RG 59, 788.5-MSP/2-555.
[611] Am Embassy Tehran to Department of State, 5 February 1958, RG 59, 788.5-MSP/2-558.

A Regional Defense System

Another key factor to the internal security of Iran and the regional defense system was arranging military talks with Pakistan, Iran, and Turkey. The goal was to bring Iran into this powerful regional defense arrangement. The United States wanted Iran to join this Middle East defense pact, but had not made any decision on increasing Iran's military aid. In order for the Shah to commit, the Shah wanted political acceptance and more military aid so that it would be well-equipped to prepare for the defense of its neighbors. The United States needed to offer explanations of what it would offer Iran if it joined the regional defense pact, but recommended that the Shah reduce some of his demands. [612]

The Shah felt that with Iran's full support of him, he could obtain social, economic, and political progress. This progress was a dream to become that *anchor point of the Western defense system in the Middle East and South Asia* and overturn Turkey. The Shah "dreamed of a well-equipped and modern Army of a half-million men under his personal control, backed by a progressive people and a burgeoning national economy, thus placing Iran, with its central and strategic location, well up in the ranks of the world's second class powers—and incidentally, making the Shah a world leader, known and feared or revered all over the globe."[613] But, he felt that he could not attain this goal because the United States did not give him enough money. Personally, the Shah was very interested in military matters-"he likes to imagine himself as winning military victories in the field some day." He wanted a big and modern Army for his own pleasure-*to play with it and woe to the person or institution which openly conflicts with his desire.* [614] The Army served as the Shah's right hand as it was the one that brought him back. The representation of the Army was the Shah. He wanted to boost morale for efficiency. [615]

---

[612] Baxter to Allen, 11 June 1955, RG 59, 788.00/6-1155.
[613] Tehran to Department of State, 11 July 1955, RG 59, 788.5 MSP/7-1155.
[614] Tehran to Department of State, 11 July 1955, RG 59, 788.5 MSP/7-1155.
[615] Tehran to Department of State, 11 July 1955, RG 59, 788.5 MSP/7-1155.

It wasn't that the United States was not interested in giving aid to Iran. In fact, it very much was since it benefited them both economically and politically. But the factors that opposed were usually the checks and balances system of the Treasury Department. This department opposed the amount of aid given to Iran. In a correspondence to the Secretary of Defense from Herbert Hoover Jr., the Under Secretary of State, additional requests of military aid of $50 million could not be granted immediately. The additional request must first be justified by evaluating Iran's existing military. Iran was not the only Middle Eastern country, as the Department of Defense stated. There were other requirements and other countries that needed money for their military policies. Congress was also getting annoyed by the increased military requests. By 1955 the United States' military assistance to Iran totaled $500 million, so if any more was given it had to be at the expense of other high priority countries in the Middle East.[616]

It said that all future military aid decisions should support the Baghdad Pact or the Middle Eastern defense pact policies. At this time Iran's main combat units were equal to five American divisions lacking firepower and mobility. The recommendation by ARMISH-MAAG was to have Iran adhere to the Baghdad Pact and have a decision reached over the Middle East defense pact. In order to maximize firepower per person, Iran needed to adhere to these policies.[617]

In light of the training program, there was an education division with 39 American employees. It was allocated $4,200,000 for the basic education and training of teachers, vocational training, and technicians. This training program trained more than 25,000 Iranians.[618] The two weak points in the Shah's government were the channel of confidential intelligence, and other agencies withholding information from each other, presenting false facts to the Shah. A concept was proposed to create a single agency with the United States' influence that would

---

[616] Hoover to Anderson, 5 August 1955, RG 59, 788.5 MSP/8-555.
[617] Dulles to Am Embassy Tehran, 9 February 1958, RG 59, 788.5MSP/2-958.
[618] American Embassy Tehran to Department of State, 11 September 1956, RG 59, 788.13/9-1156.

garner and hold all intelligence. This plan would probably not be a Ministry. The Iranian Army was too weak to take up further obligations in the Baghdad Pact.. It became the United States' obligation to provide additional training to the Iran. Iran needed a navy to claim the Islands of Farsi and Arabi and keep the boundaries safe from intruders. They also needed enough man power to hold up any aggression in the Middle East from spreading north.[619] In 1957 Congress approved $200 million as part of the president's Middle East policy. It was also determined that an amount of $30 million would be enough for Iran to assist with the president's Middle East program. There had been no final word on Iran's diplomatic relationship with North Africa. It all depended on how much capital the United States had, but perhaps a single post could be established.[620]

The new amount of $30 million to be provided to Iran was used immediately in March 1957 when Iran discussed the sale of six C-32 aircraft for Persian Air. These airplanes were military aircraft to be used for defense purposes.[621] Iran also underwent numerous training exercises. They reformed their past strategies of assigning basic trained soldiers to a unit with few officers. The problem they experienced was the shortage of junior officers or limited number of officers competent enough to lead. In order to change the order of the training, Iran increased the budget hoping that the training would improve the soldiers.[622] The other problem was that there were not enough training aides or facilities in Iran, despite promises to make more. Furthermore, conscription was poor, but the morale greatly improved because of action against Tudeh elements in Iran. When the training finally arrived in Iran from the United States, morale and motivation improved in the Iranian army.[623] There were improved techniques, progressive

[619] Reza Ansari to Prime Minister, 7 February 1957, RG 59, 788.5 MSP/2-757.
[620] H.E. Ahmad to Imperial Ministry of Foreign Affairs, 31 January 1957, RG 59, 788.5/1-3157.
[621] Department of State to Am Embassy Tehran, 12 March 1957, RG 59, 788.5522/3-1257.
[622] Department of State to Am Embassy Tehran, 12 March 1957, RG 59, 788.5522/3-1257.

training programs, and improved activities in Iran. A note by Ambassador Chapin from Ali Qoli Ardalan stated (from a translation in Persian) that: "Referring to the agreement dated October 6, 1947, between the Imperial Government of Iran and the Government of the United States of America, concerning the American Military Mission with the Iranian Army, it is respectfully proposed that the above mentioned agreement be extended until (March 20, 1958).[624]

In reply, Chapin stated, "I am authorized to inform Your Excellency that the Government of the United States of America is agreeable to the extension of the Agreement…for a further period of two years."[625]

In 1958, there were 1,000 American military personnel in Iran training Iranian soldiers. Most of them have been there since the beginning of World War II from October 2, 1942 and will stay until March 20, 1958.[626] The political situation had been very fragile in Iran. The strategic location of Iran also further complicated things. The proposal to provide immunity to Americans was seen with utter reluctance by Iranians. It was understandable because such a proposal would require a submission to the Iranian parliament, which could complicate things further.[627] It would definitely help America because of the huge employment of trainers in Iran, but Iran was reluctant to sign this unorthodox agreement signed in Spain and Ethiopia, because of their own freedom and independence. Furthermore, there would be a conflict of an extra-territorial principle benefitting the Soviet Union and secession could rise and the United States military could be weakened. The United States would be accused of setting up bases in Iran because of immunity. It would be a disaster. If the United States would negotiate, they could lose

---

[623] Department of State to Am Embassy Tehran, 12 March 1957, RG 59, 788.5522/3-1257.

[624] Department of State to Am Embassy Tehran, 12 March 1957, RG 59, 788.5522/3-1257
[625] Department of State to Am Embassy Tehran, 12 March 1957, RG 59, 788.5522/3-1257
[626] Murphy to Mammie, 31 July 1957, RG 59, 788.5/7-3157.
[627] Murphy to Mammie, 31 July 1957, RG 59, 788.5/7-3157.

their stake and settle for something less in the oil industry, so they did not intervene.[628] In August 1957, the Iranian parliament passed an Armed Forces Bill that provided the ranks of a full general, admiral, promotion grades and purposes.[629]

In response to the foreign aid program, the American ambassador noticed that Iran's oil revenues had been increasing for some time, but aid to Iran from the United States had not decreased. The Ambassador reported that he did not believe further assistance was needed. However, he imagined that psychological problems would occur with reduction of U.S. aid. Also, Iran could not get any more military aid nor receive any more equipment because of its rapidly increasing income. The lessening of aid would definitely hurt United States- Iranian relations and the dream of the Shah who dreamed of building up a large military.[630] The United States felt that the Shah's reputation depended on the amount of aid Iran received. The Department of State said, "The Shah's prestige suffers when you can do no more than chickens and turkeys and jackasses and wheat and the other things that people can't see and understand."[631] America understood that Iran received $112 million in 1957 and told Iran that "all your little programs of aid in little ways and that money to build a few roads or dams or technical schools or a university." Iran was not spending their money "right." Americans stated that Iran could be saved for Iranians and for the world if everyone sat down and discussed where the problems occurred. The Department of State said, "Let's decide how to solve this budget problem of ours, further by a loan from you or by some other means. But, please don't be tricky with us. We can't afford it, and neither can you." [632]

---

[628] Murphy to Mammie, 31 July 1957, RG 59, 788.5/7-3157.

[629] Department of Army to Department of State, 1 August 1957, RG 59, 788.5/8-157.
[630] Department of Army to Department of State, 1 August 1957, RG 59, 788.5/8-157.
[631] Stelle to Am Embassies and Consulates, 1 August 1957, RG 59, 788.5/8-157.
[632] Stelle to Am Embassies and Consulates, 1 August 1957, RG 59, 788.5/8-157.

In the days of 1957 the Shah was concerned of the dangers of Iranian independence, and was weighing Soviet offers to see if they were more lucrative, and to secure no opposition. He was concerned about the horrible situation of the Middle East and South Asia. Syria and Egypt were looking to join the pact with Jordan and Iraq. Iraq was becoming Iran's target along with the Soviet Union. If the Middle Eastern states joined the movement with the Soviet Union, the Shah had to either defend his nation or be diplomatic with Iran. He was now pondering if a reduction in his military was worthy of action and diplomatic ties could prevent an invasion if Iran. The Shah did not know what to expect from the United States. In a recent Bandung conference, a summit of all the third world leaders, the Soviets alleged that the West was pulling the Middle East into a military bloc defended by the United States.[633]

On June 14, 1957 Lt. Col. William Dean of the U.S. Military Mission visited northwestern Iran and realized the following: 1) there were no anti-British feelings 2) there was lots of equality between landowners and landless peasants 3) there needed to be a change in the tax system and 4) road conditions in northwestern Iran were terrible because large trucks used those roads and broke it. The majority of the money was spent repairing the roads. [634]

The American Immunity Debate

The jurisdiction statuses of American military personnel were still under heavy debate. Iranians were insisting that they had jurisdiction in the affairs of American personnel in Iran.[635] The Shah was very upset by Vershinen's statement released by the Soviet Union, by that Iran "could and would be knocked out by conventional weapons and ordinary missiles in event hostilities."[636] Iran felt that the Soviets had placed them in the same category as West Germany,

[633] American Embassy to Department of State, 14 June 1957, RG 59, 788.00/6-1457.
[634] American Embassy to Department of State, 14 June 1957, RG 59, 788.00/6-1457.

[635] Department of State to AmEmbassy Tehran, 25 September 1957, RG 59, 788.5/9-2557.
[636] Tehran to Secretary of State, 13 September 1957, RG 59, 788.5/9-1357.

Turkey, and other NATO countries that they wanted war with. Any country that supported or had U.S. military activities was a threat to the Soviet Union.[637] Since the policy of the Soviet Union looked to be true, Iran reevaluated its foreign policy toward the Soviet Union. Iran said, "Under such re-evaluation, Shah indicated he might be prepared to allow US establish bases in fact in Iran."[638] The Shah was preparing against the threat of Soviet Union, but he wanted to have some kind of promise from the United States that he would be backed up after saying such threatening statements to them. [639]

A very concerned report dated October 17, 1957, reported from Tehran to the Secretary of State that there was no morale deficiency in the U.S. military personnel in Iran. Some were aggrieved due to crimes they may have committed, automobile accidents, or Iran's scrutiny over U.S. military. But none of these faults was due to the internal organization of the U.S. military.[640] The Iranian Army was also going through a reorganization involving the major units of Iran. There were 15,000 combat type troops.[641] The Government of the United States would in fact come to the aid of the Iranian Army if their government engaged in the affairs of other governments. There was also ongoing debate on Article 24. The Government of Iran wanted Article 24 deleted from the ARMISH agreement. The United States admitted that Article 24 was a similar article signed by other nations who asked for U.S. military aid.[642] Article 24 was an infringement of Iran's sovereignty. It required Iran to consult with the United States before signing an agreement with a third party nation. In this agreement, all foreign policy decisions

---

[637] Tehran to Secretary of State, 13 September 1957, RG 59, 788.5/9-1357.

[638] Tehran to Secretary of State, 13 September 1957, RG 59, 788.5/9-1357.
[639] Tehran to Secretary of State, 13 September 1957, RG 59, 788.5/9-1357.

[640] Tehran to Secretary of State, 17 October 1957, RG 59, 788.5/10-1757.
[641] Am Embassy Tehran to Department of State 16 September 1957, RG 59, 788.5/9-1657.
[642] Beirut to Secretary of State, 31 October 1957, RG 59, 788.5/10-3157.

would be subject to America's approval and would need to benefit both nations. Article 24 was needed for full U.S. participation.[643]

The proposed airfields to be built in Iran were to be constructed by Morrison, Henry Kaiser, Oman, Farnsworth, and Wright, contractors with the U.S. Defense department. The facilities were to be built in northern Iran.[644] The Ambassador to Iran and USOM requested an amount of $56 million for non-military aid in 1958. The reason the United States was fearful of increasing military assistance was that Iran had already received so much money, and had a lot of money to cover their own expenses. But, nevertheless, the United States did provide increased aid in 1958, including a large construction program to build airfields.[645] It was actually on January 22, 1958, that the request to finance the construction of QOM airfield and the military construction was presented. An amount of $50 million was given to the military assistance program from the defense budget. Though for auditing purposes the construction program was listed under the defense program. If in 1959 the project was the same, the same would happen that year too. There was discussion of another $10 million from the Asian Economic Development Fund.[646]

Secretary Dulles Arrives in Iran

In the early part of 1958, Dulles left Washington D.C. in utter discontent of Iranian politics. He stated that his arrival was prompted with twenty-four hour tension. Dulles stated that the Shah felt that he was a *military genius,* and someone who wanted to build up his military and hold a dominant position in the Baghdad Pact. The Shah felt that a description of retaliatory power was not enough to convince the Soviet Union or his own people that Iran's defense was

---

[643] Beirut to Secretary of State, 31 October 1957, RG 59, 788.5/10-3157
[644] Beirut to Secretary of State, 31 October 1957, RG 59, 788.5/10-3157
[645] Tehran to ICA, 19 November 1957, RG 59, 788.5/11-1957; Tehran to Secretary of State, 30 November 1957, 788.5 MSP/11-3057.
[646] Dillon to Acting Director ICA, 22 January 1958, RG 59, 788.5 MSP/1-2258.

secured.[647] He wanted to increase missions and that required more aid. Most of the governmental ministers Dulles spoke to were concerned about Iran's economic difficulties, and could not cope with the Shah's obsession with building up his military. The Iranians had been also frustrated by American military aid given to Pakistan, Turkey, and India. Unless the United States provided promises of more military aid, Iran would withdraw from the Baghdad Pact with a neutral and cooperative policy with the Soviet Union.[648] In a dinner with more than 160 people, including all the Diplomatic Corps, many people admired Dulles and America's emphasis on peace. After numerous meetings with different ministers and the Shah, the Shah concluded that his problems were military and that a strategic and tactical base in Iran was needed. Dulles told the Shah of the new problems of weapons of mass destruction.[649] The conclusions on the topics negotiated between the Shah and Dulles were t: 1) "we would be prepared to provide some more weapons and also provide more training for their use. On the economic side, I indicated [regarding] worthy projects." The funding would come from the Development Loan Fund. If this was met, some of the Iranian oil revenues would be diverted for development and budgetary requirements.[650]

It was further on January 26 that the Shah did not discuss anything about his budgetary aid. The reason for the Shah's insistence was a potential Soviet invasion on Iran. The Soviet Union was prepared to start World War III and they would attack first on American soil. Tehran reported, "any World War likely to start off with attack on US, not only isolated invasion on Iran. War would begin on global crisis."[651] In 1958 the Shah and his wife were planning to visit Japan and Honolulu. They also planned to stop by the United States to talk about the military problem. Foster wrote to the State Department that when the Shah stopped in Ankara, he [Foster]

---

647 Tehran to Secretary of State, 25 January 1958, RG 59, 788.5 MSP/1-2558.
648 Tehran to Secretary of State, 25 January 1958, RG 59, 788.5 MSP/1-2558.
649 Tehran to Secretary of State, 25 January 1958, RG 59, 788.5 MSP/1-2558.
650 Tehran to Secretary of State, 25 January 1958, RG 59, 788.5 MSP/1-2558.
651 Tehran to Secretary of State, 26 January 1958, RG 59, 788.5 MSP/1-2658.

was worried that the Shah would drop out of the Baghdad Pact- an event that would be in fact a blow to the entire political landscape of the Middle East.[652]

America's realization of their military aid mistakes....

The United States Air Force submitted a bill of $5,196.61 involving meals of $14.95 and various entertainment exercises with Iranian officials. This bill was presented to John Janke, Chief of the Accounts Division. There were also many invoices from the Mission and other housing expenses.[653] The Assistant Secretary of Defense wrote to Roundtree stating: "We are all concerned over the inordinate demands for additional military assistance from the Shah of Iran."[654] The Assistant Secretary of Defense stated that he would find it difficult to persuade the Shah not to adopt more aid measures from the United States once he saw increased U.S. military aid to Taiwan and Japan. The Shah potentially could take the Asia Pacific aid package and undermine the United States. He blackmailed America with his knowledge of potential friendly relations with countries not friendly to the United States. In order to not succumb to the Shah's peer pressure, a State Defense action was taken by all U.S. military and civil leaders informing them of a fake increase of aid so that the United States could give aid to Japan and Taiwan. Both countries would tell the Shah that they too were boosting their military forces against a potential armed attack from the Soviet Union. The Assistant Secretary stated, "In both countries I think our officials should be urged to take all possible discreet action to prevent a glamorous display of U.S. military aid to the Shah."[655]

---

[652] Tehran to Secretary of State, 26 January 1958, RG 59, 788.5 MSP/1-2658.

[653] Department of Air Force to John Janke, 28 February 1958, RG 59, 788.58/2-2858.
[654] Assistant Secretary of Defense to Rountree, 16 April 1958, RG 59, 788.11/4-1658.
[655] Assistant Secretary of Defense to Rountree, 16 April 1958, RG 59, 788.11/4-1658.

The Shah wrote to President Eisenhower stating "it has indeed been a source of gratification to welcome to Tehran your distinguished Secretary of State."[656] The Shah also stated that "I endeavored to bring clearly to his attention the dangers to which we in Iran are exposed as well as the obligations which we feel bound to honor as loyal members of the Baghdad Pact."[657]

In a report in June 1958, the American Embassy wrote to the United States that military assistance programs in Iran were important for strengthening American objectives in Iran. The "US policy in Iran is directed toward the maintenance and strengthening of a stable regime, friendly to the U.S. - one capable of maintaining internal security and offering a reasonable measure of resistance to any threat beyond its borders."[658] The Shah was the key to America's involvement. The intentions of America were to create objective assistance to Iran, but the assistance had not been objective because of the Shah's intentions. The Shah worked to maintain internal security measures and of course strengthen his military to deal with external threats such as the threat from the Soviet Union. When Iran involved itself in the Baghdad Pact, it wanted to be the leading force and dominate the Baghdad Pact militarily. As head of the military forces in the Baghdad Pact, it led to the establishment of a United Arab Republic that allowed it to strengthen Iran's own forces as well as the forces of the Middle East.[659] The American Embassy was really worried about the amount of aid and military equipment the United States provided to Iran. The American Embassy stated "the military forces and plan would be dangerous to the regime and subsequently obstructive to U.S. aims."[660] There was a lot of resentment in Iran

---

[656] Shah to President Eisenhower, 28 January 1958, RG 59, 788.11/1-2858.
[657] Shah to President Eisenhower, 28 January 1958, RG 59, 788.11/1-2858.
[658] American Embassy to Department of State, 5 May 1958, 788.5 MSP/5-558.
[659] American Embassy to Department of State, 5 May 1958, 788.5 MSP/5-558.

[660] American Embassy to Department of State, 5 May 1958, 788.5 MSP/5-558.

because of U.S. operations. Military strength had reached a point that if there was a power imbalance, it could lead to serious political danger. There needed to be a limit on increasing troop strength in Iran without American involvement. The American Embassy reported, "the real danger that military expansion could weaken Iran."[661] It would take a 104% increase in aid to cover Iran's military expenditures for pay, allowances, food, clothing, and many other expenses for Iran's troops of 140,000 men. These military factors prompted more aid and a steady rise in expenditures due to operations and maintenance from 1957 to 1961.[662]

In July 1958 the Shah got a credit of $40 million from the Development Fund out of his visit to France -which would finance a variety of projects in the plan organization.[663] In a visit to the United States in July 1958, the Shah spoke about the situation in the Middle East and Lebanon looking at America's tactics, U.S. economic aid policies, and potential tactics of the USSR. The specifics of U.S. military and economic aid were not discussed, just points in general. There were not any new commitments made by the United States. The Shah was concerned about the situation in Lebanon because it had been invaded by Nasserism. The Shah spoke about the Iran-Pakistan relationship and how he needed more aid for defense. He continued to stress the need for more military training in Iran.[664] He told the president that Iran and Pakistan united would be better, and felt that Turkey should receive less attention. A potential meeting was to take place between Bayer, Mirza Sahib from Pakistan, and King Faisal to discuss Lebanon and the threat to the Middle East from the Soviet Union and UAR.[665] In October 1958, the U.S. government was preparing to announce military aid for 1959[666] Due to

---

[661] American Embassy to Department of State, 5 May 1958, 788.5 MSP/5-558.

[662] American Embassy to Department of State, 5 May 1958, 788.5 MSP/5-558.

[663] Department of State to Ambassador of Paris, 3 July, 1958, 788.11/7-358.
[664] Department of State to AmEmbassy Tehran, 7 July 1958, 788.11/7-758.
[665] Department of State to AmEmbassy Tehran, 7 July 1958, 788.11/7-758
[666] Department of State to Am Embassy Tehran & Baghdad, 16 October 1958, RG 59, 788.5-MSP/10-1658.

the internal situation in Iran, the State Department felt that the United States should finance an equipment program for the Iranian police. ICA also believed that the money should be given against the total already provided to Iran. The Country Team, a group of the United States, provided an estimate of $3.3 million through1965 for transportation, communications, weapons, etc. Construction of 100 police buildings throughout Iran cost an additional $5.4 million to be financed through the Government of Iran. There was an additional cost of $338,000 for riot control prevention measures. [667]

In December 1958, the United States discouraged another Iranian mission to Washington D.C. to request additional aid. The U.S. wanted to continue to maintain freedom and independence in Iran- these values had been promised continuously for the past four years. The American Embassy in Tehran reported, the "U.S. has scrupulously sought fulfill every commitment it has made Iran and is proud of contribution it has been able make to enhancing abilities of Iranian armed forces."[668] The United States provided enough land forces to defend northwestern Iran. The Soviet threats were not to give Iran more money or deter the United States or Iran from progressing. The American Embassy said that they knew Iran did not think military aid and development was the only way to success in Iran, but that economic and social developments were also in Iran's best interests.[669] On December 20, a request came in for $175 million for 1959, which was $24 million more than in 1958. The reasons given were that there was more of a deficit and more expenses.[670]

But Senator Moayed-Sabeti did not believe that any development program could be successful in Iran *"as long as half of the country's expenditures were going to the armed forces.*

---

[667] Department of State to Am Embassy Tehran & Baghdad, 16 October 1958, RG 59, 788.5-MSP/10-1658.
[668] Department of State to Am Embassy Tehran, 17 December 1958, RG 59, 788.5-MSP/12-1758.
[669] Department of State to Am Embassy Tehran, 17 December 1958, RG 59, 788.5-MSP/12-1758.

[670] Tehran to Secretary of State, 23 December, 1958, RG 59, 788.5-MSP/12-2358.

Either Iran will have to cut down on its Army or else receive considerably more military aid from abroad."[671] Many people felt that in light of nuclear bombs and a strong Iranian Army, Iran would still be helpless because of its failing economy. By this time morale was low in Iran's army and if more millions were spent, maybe the Iranian Army could improve, but at the cost of the country's entire revenues and resources, it was not worth it, according to the Senator.[672] Senator Sabeti reminded Iranians that:

> Iranians have not forgotten what happened during the reign of Reza Shah, when year after year a large part of the nation's budget was devoted to the Army. **When finally in 1941 the country was invaded, Iran's defenses folded up in a matter of hours**. If the vast sums spent on the Army had been used to build schools and dams, Iran could not have held out for these few hours, it is true…..[673]

In 1946, when it was historically told that the Iranian Army pushed out the Soviets from Azerbaijan, it was "U.S. finances and the unfavorable reaction of the United Nations that compelled the Russians to leave."[674] If Iran was attacked by the Soviets in the future, it was only the United States that could provide relief to the invasion. Senator Sabeti said, "What Iran needs is a small, well trained, and well paid force capable of ensuring internal security."[675] Though Iran received new planes from the U.S. Air Force, the Senator remarked that another Sugar refinery plant would have been more beneficial. The elite and educated felt that no additional money should be spent on Iran's army. But the Shah would not accept a smaller army.[676] In 1959, General Motors, who made a great deal of money in Iran, shipped 98 jeeps to Iran at a total value

---

[671] Department of State to Am Embassy Tehran, 17 December 1958, RG 59, 788.5-MSP/12-1758.

[672] Department of State to Am Embassy Tehran, 17 December 1958, RG 59, 788.5-MSP/12-1758.

[673] Department of State to Am Embassy Tehran, 17 December 1958, RG 59, 788.5-MSP/12-1758.

[674] Department of State to Am Embassy Tehran, 17 December 1958, RG 59, 788.5-MSP/12-1758.

[675] Department of State to Am Embassy Tehran, 17 December 1958, RG 59, 788.5-MSP/12-1758.

[676] Department of State to Am Embassy Tehran, 17 December 1958, RG 59, 788.5-MSP/12-1758.

of $104,000 with a unit cost of $1065.[677] Ankara wrote to the Secretary of State stating that military aid to Iran had been drastically reduced and it was "our wish to rapidly secure for Iran a tangible and substantial amount of military aid as a matter of urgency." In December 1958, the Assistant Secretary of Defense wrote that U.S. Mission agreements would be extended on condition that the "U.S. military personnel stationed in Iran not be subjected to criminal jurisdiction by Iranian authorities and therefore, our military authorities in fact, exercise exclusive criminal jurisdiction over such personnel.[678]

The year of the Military crisis

In February 1959, Iran's only five star General, Abdullah Hedayat, suffered a heart attack and was incapacitated because the Shah was negotiating with the Soviets. General Bakhtiar was also suffering, so a leader from SAVAK- either Brigadier General Hassan Pakravan or General Alavi-Kia- would resume power of Iran if the Shah had a heart attack or was assassinated.[679] The Soviet and Iranian negotiations had definitely increased tensions due to the internal situation of Iran. Iran's security interests and the Shah's own ideas of development, if kept low-key, may be more successful.[680] In response to the Defense Department receiving exclusive jurisdiction, the chances were slim, but Iran understood that exclusive jurisdiction would affect the stability of the Shah's regime. In 1958, Iran proposed to have roughly $160 million for aid for the year 1959. In response, the United States was to give $156.2 million, which was prior to a commitment of $28.6 million for support. Then Iran dropped the figure to $109.6 million and the difference of $46.6 million occurred. The United States was adamant not to pick up the remaining tab.[681] In a

---

[677] Explanatory note on Price Differentials, 20 June 1958, RG 59, 788.58/6-2058.
[678] Assistant Secretary of Defense to Assistant Secretary Near Eastern South Asian and African, 10 December 1958, RG 59, 788.58/12-1058.
[679] Am Embassy Tehran to Secretary of State, 7 February 1959, RG 59, 788.5-MSP/2-759.
[680] Department of State to AmEmbassy Tehran, 11 February 1959, RG 59, 788.5/2-1159.
[681] Lincoln & Perkins to Mr. Jones, 5 May 1959, RG 59, 788.5/5-559.

subsequent meeting on February 12 with Iran and the Soviets, the President of the United States, Turkey, Pakistan, and Prime Minister MacMillan sent messages to the Shah to stick with the western alliance. On the night of February 11, it was an unclear whether the West had won their proposals and that the Soviet delegation left Iran on February 12. The Shah's concerns as discussed in the negotiation were to prevent the rise of troops in Iran to go against the Shah, Turkey, and Pakistan entering SEATO, and the remaining two divisions for Iran were refused.[682] In June 1959 Iran requested destroyers. These war ships were part of the military assistance program.[683] In November 1959, there was a $35 million project to build the Khaneh barracks, the largest of its kind. It would encompass 652 buildings, 50 million bricks, and 450,000 square meters. As the project neared completion, the amount of potential employees declined. There was a skeleton staff. This was due to the low Kurdish population working in the barracks, since most of the employees were from local Kurds. It would be ready for occupancy on December 31, 1959.[684] The United States hence was able to secure a regional defense arrangement in Iran and were able to pull Iran away from the negotiations and influence of the Soviet Union towards the end of 1959. This regional arrangement was maintained with more U.S. military bases across Iran especially in the north. Also, the U.S. military missions received an extended mandate to continue their training and resource support to the Iran Armed Forces.

Concluding Part

The Soviet Union in the 1950s

The Soviet Union was indeed a threat to democratic peace and the democracies of the world. The ideology of communism could have weakened America and destroyed productivity.

---

[682] Department of State to Am Embassy Ankara, Karachi, Tehran, 12 February 1959, RG 59, 788.5/2-1259.

[683] Special Assistant For Mutual Security Coordination to Lathran, 4 June 1959, 788.5621/6-459.

[684] Tehran Consulate, Tabriz to Department of State, 23 November 1959, RG 59, 788.5/11-2359.

Another World War could have began that could have wiped out the entire planet. George Kennan relayed that the Soviet Union posed a geo-political problem. The problem and fear of the Soviet Union was mainly the potential of another war. The Soviet Union had great military strength that could have in fact caused a cold-blooded war. After World War II, the United States learned from its tragedies, and could not financially bear the burden of another world war. There were only five areas of the world that had great military strength, enormous man power, expensive weapons, and an ability to reach the frontier of the enemy very quickly. All of them were in the Northern Hemisphere. They were: the United States, Japan, and England (America had influence), Germany, Austria, and the Soviet Union.[685] Kennan said, "I repeat, nowhere outside these five areas can military industrial strength be produced in this world today on what we might call the grand scale."[686] Kennan did not refer to China because in 1954, China had land mass, but no military strength. The goal was to prevent the Soviet Union from acquiring China's land mass and use it against the United States.[687]

The physical and military power of the Soviet Union was weak before 1939, but it had acquired the Baltic states, eastern Europe, and eastern Germany. Due to this large land mass, Kennan believed that the Soviet Union was a larger threat to the United States than we assumed in the 1950s. The Soviets believed that they always needed to have an enemy well-matched against their power, and the United States fulfilled that description.[688] Though they knew another war may be too costly for them, they were not afraid to answer to the thought of holding a war against a major capitalist nation like the United States. It was true that communist influence declined since the 1930s, but the major foreign communist parties were working toward a

---

[685] George Kennan. *Realities of American Foreign Policy.* (Princeton: Princeton University Press, 1954),64.

[686] George Kennan. *Realities of American Foreign Policy.* (Princeton: Princeton University Press, 1954),64.
[687] George Kennan. *Realities of American Foreign Policy.* (Princeton: Princeton University Press, 1954),69.
[688] George Kennan. *Realities of American Foreign Policy.* (Princeton: Princeton University Press, 1954),69.

revolution of a nation and potential control of a nation. That is how the Soviet Union expanded their power. China was the only recent victory of a huge acquired land mass turned communist. Kennan reported, "We all recognize that any further aggression of Soviet Power will represent a still greater danger." In order to weaken Soviet power, Kennan wrote in 1954 that an overthrow in either all or part of the Soviet Union would be beneficial. Kennan said, "it implies that this overthrow should constitute an active aim of western, and particularly American, policy- that the main impulse to it, should come from without and from us."[689] George Kennan wrote: "I can conceive that Soviet power will some day recede from its present exposed positions, just as it has already receded in Finland and Yugoslavia and northern Iran."[690]

Conclusion

In 1991 Boris Yelstin and his daughter were standing by the television set wanting to watch something different. Each channel was showing swans on a lake. Yelstin's daughter went to Boris and informed him that every channel was showing swans. Boris Yelstin got the signal. The Soviet Union was about to experience a revolution. Quickly he grabbed his coat, informed his advisors, got on a tank and drove to the Capitol. There was another general who also figured out that this would be the best moment for a revolution. He too grabbed his troops and marched into the Capitol. In ten minutes Yelstin arrived at the Capitol and pointed the tank gun at the opposing General and his troops. Immediately, the opposing general surrendered. Yelstin lifted the hood of the tank, pulled his head out, and pronounced himself the new President of Russia. If Boris Yelstin had been one minute later, the fate of the Soviet Union would have continued under another communist martial law. Democracy prevailed in 1991.

---

[689] George Kennan. *Realities of American Foreign Policy*. (Princeton: Princeton University Press, 1954),77.
[690] George Kennan. *Realities of American Foreign Policy*. (Princeton: Princeton University Press, 1954),79.

But, what happened to the Soviet Union? The Soviet Union was a powerful nation, a state that fostered bi-polarity and was an active member of the Cold War since 1945. Political scientists and historians knew the Soviet Union was going to collapse. They began the Cold War with huge political, economic, and military influence in the Middle East. The key to their hegemony and their victory in the Cold War was to have a stronghold in Iran. It was to control Iran's oil and exploit the West with dependence to oil owned by the Soviet Union. The plans of both Great Britain and the Soviet Union failed when the United States intervened in the negotiations of the oil settlement of Iran. When Mossedegh nationalized oil, the oil revenue going to Great Britain and the Soviet Union was next to nothing. The United States helped lead the overthrow of Mossedegh, install the Shah, and began showering the country with millions upon millions of dollars. President Eisenhower had an American foreign policy, the Eisenhower doctrine, which was to provide financial aid to the third world. It was an economic policy that promised aid to those countries easily influenced by Communism. It was also to provide armed forces to those places of the world that battled against communism. The Middle East, especially Iran, showed keen interest in banning communism and wanted foreign aid to disavow against any lucrative offer from the Soviets. If the world's largest oil supply was to go to the Soviets, then it would create dire economic consequences to the West and the United States. In return, the United States improved its banks, its automobile industries, earned profits from different Iranian monopolies and was earned more than $9 billion a year in oil revenues.

Caught Between Ambitions was a story searching for the truth of what happened in the 1950s. Its goal was to show American development policies in Iran. But there was a statement in the chapters preceding this conclusion that the Shah was a blockade against development. If this is true, then development policies of the United States were simply political: to have hegemony in the Middle East and defeat the Soviet Union and Communism; economic: to control the oil, and receive profits from Iran's monopolies and exports; and military: to create a regional defense arrangement against and prepare for a potential invasion of the Soviet Union. During the Pre-Revolution era (1950-1951), politically, the U.S. wanted to initiate an Iranian negotiation. Economically, Iran needed aid and the U.S. wanted oil. Militarily, Iran wanted to improve their military infrastructure while the United States wanted to continue their U.S. military missions in Iran. The political development policy's goal between 1951 and 1953, was to stop communism and weaken the Soviet Union. With America's first encounter with Iran as a negotiator of the oil settlement, they wanted to control the oil, to get cheap oil, and a flow of 675,000 barrels of oil westward. Iran began some earlier trade policies with the Soviets to find out what exports they had and how to weaken them by creating a monopoly over those same exports- which occurred later. On a path to modernization, the United States cooperated with Iran to achieve some kind of oil settlement that would weaken the influence of both Great Britain and the Soviet Union. Iran was having a bad time in their infrastructure and they needed an outside intermediary that could grant them the independence they needed. Nationalization of oil was the single most terrible decision that affected Iran. It nationalized the oil industry weakening both Great Britain and the Soviet influence, but it was expected that nationalization would prompt less foreign aid into Iran. Iran would then become debt-forsaken, ask for bail out, and would not be able to find one. When the Shah wanted Mossedegh to remain in power and supported his nationalization of oil policies, it was a plan to build up enough resources to get rid of him in the future. It was nationalization that actually helped the overthrow of Mossedegh, which the United States wanted. Nationalization weakened communist influence and also placed the man they wanted in power. It was all a façade when nationalization actually occurred. If nationalization had never occurred, Iran would have been a rich and different country today.

The economic developments from 1951-1953 encompassed a degree of trying to gain control of Iran's oil. Oil diplomacy was the impetus to American involvement and it was the control of oil that shaped the United States' economic policies with Iran. When Iran was in heavy debt without any money in the banks, it came to the United States for obvious help and the United States gave them an emergency package of $45 million, thinking no more than $60 million would be provided to them. The nationalization of oil soon turned into an oil consortium agreement. The United States wanted control of the economy and wanted to end Soviet and British influence. During the oil consortium agreement, America also investigated investment opportunities in Iran. There was an initial seven year plan requesting $250 million from the United States for development purposes. Iran began exporting sugar, an item they used to depend on getting from the Soviet Union. Iran built many plants and also invested in opium plants as well shipping opium to the United States State Department. The goal was to economically weaken Soviet influence.

Military developments from 1951 to 1953 were mainly focused on creating a regional defense arrangement to prepare for an attack against the Soviet Union. During this time, the United States gave enormous amounts of military aid, training, and defense packages. They wanted to deter the Soviets from invading or touching Iran's borders. At one point, there was not any food, yet the money was being spent on military improvements. There was lots of training provided by the U.S. Air Force against the Soviet Union and construction of air fields and bases around Iran to be ready for an attack.

In the second revolution of 1953 to 1959, the goal of political policies in Iran was to align itself to America's policies. The foreign policy was to depend on America. America had achieved victory in the Regional Cold War. They wanted to maintain their hegemony in the Middle East. This time period was known as the *Quiet Period* in history. Also, Iran received more aid for their continued support of denouncing communism. This was a period when the United States was careful, along with Iran, to prevent communist encounters and influence. Though, some influence and meetings occurred, the United States kept Iran under its wing. There were a lot of good reports of the Shah, both from the press and the State Department. The goal of economic developments was also to prevent communism. The Eisenhower doctrine was famous in integrating American foreign policies to third world nations who would cease support of communism in exchange for foreign aid. The United States did not want to lose a state to communism or spread communism to the masses in an effort to prevent attack on the American frontier. Also, Eisenhower was ready to provide armed forces to regions that needed them. The second year plan was integrated as a $900 million package to improve infrastructure, increase oil revenues and military aid. The goal was to keep the oil on the western side of the Iron Curtain to in fact win the Cold War. The economic aid package was close to $1 billion. The United States wanted cheap oil and began allowing banks such as Bank of America to invest in the Foreign Bank of Iran and get rich. The military developments of the post-Mossedegh era were primarily to make U.S. Defense systems, and prevent attacks on U.S. and Iranian soil. During this era, there was lots of aid for training, and classrooms built for Iranian Army education. Iran joined the Baghdad Pact, a security bloc against the Soviet Union. It became the leader and most powerful military nation in this bloc. The United States did not want them to withdraw from the Baghdad Pact since it would politically hurt them and potentially invite communist influence

into Iran. The Shah spent most of his money on the military and less on economic developments and infrastructure. His people and the Americans were deeply upset, but still gave him more than $110 million in 1959. There were more than 190,000 men in Iranian troops and the United States had given them more than $535.4 million.

There was an incident in the time period of 1958 where Iran began negotiating with the Soviets for bilateral agreements and to prevent an attack on Iranian soil. There was a lot of commotion about the assassination of the Shah, cutting off aid, losing hegemony in the Middle East and having a stronger communist world. But the problem was the Shah was only interested in money for his military. He did not care if he was communist or democratic, though internally he would say he was against communism, as long as he received military aid. The United States was worried, not economically or that it provided enough military aid and training to be used against them, but mainly, that they would lose the Cold War.

A 1950 correspondence stated that Iran was needed to win the Cold War. Iran was a nation with an abundant supply of oil coming up for grabs in the Middle East and the potential to be leader of the entire region. It was Iran who was to grant the hegemony the United States needed to off-balance the power of the Soviet Union and win the Cold War. N.Saifpour Fatemi of Princeton University also stated that Iran was a rich nation that was important in the stakes of power, money, and military dominance in the region. The entire Middle East was the region that could solidify the hegemony the United States had wanted.

It is quite interesting how Iran, a third-world Middle Eastern nation, helped win the Cold War. The Cold War was heavily participated in by mainly two actors: the United States and the Soviet Union. Both actors competed in the 1950s on different levels to get ahead of each other in political, economic, and military might. But, the Soviet Union did not know that economic aid to a third-world country not supporting Communism could actually hurt their chances of winning the Cold War. Iran was very strategic because it was powerful in the Middle East, had strong defense from the north, and also was influential in South Asia. No one imagined that a regional Cold War victory would set the power dynamic off for the upcoming years.

In the years of the 1950s, the Soviet Union tried to settle on some kind of inner benefit, negotiation, or have the Iranians agree on a lucrative offer to gain some kind of influence with the Shah's regime. But nothing prevailed. With the fall of Mossedegh and the installation of the Shah, the United States had already defeated the Soviet Union by August of 1953. It was August of 1953 that impacted the second revolution- a revolution that changed the face of history. In the second revolution, the United States had already won the regional Cold War victory and the remaining years secured the newly acquired kingdom of the United States. Despite Soviet propaganda and an almost complete loss of the United States handing over its victory to the Soviet Union, the United States was able to maintain its influence in that region until 1979 when the Iranian revolution occurred and ended all Western and American influence. Fatemi taught us that unless grievances of the population are not met and changes in the political and economic structure of the country are not dwelled, then there cannot be stability in that state. Fatemi foreshadowed the fall of Iran in 1979 on the basis of population grievances. The defense system we wanted to create hence was probably never created because there was no unity in the country supporting the American developments. The Middle East will be a challenge to the United States unless the United States really *create partnerships, a common interest, and settle all disputes and conflict.* This is what the goal of American foreign policy should be in Iran and it is only these recommendations that will allow American hegemony in the Middle East to flourish once again. After 1979, Iran was an enemy to both the United States and the Soviet Union. Since hegemony was to secure Iran to potentially own the Middle East, the Soviet Union could not do it while the United States had won. The victory of the Regional Cold War perpetuated the strength of the United States in the years after 1959, while history saw a decline in power, economics, and military in the Soviet Union. The reason:

Caught Between Ambitions: The U.S. and Iranian Development Policy to win the COLD WAR.